Studies in the Information Economy:
Urban and Regional Development

Edited by John Goddard, Director
Centre for Urban and Regional Development
Studies,
University of Newcastle upon Tyne.

Understanding Information

UNDERSTANDING INFORMATION BUSINESS, TECHNOLOGY AND GEOGRAPHY

Edited by KEVIN ROBINS

Belhaven Press
London and New York

© Editor and contributors 1992

First published in Great Britain in 1992 by
Belhaven Press (a division of Pinter Publishers Limited)
25 Floral Street, London WC2E 9DS

British Library Cataloguing in Publication Data

A CIP catalogue record for this book is available from the
British Library

ISBN 1 85293 109 4

For enquiries in North America please contact
PO Box 197, Irvington, NY 10533

Library of Congress Cataloging in Publication Data

Understanding information: business, technology, and geography
edited by Kevin Robins.
        p.   cm.—(Studies in the information economy)
    Includes bibliographical references and index.
    ISBN 1-85293-109-4
    1. Information technology—Great Britain.   2. Information services
industry—Great Britain.   I. Robins, Kevin.   II. Series.
HC260.I55U53   1992   91-40511
338.4′702′0941—dc20   CIP

Typeset by GCS, Leighton Buzzard, Bedfordshire
Printed and bound in Great Britain by Biddles Ltd of Guildford and
Kings Lynn

Contents

List of Figures

List of Tables

List of Contributors

Asu Aksoy is currently working as a consultant in Istanbul. Before that she had worked at CCIS, at SPRU and at the Centre for Urban and Regional Development Studies.

Marion Banks works at the School of Information Studies, Polytechnic of North London, and was formerly a researcher at CCIS. Her research interest is in the area of new media and European communications issues.

Tim Brady joined SPRU in 1980 to work on the implications of technological change for skills and training. In 1987 he joined the Sussex PICT team on a project examining software activities in the UK. In October 1991, he moved to the School of Management at Bath University to work on information systems and value chains.

Ken Ducatel is Lecturer in the Management of New Technology in Science and Technology Policy at the University of Manchester. He was formerly a PICT research associate in CURDS. He is co-author of *Transport in the Information Age* (Belhaven Press, 1991).

Harry East is a Senior Research fellow at CCIS. A chemistry graduate, he has worked in information service development and related research in industry, international organisations and academia since 1961. He is a Fellow of the Institute of Information Scientists.

Vicki Forrest is a former Research Fellow at CCIS where she was concerned with online database expenditure in the UK. She holds a Master's degree in Information Studies from Sheffield and a Geography degree from Cambridge. She currently works in the regional planning department in the North Yorkshire Authority.

Andrew Gillespie is a lecturer in Human Geography and researcher in the Newcastle PICT Centre. His research interests focus on communication technologies and urban and regional development.

John Goddard is Professor of Regional Development at the University of Newcastle upon Tyne, and director of the Newcastle PICT Centre. He has written widely in the area of new technologies and regional development.

Bernard Harbor graduated from the School of Peace Studies at Bradford University in 1985. Between 1985 and 1986 he worked for the Greater London Council on an arms conversion project for trade unions at British Aerospace's factory at Kingston. He then worked for the Armament and Disarmament Information Unit (ADIU) at SPRU before joining the PICT programme in 1988. In 1990 he joined the research department of the Transport and General Workers' Union (TGWU).

Gareth Locksley works in the Directorate General for Competition (DG IV) of the Commission of the European Communities. He previously worked at CCIS, City University and the University of Technology in Sydney. He is the editor of *The Single European Market and the ICTs* (Belhaven, 1990).

Mark Matthews is a technology policy analyst and founder member of the Economic and Technical Change Research Group in the School of Social Sciences, University of Sussex. He previously worked as a Research Fellow at SPRU.

Ian Miles is Associate Director of PREST (Programme of Policy Research in Engineering, Science and Technology) at the University of Manchester, where he is carrying out studies focused on information technology, environmental issues, and research management. He was at SPRU from 1972 to 1990.

Kevin Robins is a lecturer in Geography and researcher in the Newcastle PICT Centre, where he is doing work on the audiovisual industries in urban and regional development.

Ian Rowlands is a former Research Fellow at CCIS. Previously he was an Information Officer for Pira, the UK Technical Centre for the Paper and Board, Printing and Packaging Industries; following that he was a senior consultant for Solon Consultants, Information Science Consultancy, London. He now works at the Policy Studies Institute, London.

William Walker is Senior Fellow at SPRU. His main fields of research are nuclear non-proliferation policy, industrial performance and the defence industries.

Series Editor's Preface

This book is the product of research undertaken in the three initial centres established by the UK Economic and Social Research Council through its Programme on Information and Communication Technologies (PICT). The three centres are the Centre for Communication and Information Studies (CCIS), at the Polytechnic of Central London, the Centre for Information and Communication Technologies (CICT), within the Science Policy Research Unit at the University of Sussex, and the Centre for Urban and Regional Development Studies (CURDS), at the University of Newcastle upon Tyne. More specifically, it is one of the many outputs of a project designed to bring all three centres together and entitled 'Mapping and Measuring the UK Information Economy'.

The roots of the project can be traced to work undertaken at OECD which sought to define the scale of the 'information sector' in member countries in terms of such measures as the deployment of 'information capital' and 'information labour'. The first aim of the PICT work was to begin the task of measuring the UK information economy in terms of the spread of information and communication technologies and information occupations in all sectors and regions and the growth and locations of the autonomous tradeable information sector. The second, and more important, aim was to map in theoretical terms how the information economy might be conceptualised.

The three centres were brought together because of complementary interests in information (CCIS), technology (CICT) and the communication of information over space (CURDS). These interests are reflected in the structure of this book. For CCIS, the key issue concerned the 'business of information'; information as a commodity, an industry and a sector. What was significant for the CICT team, in contrast, was the fact that information processing, manipulation and storage had become increasingly mediated through new technologies. For them it was the microprocessor revolution that had made possible the information economy. For CURDS the key agenda concerned the implications of information transactions for space and place, that is to say the 'geography of the information economy'. From this perspective the communications aspect of new technology is central.

Linking the work of all three centres was a growing realisation that little was to be gained from a static measuring of the state of the information economy unless it was based on a thorough understanding of the role of information, and of information and communication technologies in contemporary economic change. Measuring the state of the information economy would be of limited value to policy-makers if the mechanisms underlying its emergence were not understood. At least four different approaches to developing such understanding have been identified in this volume — the notion of the transformation from industrial to a post-industrial society as originally postulated by Daniel Bell; the techno-economic paradigm perspective of Freeman and Perez which places considerable stress on the diffusion of a new 'heartland' technology; the flexible specialisation approach of Sabel and Piore in which information and communication technologies underpin new and more flexible forms of work and industrial organisation; and the ideas of Aglietta and Boyer of the French Regulation school which points to major shifts in both the economic system and its social and institutional framework.

The contributions to this volume highlight the strengths and weaknesses of each of these approaches and point to the convergences between them. This is achieved by means of combinations of theoretical argument and empirical research. No attempt is made to produce some grand synthesis. One key lesson of the joint project is that such grand syntheses are fraught with dangers — including technological determinism and/or over-optimism about the future. Promoting the spread of new technologies and of the tradeable information sector is not a panacea that on its own will bring about the growth of lagging national or regional economies. While there are strong forces for economic restructuring in which information activities and information and communication technologies are deeply implicated, these changes are being worked out within the framework of an already highly differentiated economy. The result is strong elements of continuity as well as of change. Policy-makers will therefore have to look to both the threats and opportunities for economic development highlighted in the chapters of this volume.

John Goddard
University of Newcastle upon Tyne
August 1991

1 Making sense of information
Ian Miles and Kevin Robins

A new age?

> A new civilisation is emerging in our lives, and blind men everywhere are trying to express it (Toffler, 1980, p. 23).

> The world has entered an information age in which information is fast becoming the critical resource upon which individuals, organisations and nations rely for their own development and their place in the sun (Weissman, 1987).

> Today's sophisticated technology only hastens our plunge into the information society that is already here (Naisbitt, 1983, p. 13).

These heady quotations could be multiplied a thousandfold. This would, no doubt, please their authors: what better evidence that we are entering a new information age than the promulgation of texts around the globe, written by proponents of information industries, and read avidly by others in these industries?

The fact that the quotations are breathless, and that they come from interested parties rather than dispassionate social scientists, does not mean that we should discount them. Indeed, we believe that it is important to consider such pronouncements seriously — which means weighing up their evidence, examining their explanations, and cocking a critical eye at their policy conclusions. Discussion of the information age may well have elements of fashion in it, but these authors are trying to give us perspectives on phenomena that are real enough — indeed, some of these phenomena are so apparent in our work and everyday experience that people might be excused for grasping at straws in the effort to understand them. Consider just a few of the trends that might be adduced as evidence that there really is something important going on:

— According to OECD calculations, by the beginning of the 1980s over 40 per cent of Australian, British and US occupations were 'information occupations'.

— Information technology firms were among the world's biggest. IBM's revenues in 1985 were nearly $50 billion (in which year the entire output of the UK information technology industry — excluding British Telecom — was nearly £7 billion).
— It is now common to talk of 'embedded computers', microelectronics systems incorporated within all sorts of everyday products; these are often considerably more powerful than the largest and most advanced computers from the valve era.

But what is really going on? Do these trends have anything in common, and if so, what? This book represents a range of studies which address these questions in different ways. Some of the studies explore developments in particular sectors of the economy, others present more general overviews; some are concerned with the use of information, some with information technology. But they all share a conviction that important changes are under way, even if these are not necessarily as portentous as suggested in our opening quotations, or are perhaps significant in ways other than implied in those visions of the information society.

Current change: is there an information economy?

The term 'information economy' is used in this book — rather than more grandiose terms such as 'information age', 'information society', or even 'information millennium' — since our focus is on changes in economic affairs. We shall not be concerned with broader issues such as privacy and civil liberties, new technologies in the home, computer culture, and so on. While these topics may have considerable influence on our quality of life in the future, it will be apparent that a large number of theoretical and method-ological challenges are posed even within our limited range of subjects.

Does it make sense to talk about an 'information economy'? Is it a useful way of thinking about current or emerging developments?

In many ways, all human societies have been information economies, in that all economic activities depend upon human beings and their abilities to bring information to bear on their tasks. The term 'information economy' is, from this perspective, of most value as a way of directing attention to this fact — and of opening up a number of questions related to it. How has the role of information in economic affairs changed over time, and how does it vary across societies? Is information itself becoming a new type of phenomenon in the economy, for example as it is turned into a commodity by being offered for sale by consultants or on databases? What social and economic power is associated with access to information of different sorts?

A range of research topics quickly emerges from a focus on information; and, indeed, the 'economics of information' represents a flourishing literature which has just this concern. This literature has mainly dealt with rather narrowly economic issues, for instance the peculiar properties of information as an economic resource (such as the ability to reproduce it at very low cost, to share it without the original owner losing it, and so on). More sociological and political science perspectives on the role of information in our societies may be gleaned from the literatures on mass media, cultural studies, communications policy and the like (for example, Slack and Fejes, 1987; Mosco and Wasko, 1988; Garnham, 1990; Mosco, 1989; Finnegan *et al.*, 1988).

But greater claims are being made, as demonstrated in the quotations with which we began. The term 'information economy' is often used in such a way as to suggest that information has now become, or is in the process of becoming, even more central to the functioning of economy and society. There are, it is argued, special, qualitatively distinctive, features about the nature and role of information in contemporary economies. And these, it is suggested, warrant the use of 'information economy' to denote a new *phase* or *stage* in economic development (which can be contrasted to earlier stages), rather than pointing to a *historical universal* (whose varying manifestations may be analysed). The 'information economy' is seen as a new and unprecedented kind of social and economic formation.

What are the specificities of current developments that justify the application of the term? On this there are considerable disagreements. First, some commentators deny that any transition between stages is occurring. Second, some argue that while a profound change is under way, 'information economy' is an inappropriate label — and there is no shortage of alternative terms, such as 'post-Fordism', 'information capitalism', the 'third technological revolution', the 'Third Wave', etc. Third, even among those using the term 'information economy' and similar terms, there are important disagreements as to the key features of the phenomenon they are seeking to label.

On the first two areas of debate, our position will be rather pragmatic. We believe that there are significant changes currently under way, and it is our view that the matter is best approached by a combination of theoretical argument and empirical research. The following chapters of this book set out to develop such a combination, though some are weighted more in one direction, some in the other. The proof of the pudding is in the eating, then: the utility of focusing on change — and on continuity — will be displayed below. As for how we should label the change, 'information economy' is used because it is a widely familiar term which carries few theoretical associations. In contrast, most other terms carry connotations concerning which we have not sought to develop consensus among our diverse contributors.

This brings us to the third area of debate: just what is being talked about? Concepts — whether we are talking about 'electrons', 'species', 'social classes', or 'information economies' — are theoretically weighted. The way we understand such terms depends upon our models of the world. Sometimes an area of enquiry has reached a high level of agreement about fundamental concepts (though these will have been the subject of dispute in the past), and may be arguing only about the details of the concepts or about secondary concepts. But in the social sciences there is often intense disagreement about crucial concepts — for instance, 'class', 'value', 'ideology', 'power', even 'society' and 'economy'. This disagreement does not render discussion and research about the topics signified by the terms irrelevant; rather it means that we will argue about how best to proceed.

The next four sections of this introductory chapter outline approaches to the information economy which have been influential in recent debates, and which have, to different degrees, shaped the studies in this volume. We begin with approaches that relate the information economy to the quantitative, and perhaps qualitative, change in the role of information in economic affairs. We then consider approaches that are grounded in the implications of new information technology, which is treated as permitting radically different ways of organising production and as yielding new products. In some respects these approaches are complementary: one focuses on changing demand for information and particular uses of information, one on the technological change that permits the supply of information and its applications. The third perspective focuses on the potential of new information and communications technologies to promote greater 'flexibility' in the functioning of organisations, industries and economies more generally. The fourth approach sets out to interpret long-term economic developments in terms of movement between different systems of 'economic regulation' in which forms of production and consumption are related together in characteristic ways. It relates the use of information, communication and technology to broader patterns of change that involve social, cultural and political activity, as well as purely economic development.

From post-industrial society to information society

The term 'post-industrial society' became prominent in the late 1960s and was widely accepted in the 1970s as a useful way of describing developments in Western societies — and the approach was echoed in some Eastern European quarters as well. As with the ambiguity about whether we already have information economies, or whether these are something to anticipate for the twenty-first century, there was some uncertainty as to whether post-industrialism was a description, a prediction, or even a prescription.

In some cases, the term was seen as applicable to many Western societies already — they had become post-industrial as a result of changes in the economy that meant that the proportion of workers in service sectors had grown larger than that in manufacturing industries (which tended to be regarded as the 'real' industry). This decline of manufacturing in the employment mix was complemented, furthermore, by an increase in the share of white-collar workers, and a decline in the share of direct production workers, even within manufacturing industries. Associated with this was a move away from the sorts of social conflict which characterised industrialisation, and which derived in large part from the alienating and exploitative nature of factory work, and the class-based ideologies to which it gave rise.

Not all commentators considered that post-industrial society was already here. The classic and seminal text, Daniel Bell's *The Coming of Post-Industrial Society* (1976) was subtitled *a venture in social forecasting*. The full emergence of post-industrial society, it was argued, would be associated with substantial changes in social relations: for instance, the ownership of capital would no longer be the main source of social power. Instead, reflecting the importance of knowledge-based activities in the economy (signified by the growth of white-collar jobs, and institutions involved with planning, research and development, etc.), knowledge itself would become the organising principle.

These perspectives were subject to exacting criticisms. It was argued that the numerical decline in manufacturing employment in no way diminished the importance of this sector as an engine of economic growth and as the base for many services activities. It was also pointed out that the post-industrial approach tended to depict the growth of services as the result of an inexorable shift in final demand away from goods and towards services, whereas in fact much of the development of final demand in recent decades has involved the replacement of services by consumer goods (cars replacing public transport, washing machines replacing laundries, for example). It was also stressed that access to knowledge (and to the means of producing and disseminating knowledge) is itself facilitated by the ownership of material capital.

But disillusion with the post-industrial approach was probably accelerated as much by social and economic developments as by intellectual critique. New waves of political and industrial conflict in the 1970s demonstrated that the 'end of ideology' had not yet come. The economic problems of the 1970s and 1980s showed that the management of mixed economies was by no means as easily tackled by Keynesian means as had been expected — and similar disillusions began to set in about many other planning institutions, for instance town planning. In the wake of these developments, a neo-conservative political economy swept to power in many Western countries, intent on reining back the welfare state institutions that had contributed a major part of service sector employment growth, and exhibiting considerable contempt for many of the taken-for-granted features of post-industrialism, such as strong planning bodies, greater equality and, not least, the irrelevance of material wealth.

Elements of the post-industrial view do live on in many of the accounts of the 'information society'; but there are significant updatings of the account. It is interesting to note that while post-industrial theory was mainly a US and West European approach, information society theories have been particularly associated with Japanese commentators, with the USA following behind and Europeans providing, on the whole, few original contributions.

Now, the terms 'information society' and 'information economy' are used with a range of very different emphases. Some accounts of the information society focus on technological change, and will be discussed in the next section. The most elaborate exposition using such a term, however, closely mirrors the post-industrial viewpoint. Rather than the service sector and white-collar work being seen as the wave of the future, however, it is the 'information sector' and 'information work' whose growth is considered to be central. This neatly deals with one objection against the post-industrial account. This criticism was that it adopted too much of a homogenising approach to services (effectively treating them as forming one huge sector).

When looked at in more detail, services appear to be quite diverse. Indeed, some services have been expanding, while others have been declining; the post-industrial view was embarrassed by the decline of many consumer services (employment in public transport, hairdressers, etc.) and the surging growth in many producer services (advertising, consultancy, financial services, etc.), neither of which accorded with the view of post-industrial development being driven by a shift away from material concerns towards 'higher needs' in consumer demand.

The new emphasis on information activities suggested that services in general could be segmented between information services (mainly growing) and traditional services (often in decline). On such a basis, many analysts followed the influential initiative of Marc Uri Porat (1977), who had proposed a statistical framework for classifying information activities — a new classification for economic statistics. The OECD, for instance, produced data for a range of Western countries depicting the growth of these activities. Compared to the post-industrial account, this seemed to be an approach that grappled with at least one of the main features differentiating various types of services: some are oriented to servicing material goods, or to dealing with the physical or biological state of people (these are often very dissimilar processes, of course, but the Porat approach collapses them together), while other services are oriented to handling intangible outputs — to providing information or communications facilities. In the Porat approach, these information service jobs are classified together with jobs that involve producing information technologies (understood as including not only computers and telecommunications, but also printing presses, mass media and any other devices dedicated to handling information in some form).

This approach to the information society carries many features of the post-industrial approach. The rationale for demarcating a new stage in economic affairs is based upon shifts in economic structure, shifts in which a new sector of the economy, and a range of new jobs, becomes prominent in economic and social life. Information work and information products are central attributes. In part, at least, these trends are being driven along by shifts in demand. And the trends have important implications in that new types of work relation and new social interests are promoted by information work, although there is less unanimity in information society accounts than was typical for the post-industrial perspectives — especially among European commentators.

For instance, for post-industrialists, the continued growth of services was expected to mop up jobs displaced from manufacturing: information society accounts sometimes argue that new information jobs will replace jobs lost through the automation of other sectors, but there are many commentators who are more equivocal about this, pointing to the scope for job losses in services due to the application of new technologies. Also, while strong echoes can be found of the view that knowledge will displace material capital as the basis of social and political power, information society accounts sometimes prefer to stress inequalities in information access and production; for example, talking of the 'information-rich' and 'information-poor'. Perhaps this debate as to whether the information society trends are to be viewed as positive or negative reflects the changed economic climate of the 1980s and 1990s; perhaps it reflects the presence on the academic scene of researchers influenced by the radicalism of the late 1960s and early 1970s. In either case, the developments that helped to undermine post-industrial theory continue to give rise to scepticism as to the millennial views of the information society perspective.

Technological revolutions

The second approach we wish to discuss here is sometimes referred to as the neo-Schumpeterian approach. This label indicates the strong influence on many recent researchers of the economist Joseph Schumpeter, whose works in the 1930s and 1940s presented long-term perspectives on economic development. Schumpeter had paid particular attention to the so-called Kondratiev waves: long cycles of faster and slower growth, lasting perhaps 40 or 50 years, which many analysts have claimed to detect in long-run economic statistics. The existence of these long cycles remains fiercely contested among economic historians and statisticians; but the re-emergence of major economic problems in Western countries in the 1970s, slap on target in terms of long wave predictions, led to an upsurge of interest in the field after a long period of neglect. In some ways, then, the crises that helped undermine the post-industrial account did lead a new generation of economists to analyse the dynamics of long-term change, to return to questions that had become submerged in the post-war boom period, when it was fashionable for economists simply to model states of equilibrium and ignore structural change.

The recent literature on technological revolutions began very much in the context of efforts to account for these (alleged) long cycles. Many candidates for *the* causal force were suggested, with some commentators arguing that only a multi-causal explanation would suffice. Several accounts focused on technological factors.

One type of technological explanation rested on the construction of major new infrastructural systems, such as railways, roads, electricity systems — and, perhaps, telecommunications in the current period. Such construction takes considerable time to accomplish completely, and can stimulate innovations which make use of the infrastructure to create economic growth around new market and geographical areas. Its results unfold slowly over a long period until there begins to be some 'saturation' of the infrastructure's capabilities: this is the mechanism responsible for long cycles. Another, though not unrelated account, draws attention to clusters of innovation of a less co-ordinated kind, rather than to those surrounding a few physically large innovations. Some authors (e.g. Mensch) attempted to identify clusters of basic inventions that have occurred at distinct points in history, with waves of growth-inducing innovations surging up in their wake. Others (e.g. Freeman) criticised this view, arguing that the rate of invention shows far less fluctuation over time than is claimed: what varies, for them, is the propensity of entrepreneurs to exploit potential technological advances so as to generate innovations.

This latter approach began to direct attention toward technological revolutions as a possible factor behind long cycles. As research into this topic gathered momentum — and as the threat of another Great Depression appeared to diminish — the question of long waves began to recede. Whether or not there are more-or-less regular cycles in Western economies, it is now argued that there have been successive 'shocks' to these economies associated with major new technologies. Long waves are now interpreted, if considered at all, in terms of the succession of 'new technology systems' or 'techno-economic paradigms' associated with 'technological revolutions'. Let us consider what these terms mean.

According to a particularly explicit account by Carlota Perez (1983), a technological revolution involves the diffusion of a new *heartland* technology, which substantially affects the utilisation of a key element of a wide range of productive processes. A heartland technology is a technology which is employed across many production processes (such as the electric motor — or, now, the microprocessor). For a new heartland technology to diffuse widely it has to offer economic benefits (reduced costs, improved quality) in both economically and politically acceptable ways. A 'revolutionary' heartland technology is one that offers the possibility of dramatic changes in production costs and methods, so that it is applied widely and rapidly. This is associated with changes in the perceptions of managers, engineers and workers, of the relative costs and capabilities of different factors of production. Something that was previously out of the question now becomes economically or technically possible; some skills become unnecessary while others need to be cultivated; the goods and services on offer from upstream industries change, as may the demands of downstream industries.

A technological revolution occurs when the potential of a new revolutionary heartland technology is exploited — not only across a wide variety of production processes (in the case of information technology, these are often described as factory and office automation, for instance), but also in a wide variety of products. These new products will include intermediate goods and/or services being used in the production processes (e.g. robots, business information services), and others that are final goods and/or services being supplied to consumers (e.g. Compact Disc Players, new services like Prestel and Minitel). The 'swarming' of innovations in a technological revolution involves the generation of many new products — indeed, the creation of clusters of new products as innovations are built upon innovations, all of them capitalising on the possibilities offered by a new heartland technology. Schumpeter talked of 'gales of creative destruction', wherein innovations challenge and undermine many existing branches of production, sets of skills, occupational structures, user-supplier relations and social and economic institutions.

The complex of changes that are enabled by a technological revolution is sometimes referred to as a 'new technological system' or 'techno-economic paradigm' (again, there has been a proliferation of labels here, addressing similar but not quite identical concepts). In some interpretations, the changes made by myriad economic actors lead to change at the level of the whole economy — the creation of new industrial structures, training systems, social institutions, and so on. Others delimit the notion more to change in production processes, perhaps even in single industrial sectors or — in some cases — in specific firms.

New information technology (IT) is held to be the latest revolutionary heartland technology — and one which opens up opportunities for change on a very wide scale. Earlier technological revolutions were based around transformations of our capacities to process energy, inorganic materials, organic chemicals, and the like. But many production processes do not substantially involve these sorts of activity which manipulate matter and energy. Office work, for instance, is very much a matter of manipulating, that is processing, information.

In fact, all tasks to which human labour is applied inherently involve some measure of information-processing. This might be in terms of receiving instructions (communication), checking to see what state the materials are in (perception), performing calculations or other mental acts (transformation or information), or whatever. New information technologies can be brought to bear cheaply and efficiently on these activities. They are distinct from previous technologies which carry information (books, telegraphs), or which, much less commonly, allow it to be manipulated (slide rules, early calculating machines and computers). Microelectronics has emerged as a new heartland technology which provides dramatically cheapened capacities to store, manipulate and communicate information. Around microelectronics, related information and communications technologies are the centre of rapid increases in performance and capability: fibre optics, satellites, optical discs, even software. Thus devices carried in people's pockets and sold as mass consumer goods now outperform whole roomfuls of equipment that represented the state of the art in computer science a few decades ago.

The neo-Schumpeterian approach to the information economy, not surprisingly, places heavy weight on IT and the exploitation of the opportunities it provides. It is this that makes the 'information economy' a new stage in development; our economies are being restructured as the use of IT becomes pervasive, as IT sectors become of crucial strategic importance, as new products and processes are experienced in work and everyday life situations. A new technological system is being forged: the role of information in this system is shaped by the applications of IT.

From this perspective, an emphasis on information activities as proposed by the information society approach is problematic. First, it does not point to the transformation of information-processing by IT; information workers are counted up as if someone using a quill pen is equivalent to someone controlling a supercomputer. New IT is confounded with traditional technologies and human information-processing (postal deliveries, for instance).

Second, it may divert attention away from the application of IT to tasks other than specialised information activities. Not only information workers process information: office workers may be affected by the use of word processors, but, equally, factory workers are affected by the use of robots.

Flexible specialisation

'Flexibility' has become something of a buzzword in recent years. We hear talk of the flexible firm, the flexible labour force, flexible management, and so on. Several different uses of the term are being made — for example, calls for a more flexible labour force may be pleas for more willingness to accept short-term contracts or to abandon trade union demarcation practices, or they may involve arguments that new skill combinations will be required, or that retraining facilities should be introduced. The term 'flexible specialisation' has gained some popularity as a view of the future of organisations (a new techno-economic paradigm for the firm?) which relates very much to the information economy literature, while distancing itself from (at least the cruder) appeals for workers to be flexible so as to meet their firms' requirements better.

The best-known proponents of this case, Michael Piore and Charles Sabel, actually come from backgrounds of research in labour market and organisational change. In their highly influential book *The Second Industrial Divide* (1984) they argue that a new phase of industrialisation is being entered (rather than a post-industrial society), and that its outlines can already be seen in some advanced companies and regions. This new phase they describe in terms of a shift from a type of industrial system based on mass production (and mass consumption) to one based on flexible production (and customised consumption). Whereas mass production is based on the use of special purpose machines and semi-skilled workers to produce standardised goods, flexible specialisation uses flexible, general purpose machinery and multi-skilled workers to produce customised goods for particular and changing markets. They argue that flexible specialisation is the appropriate model for industrial development in consequence of changes similar to those depicted in the two perspectives summarised above.

Flexible specialisation is the new paradigm for both demand and supply-side reasons. On the demand side, there are substantial changes occurring, so that both industrial and consumer users are typically requiring more varied products. Rather little evidence is supported for this case other than management say-so (and this belief about demand change is certainly widespread among industrialists), and many economists have strongly criticised their argument about the saturation and breakup of mass markets. According to Karel Williams and his colleagues (1987, p. 427), 'if Piore and Sabel believe mass markets are breaking up that is because they are conceptually confused about what is going on and crucially fail to draw the distinction between simple product differentiation and market fragmentation' (cf. Elam, 1990). However, Piore and Sabel continue to argue the case that the call for relatively small runs of products, and for rapid adjustment to volatile markets, necessitates flexibility and specialisation on the part of firms.

On the supply side, Piore and Sabel put greater emphasis on information and communications technologies and on technological dynamism. ICTs permit greater use of market intelligence: information can be fed from cash registers to warehouses, and to the design staff in factories and head offices, so that market trends can be quickly identified and responded to. The classic reference here is to the example of Benetton. New IT-based equipment can be rapidly reprogrammed, allowing for so-called economies of scope to become important alongside the traditional economies of scale — firms can quickly change their products, even customising them to specific customers. The technology allows flexibility, and firms will necessarily be pushed in this direction as competitors use the possibility to gain an edge. Even in non-competitive areas, such as public services, consumer pressure for flexibility may grow as a consequence of experiencing it elsewhere.

The ideas developed within the flexible specialisation thesis have been taken up very actively, in particular in policy circles as a way of 'reversing industrial decline' (see Hirst and Zeitlin, 1989a, 1989b; Zeitlin, 1989). Pointing to successful areas like Baden-Württemberg in Germany and Emilia-Romagna in Italy, it is argued that this new technological paradigm offers a way beyond the crisis-ridden state of the British economy, for example. In this perspective, great emphasis is put on the importance of institutional regulation at both the micro (firm, region) and macro (national, international) levels of the economy. Of all the various ways of looking at the economy, the flexible specialisation thesis has been most attentive to questions of space and place, and has therefore been of particular interest to those concerned with the geography of the information economy and with regional development issues. Sabel, particularly, has emphasised the possibilities that flexible specialisation offers for the 're-emergence of regional economies', while others have seen it as a potential solution to the problems of less-developed countries (see Sabel, 1989; Hirst and Zeitlin, 1989a; Murray, 1991; Schmitz, 1989).

The characteristics of flexible specialisation are described in different ways by different proponents of the idea, but (in contrast to much of the general advocacy for 'flexibility') it is common to find stress on: small and decentralised firms, sometimes networked together by ICTs; highly skilled workers, involved in a kind of new technology artisanship; high levels of retraining; high levels of innovation and product change; integrated information systems relating markets to design and production; co-operation and collaboration between firms, including the use of collective services; geographical clustering of activities.

Whether we should treat flexible specialisation as a distinctive approach to the information society or whether it is actually a variant of the neo-Schumpeterian perspective, its very appeal and popularity make it an approach that should be noted.

Regulation theory and post-Fordism

The fourth perspective on the 'information economy' agenda that we shall consider describes it in terms of the transformation from a socio-economic era called 'Fordism' to one referred to as 'post-Fordism'. The original approach was developed by the French Regulation School of economists, notably Michel Aglietta (1979), Alain Lipietz (1987) and Robert Boyer (1986) (for an overview, see Jessop, 1990). Within this perspective, new technology has not been seen as the central object of analysis: the approach is a broader political economic one, concerned with more general patterns of economic and social change, with technologies as only one element within this overall dynamic. Nor has technology been considered to be a *determinant* of economic and social change: new technologies, within this perspective, are seen as being compatible with a range of new models of economic and social development.

The Regulation approach sees the current period in terms of what it describes as the 'crisis of Fordism'. Fordism is a concept used to describe the economic system (the 'regime of accumulation') and the social and institutional framework (the 'mode of regulation') that have structured capitalist economies since the late forties (the chronology differs between national economies). In concrete terms, Fordism has been a form of economic growth centred around mass production and consumption, and based on the exploitation of economics of scale in the manufacture of standardised goods. The regulatory system that supported this has been the interventionist and welfare state elaborated through the policies of Keynes and Beveridge, for example. In the mid-1970s, it is suggested, this Fordist regime became destabilised for a number of reasons, including declining productivity, wage demands, market saturation, increasing cost of raw materials, structural over-capacity, increasing costs of public services. Fordism both as an economic system and as a social and institutional framework was no longer viable, and had to be replaced by a successor regime. In Britain, for example, the restructuring process of the 1980s, associated particularly with the period of Thatcherism, is seen as the way in which this (tentative) process of change was unfolding. Post-Fordism was associated with increasing privatisation and liberalisation of the economy and with a breakup of the welfare state and welfare service provision.

Regulationists have, for the most part, been reticent about what a post-Fordist regime would actually look like. In their view, the shape and nature of any successor to Fordism is likely to be contentious and contested and could assume a number of different forms. Others have been more forthcoming in speculating on the nature of the new regime (often a kind of polarised invasion of Fordism). Michael Rustin outlines the ideal types of Fordist and post-Fordist production and regulation as found in Table 1.1. He emphasises, however, that post-Fordism could turn out to be more or less democratic: a very desirable and decentralised form of society, or a repressive and centralised one.

Rustin plays down the importance of new technologies in shaping this successor to Fordism. 'It is clear', he argues, 'that the shape of this environment is not and will not be determined by new technologies alone.'

Table 1.1 *Ideal types of Fordist and post-Fordist production and regulation*

Fordism	*Post-Fordism*
low technological innovation	accelerated innovation
fixed product lines, long runs	high variety of product, shorter runs
mass marketing	market diversification and niche-ing
steep hierarchy, vertical chains of command	flat hierarchy, more lateral communication
mechanistic organisation	organismic organisation
vertical and horizontal integration central planning	autonomous profit centres; network systems; internal markets within firms; out-sourcing
bureaucracy	professionalism, entrepreneurialism
mass unions, centralised wage-bargaining	localised bargaining, core and periphery work-force divided; no corporation
unified class formations; dualistic political systems	pluralist class formations; multi-party systems
institutionalised class compromises	fragmented political markets
standardised forms of welfare	consumer choice in welfare
prescribed 'courses' in education	credit transfer, modularity, self-guided instruction; 'independent' study
standardised assement (O level)	teacher-based assessment (GCSE) or self-assessment
class parties, nationwide	social movements; multi-parties; regional diversification

Source: Rustin, 1989, pp. 56–7.

Technologies must be seen 'as resources or means of power, not as causal agents in their own right' (ibid., p. 60). Others have given more emphasis to the role of new technologies in the process of transformation to post-Fordism. Annemieke Roobeek (1987), for example, sees post-Fordism in terms of the emergence of a new 'technological paradigm'. In her view, which tries to combine the Freeman-Perez type of analysis on technological paradigms with a Regulation perspective, 'the new core technologies can be seen as the main catalysts that hasten the conceptualisation of a post-Fordist regulation' (p. 130). If the original approach de-emphasised technologies, then more recent attempts have sought to reinstate them within the dynamics of the shift from Fordism to post-Fordism.

We can see this as a consequence of an increasing convergence of the

Regulation approach with theories of flexible specialisation and neo-Schumpeterian approaches (for example, Mahon, 1987). This is particularly notable in the volume edited by Giovanni Dosi, Christopher Freeman *et al.*, 1988, *Technical Change and Economic Theory*, in which Regulationists (Boyer) and neo-Schumpeterians (Freeman, Perez) distinctly converge. There have also been convergences between theories of post-Fordism and the flexible specialisation thesis. If some proponents of the flexible specialisation thesis, like Paul Hirst and Jonathan Zeitlin (1991), have insisted on keeping their distance, seeing post-Fordism as marred by technological determinism, others have sought to overlay the two perspectives, describing post-Fordism in terms of an emerging regime of 'flexible accumulation'. We might also note in passing that, in a recent essay, the grand theoretician of post-industrialism and of the 'information society', Daniel Bell, has himself taken an interest in the flexible specialisation thesis (Bell, 1989).

The points of convergence are interesting, and it may well be that these various approaches can, and will, be synthesised. As yet, however, this remains an aspiration rather than an achievement. Thus, although the notion of 'technological paradigms' is used in both approaches, what must be acknowledged is that it means quite different things to Piore and Sabel than it does in neo-Schumpeterian theory. Similarly, concepts of 'crisis' and 'historical shift' are used very loosely and vaguely, as are notions of historical 'phases' or 'stages'. There is often, for example, an unsubstantiated assumption that regimes of accumulation correspond to Kondratiev waves. There is also a great deal of confusion about the object of analysis: at times it is the labour process or industrial organisation, whereas at other times it is the macro-economy or even society as a whole.

Understanding information

In their different ways, these various theoretical perspectives all shed light on the role and significance of information in contemporary change. Through their different insights, we have come to understand more fully the way in which information has emerged as such a pervasive force in economy and society (information labour, information technologies and infrastructures, information flows, information goods and services). No single approach to the information economy is likely to encompass these developments in their entirety. The attempts to develop some convergence between the four approaches reflect a will to move towards a more comprehensive and systematic analytical framework, but, as we have suggested, they remain tentative steps — a far cry from any general theory of the information economy. The authors in this volume have drawn on one or more of these theoretical perspectives as has been appropriate to their particular objectives. It is far from certain that any over-arching theory will emerge: for the moment, at least, it seems more productive to allow competing theories to work with and against each other.

The four approaches we have been discussing — post-industrialism, neo-

Schumpeterianism, flexible specialisation and Regulation theory — provide useful 'tools' for understanding the information economy. But we must be aware that they are themselves not without problems. If each illuminates particular aspects of the 'informatisation' of society, each also has significant limitations and 'blind spots'. There are some more general problems that can occur across all of the four perspectives, relating to the theorisation of both technology and social change. These are problems that merit careful attention.

As to technology, there is always a danger of falling into a perspective of technological determinism, reducing all economic and social change to being expressions of technological causes and determinants. This, of course, is always going to be a risk in a research area which is centrally concerned with new technologies (and it is to counteract this temptation that many researchers have focused on the 'I' rather than the 'T'). Post-industrialism and neo-Schumpeterian theory have been particularly criticised on this account, though it can also mar the other two perspectives.

To some extent there have been conscious attempts to work against the temptation of technological determinism. Thus, within the neo-Schumpeterian perspective, Freeman and Perez have sought to emphasise that techno-economic paradigms are to be seen in the context of a socio-economic and institutional system. The danger, however, is that the socio-institutional remains subordinated to the techno-economic: techno-economic change brings about socio-institutional adaptation and adjustment; with techno-economic change old social relations and institutions become anachronistic and have to adjust (albeit with a 'time lag') to the conditions of the new paradigm. The social is taken into account but in a functionalist and derivative way. The challenge is to avoid collapsing the social into the technological. As Robert Boyer (1988, p. 67) puts it, 'a major challenge is to see if one can distinguish clearly between two dynamics — one concerning institutional forms, and the other the technological system — and then to investigate their *ex post* compatibility'. Or, as Michael Rustin (1989, p. 63) puts it, in the context of theories of post-Fordism: 'One needs to see Fordism and post-Fordism as specific, willed resolutions of conflicts at the level of social relations, not as the automatic outcomes of the technological imperatives of "mass production" or its information-based successor.' It is necessary to work against the temptations of technological determinism.

The second general problem that potentially affects all the theoretical perspectives relates to our understanding of social and economic change. Within all the perspectives, there is a tendency to look at historical transformation in terms of the shift from one 'phase' or 'stage' of development to another: from industrial to post-industrial society; from one long wave to its successor; from mass production to flexible specialisation; from Fordism to post-Fordism. This change is frequently seen in terms of a movement from the bad old days to the bright new times that are waiting for us. If the past was marked by centralisation, concentration, massification, standardisation, and so on, then the future will be its antithesis, a new era of decentralisation, flexibility, customisation and diversity. This, of course, strikes responsive chords, appealing as it does to an age-old desire to believe in the future and in progress.

This notion of change is clearly simplistic and schematic, however. For one thing, there is an over-emphasis on change, and a failure to recognise continuities over time. Rather than seeing economic and social change in this linear way, a more appropriate metaphor might be one of cumulative developments in which new developments form as 'layers' across the old, with new and old always co-existing. The linear perspective strips social and economic development of its complex and contradictory character. Counter-vailing and divergent processes are not taken seriously in their own right, but tend to be dismissed as anachronistic and residual elements of the old era (industrialism, Fordism, mass production, or whatever). Certain (supposedly emergent) tendencies in the present are then absolutised and projected forward as the paradigm for the new era (post-industrialism, post-Fordism, flexible specialisation), and it is in the light of this ideal-type projection that contemporary developments are measured. Within this evolutionary scheme, the nature of future developments has become a foregone conclusion.

To understand the nature and direction of contemporary change is nevertheless a fundamental agenda. As Peter Stearns (1984, p. 685) argues, 'Our ability to locate ourselves in a past-present-future continuum is not a sterile exercise in contemporary periodisation: it affects how we plan for the future.' In planning for that future, an understanding of information, information technologies and the information economy will prove crucial, and must be a priority for social science research (see Moore and Steele, 1991). The attempts to map and measure the information economy within the Programme of Information and Communication Technologies (PICT) aim to contribute to both the social science and the policy agendas.

Understanding information and PICT

The chapters in this book come from work undertaken within the framework of the UK Economic and Social Research Council's Programme on In-formation and Communication Technologies (PICT). More specifically it represents some of the output from the project on 'Mapping and Measuring the Information Economy' that was jointly undertaken by three of the PICT centres: the Centre for Communication and Information Studies (CCIS) at the Polytechnic of Central London; the Centre for Information and Com-munication Technologies (CICT), based at the Science Policy Research Unit, University of Sussex; and the Centre for Urban and Regional Development Studies (CURDS) at the University of Newcastle upon Tyne.

The book has been organised into three sections, reflecting the different approach to mapping and measuring the information economy undertaken by each of the centres. The key agenda is how to understand information. How extensive is the role of information in contemporary UK economy and society? What is its significance? How is it changing that society? The three centres provide different perspectives on these questions. If PICT's concerns are with ICTs (information and communications technologies), then CCIS focuses on the 'I', CICT priorities the 'T' and CURDS takes up the 'C' in that formulation. These different approaches provide the basis for the three sections: the 'business of information'; the 'technology of information'; and the 'geography of information'.

For CCIS, the key issue concerns the 'business of information': information as a commodity, an industry and a sector. What is significant for the CICT team, in contrast, is the fact that information processing, manipulation and storage has become increasingly mediated through new technologies. For them, it is the 'microprocessor revolution' that has made possible the information economy. For the CURDS researchers, the key agenda concerns the implications of information transactions for space and place, that is to say the 'geography of the information economy'. From this perspective, what becomes central is the communications aspect of the new technologies.

Centre for Communication and Information Studies

In focusing on information as a business, CCIS takes up the agenda set out in 1983 by the Cabinet Office's Information Technology Advisory Panel in its report, *Making a Business of Information* (ITAP, 1983). The ITAP report (which was actually a significant factor in the development of the PICT research agenda) emphasised that 'the provision of information is an increasingly important commercial activity' (p. 7) and argued that the expanding 'tradeable information sector' would become ever more important to the success of the UK economy. New technological developments, it stated,

> are bringing together hitherto disparate activities in information supply. The same intellectual property may now be exploited in books, films, video cassettes and interactive computer programmes. There are new opportunities — through cheaper and better telecommunications services: teletex, rapid facsimile, satellite links, etc. — for the supply of information from the United Kingdom to the rest of the world. This is already a substantial source of overseas earnings. With greater recognition from both Government and the private sector, and vigorous exploitation of technological developments, it could become even more significant (p. 7).

In the context of concerns with IT as they were being developed in the early eighties, the ITAP argued in favour of an emphasis on the I of IT, and not the T (p. 8):

> The nation has over the past year become much more aware of the significance of IT — in part of the vigorous promotional efforts initiated by Government — indeed the very existence of the Panel is a consequence of the Government's recognition of the importance of IT. Emphasis has, very rightly, been placed on the devices associated with IT — the fibre optics, home computers, advanced telephones

etc. — and their capabilities. That has introduced people to potential applications. Now there needs to be a complementary element in Government and company thinking, for equipment is only as valuable as the information that it handles (p. 39).

In line with this emphasis, the ITAP report made three central recommendations:

i. Government should recognise the current economic significance of the tradeable information sector, and the opportunities for future growth and take its interests into account in policy information.

ii. Those already active in information supply — in publishing, broadcasting, film-making etc. — should closely examine their present activities to identify how new technology is eroding previous distinctions between their particular interests and others with which they may previously have had no contact, and should prepare business strategies accordingly.

iii. Those wishing to stimulate or participate in new business activities should note the many opportunities now being opened up through the use of new technology for the supply and analysis of information, which are suited to an entrepreneurial approach (p. 9).

It is this emphasis that is recognised in the four chapters written by the CCIS contributors to this book. Their argument is that information is a business, that it is a rapidly innovating business, and that it is now a big (and growing bigger) business.

If information is a business, then it is a very particular kind of business — in Gareth Locksley's phrase it is 'funny peculiar'. Information as a commodity is different from more 'traditional' industrial commodities. As Locksley argues in his chapter, the information commodity is 'immaterial' and is not consumed in use. Because it depends on creative input it is also the case that its success within the market, that is the scale at which it will be consumed, is highly unpredictable. What also distinguishes it is that the costs of production are skewed towards the first copy, with low costs of reproduction. In addition, it is possible to repackage the information commodity and to sell it across different markets (the 'cascade' strategy).

This particularity of the information commodity then becomes fundamental to the organisation, methods and dynamics of firms involved in the business of information. The nature of its product has powerful implications for the structure and segmentations of the sector. Locksley makes an analytical distinction between four separate information activities: production/innovation/creation; packaging/publishing/reproduction; distribution/transmission/diffusion; marketing and servicing. In her chapter, Asu Aksoy develops this typology more systematically. Her objective is to outline the relationship between these different functions and to suggest how this then has implications for the organisation of information businesses. For example, she emphasises that in this sector it is not production, but rather packaging and distribution that are the key elements. Aksoy goes on to outline the market structure for each of these activities: the number and size of sellers and buyers; barriers to entry and exit; the extent and character of product differentiation; the extent of competition; and so on. What she emphasises, however, is the significance and the extent of integration between activities.

This, too, is the paramount observation in Marion Banks' chapter. Focusing particularly on the media component of the information and communications industries, Banks draws attention to the scale at which integration has taken place. The economic and operational structure of this industry, she argues, necessarily leads to concentration and centralisation of ownership and control. Economies of scale give larger concerns a powerful advantage. Control over the key nodes of the information business (particularly distribution) becomes a further strategy for achieving a monopoly position. And cross-media ownership which provides economies of scope, that is to say control over different product lines, becomes a further mechanism for achieving a dominant position in the sector. These have been the strategies behind the empires of Murdoch, Maxwell, Bertelsmann and Berlusconi. As Asu Aksoy argues, 'the way to attain flexibility in the information business is, actually to integrate, to increase the portfolio of information products in order to be able to add value, and to widen the possible channels of distribution'.

In their chapter, Harry East, Ian Rowlands and Vicki Forrest take up these issues with reference to a particular case study, online database services. In their account, they show how this particular electronic commodity has emerged as a consequence of both technological and market developments, and they explore some of the dilemmas in making a business of this particular immaterial product. What East *et al.* also observe is that in this activity, as in other information and communications activities, competition has been associated with growing integration. They observe that integrated US companies now dominate world trade in outline information, whilst European producers have been driven to look for niche markets, such as financial, scientific and patents information. The key to a financially viable online database sector, they emphasise, 'hinges on the potential for far greater economies of scale', and in consequence, what we are seeing is 'a tendency towards consolidation with large producers becoming even larger, and an increase in acquisitions and producer-vendor mergers'.

One central policy question emerges from all the CCIS contributions, and this concerns the balance between market-forces and regulation in the information and communications business. What they express is a concern about any ideal of unfettered competition and privatisation. Is it the case that diversity and choice in the provision of information may be increased by the liberalisation of broadcasting and other information and communications media? Or is there, rather, the possibility that the opposite may occur? The CCIS researchers fear that the latter is the most plausible scenario, with corporate integration and concentration militating against consumer interests. They draw attention to the potential conflict between rational business strategies, on the one hand, and questions of public interest, on the other. Locksley argues that increasing integration and oligopoly within the information sector could lead to a *Pravda* model of information provision. What needs to be considered are the appropriate regulatory measures to ensure that both public and private interests are both taken into account.

Centre for Information and Communication Technologies

In the second part of the book, the CICT researchers focus on the technological dimensions of the information economy. Based within the Science Policy Research Unit, CICT has been influenced by the neo-Schumpeterian framework developed there by Christopher Freeman, Carlota Perez and other researchers. This approach is used to criticise and improve on theories of post-industrial society as developed by Bell, Porat and Machlup. Within this perspective, IT is seen as the basis for a 'technological revolution', or in a different terminology, it is the basis for a new long cycle, or Kondratiev wave, of economic development. According to Freeman and Perez, such technological revolutions, or changes in 'techno-economic paradigm' are 'so far-reaching in their efforts that they have a major influence on the behaviour of the entire economy':

> A change of this kind carries with it many clusters of radical and incremental innovations, and may eventually embody a number of new technology systems. A vital characteristic of this . . . type of technical change is that it has pervasive effects throughout the economy, i.e. it not only leads to the emergence of a new range of products, services, systems and industries in its own right: it also affects directly or indirectly almost every other branch of the economy, i.e. it is a 'meta-paradigm'. We use the expression 'techno-economic' rather than 'technological paradigm' because the changes involved go beyond engineering trajectories for specific product or process technologies and affect the input cost structure and conditions of production and distribution throughout the system (Freeman and Perez, 1988, p. 47).

The CICT research seeks to explore the implications of this radical economic and social transformation, taking technology very seriously, and making questions of technological change and innovation central to their analysis of the British economy. A major concern has been about the extent to which the 'British disease' — the relatively slow growth and poor economic performance of the UK — reflects a problem with translating scientific and technological ingenuity into successful innovations, rather than (as other popular accounts would have it) stemming from a militant work-force or from consumers and pressure groups resistant to change. The question of technology, they argue, is fundamental to analysing the economy and economic recovery in Britain, and a good understanding of technology must be central to any analysis of the emerging information economy.

Social science in general, however, has not been very good at dealing with technology. A great deal of social science thinking mirrors everyday notions, with technological determinism of one kind or other limiting the appraisal of technological change. The development and diffusion of technologies is often treated as if it were fairly inevitable: as human knowledge grows, superior technologies displace earlier ones — this is progress. And technology is seen as having 'impacts': it leads directly to specific sorts of social consequence. These ideas (and other aspects of technological determinism) are widely criticised by social scientists, but alternative views of technology are also often equally unsatisfactory. Some commentators view technology as simply an epi-phenomenon of social affairs, as if it were something that could accommodate magically to new demands (be they changing factor prices, as in neo-classical economics, or managment intentions, as in some Marxist accounts).

These two extreme (but common) approaches both fail to take technology sufficiently seriously. In the one treatment it 'falls from the sky': technology has its own logic which is imposed upon social affairs. In the other it is merely a by-product of social affairs, posing no particular problems of its own. A more sophisticated approach is to take technology not just as devices, but as sets of social practices (the knowledge and skills that are the '-ology' of technology), some of which involve working on and through the non-living physical world; and where these social practices are seen as being in dynamic relations to other social practices (so that instead of talking about 'technology and society' we would talk about 'technology in society'; instead of talking about the 'impacts of technology' we would talk about the co-evolution of technological and other social practices).

But even when such an approach is proposed, there is typically rather little effort to look in detail at the specific issues raised by different technologies — whether these are information technologies as compared to energy tech-nologies, new information technologies compared to traditional means of communication, or everyday incremental innovations compared to re-volutionary technological changes. While there have been good descriptive studies based on an awareness of the social embeddedness of technology, there has been little effort to theorise technologies, and to relate this to the varied implications of the variety of concrete technologies in application.

Such considerations inform the three CICT chapters, which draw upon various elements of SPRU's past work in an effort to illuminate the 'information economy'. In the first chapter, Matthews and Miles are concerned to differentiate *new* information technology from traditional information and communications technologies. They argue that a new heartland technology, microelectronics, makes it possible to apply IT across the whole economy, and that the term 'information economy' might be most usefully applied to this process. Using British official statistics, they trace out some of the implications of this approach, showing that while the statistics are limited, they can still be used to outline important developments.

One of the main problems with available statistics is that their focus is rather off-centre in comparison with 'where the action is' in the information economy. Increasingly, software, rather than hardware alone, is the key to IT applications, and increasingly these applications are in services rather than in manufacturing — yet our statistics focus on the more familiar, more readily measurable factors. Brady's chapter draws attention to the software side of IT development, and draws on new data which identify where software activities are happening in the British economy. As IT is becoming more pervasive, so the production and maintenance of software is becoming an activity that is no longer confined to specialised hardware and software producers, but is spread across organisations of all types. Brady discusses what is developing and how.

These two chapters discuss key contours of the information economy. But their focus is on the civilian economy, and it goes without saying that IT has major military applications — from 'smart' missiles to 'command, control, communications and intelligence systems'. This became all too clear during the Persian Gulf War. While IT development is now being driven along in large part by commercial applications, many of the key innovations in computing and microelectronics were made by defence laboratories and contractors. Even today in Britain the bulk of government research and development funding goes to military programmes, so the influence on IT activities will be profound. Harbor and Walker show that it is possible to bring social science analysis to this traditionally secrecy-shrouded area, and provide an informative and perhaps surprising picture of the defence electronics industry today.

Each of these studies demonstrates the scope for applying statistical analysis to questions of the role of IT in an advanced industrial society. They show that it is necessary to think about technology seriously, to draw distinctions among technologies, and to relate this task to broader social scientific analyses. They do not claim to have provided a comprehensive account of the information economy in these studies, but they have set out some useful approaches to understanding the social, economic and historical issues — alongside the technological ones — that confront Britain as an information economy.

Centre for Urban and Regional Development Studies

In the third part of the book, the CURDS researchers focus on some of the geographical implications of new information and communications technologies. In most of the literature on post-industrial society and the information economy, there has been a breathtaking disregard for questions of space and place. Indeed, it has been commonly assumed that ICTs will bring about such a compression of time and space that they will, thereby, transcend the frictions of geography once and for all. There has been a tendency to conjure up images of world-wide data banks and services, and to imagine the possibility of instantaneous communication within a 'global village' made real. Within this kind of futuristic scenario, it is assumed geographical divides — centre/periphery, city/heartland, North/South — will become a thing of the past as all places gain equal and immediate access to information networks and resources.

The CURDS contributors radically question this sort of wishful and idealistic scenario. Within the information economy, they argue, geography will continue to matter. The spatial dynamics of economic and social transformation are of the utmost importance and are a crucial issue for research on information and communications technologies. 'Space' is a complex and multi-layered concept. As Doreen Massey writes:

> It includes distance, and differences in the measurement, connotations and appreciation of distance. It includes movement. It includes geographical differentiation, the notion of place and specificity, and of differences between places. And it includes the symbolism and meaning which in different societies, and in different parts of given societies, attach to all of these things (Massey, 1984, p. 5).

The geographical transformations associated with the new information and communications technologies are being felt in all these dimensions. The information economy involves new spatial forms for the organisation of industrial and economic activities; new patterns of location and of territorial configuration; new dynamics of unevenness in the development of places; new kinds of relationship between cities, regions, nations and so on; new meanings and senses of place. Inevitably, the process of change will be complex, a matter of both breaks and continuities, and its eventual outcome remains uncertain.

In its research into information and communications technologies, CURDS has been concerned with both the 'I' and the 'T', but also very much with the 'C'. Communication is absolutely central to any analysis of the geography of the information economy; to the understanding of how economic structures and activities are organised across space; and to analysing the relationships and interrelationships of particular places and territories. In developing this research agenda, CURDS has focused particularly on the changes taking place in organisations, looking at both intra-organisational and inter-organisational transformations. How is organisational behaviour changing? Towards greater decentralisation, or centralisation? Are different components of the value chain becoming more integrated or dis-integrated? What now governs decision-making about location? The study of organisational change provides a basis to explore the geography of the information economy.

An important aspect of organisational change has been the increasing growth of computer networks. As John Goddard argues, computer networks facilitate capital and labour flows across space, thereby creating 'the possibility of new organisational geographies — what work is done where — and offering new possibilities for the way territories — markets and administrative areas — are managed'. The analysis of computer networks has been a central aspect of the empirical work undertaken at CURDS, involving both original survey work and the analysis of existing data, particularly the Workplace Industrial Relations Survey (WIRS). What these data reveal are significant inequalities within the UK space economy, as both John Goddard and Ken Ducatel make clear.

CURDS research has very much sought to avoid a deterministic account of technological change. What must be emphasised is that, if ICTs have created possibilities, they have not determined the trajectory of development. Technology is one variable in the dynamics of economic and social change. In the light of this conviction, the CURDS work has developed around a political economy approach to the information economy. As Kevin Robins and Andrew Gillespie argue, the 'post-Fordist hypothesis' offers perhaps the most complex perspective on contemporary change, and it has also been attentive to the geographical manifestations of change. What emerges from this perspective is the observation that the information economy is associated with increasing globalisation, and, particularly, with new forms of encounter between the global and the local.

In their chapter, Robins and Gillespie are concerned to develop the elements of a geographical analysis of the information economy. In their view, post-industrial theory and the neo-Schumpeterian perspective offer only limited help, whereas the flexible specialisation thesis and the Regulation approach offer a good starting-point. They ask two key questions: What kinds of organisational restructuring are being brought about by the new ICTs? What are the implications for particular places and territories? In trying to address these issues, they are critical of economists (Piore and Sabel) and geographers (Scott and Storper) who suggest that we are moving towards an era of 'flexible specialisation' or 'flexible accumulation' centred around flourishing regional and local economies. Robins and Gillespie develop the outlines of an alternative map of the information economy, centred around a more complex and variegated picture of globalisation and localisation.

Ken Ducatel's chapter looks specifically at the technology of computer networks as they have developed in Britain. Ducatel argues that there is a need to understand the logics shaping these new systems if we are to intervene in their future development. To this end, he undertakes a detailed analysis of the WIRS data, based on a survey of around 2,000 establishments in the public and private sectors. Ducatel seeks to 'open the black box' to see how this new technology has initially been used, and how it has been differentially adopted from sector to sector and from region to region. His findings — which include hierarchical rigidities within organisations and also signs of deepening regional separation — give cause for concern. What this raises is the question of whether market dynamics should be counteracted by certain forms of government and local government action.

In the final chapter, John Goddard brings together a number of the theoretical and empirical strands of the CURDS research. He presents case studies of the development of computer networks, which supplement Ducatel's analysis of the secondary data, focusing particularly on the territorial mapping of this new technology. Like Ducatel, he finds evidence of geographical unevenness, with a distinct skew to London and the South-East. Goddard goes on to link demand for computer network services to the question of telecommunications infrastructure provision, arguing that tele-communications regulation should take into account different patterns of demand in order not to work against the interests of peripheral regions. A third focus in this chapter is on one particular industry within the tradeable information sector, that is broadcasting. Again there is evidence of con-centration and centralisation in London and the South-East. These various observations lead Goddard to observe that 'there are dangers of global integration proceeding hand in hand with regional and local disintegration, of islands of economic growth in the network economy and economic decline of the network'.

It is this policy agenda that is central to the CURDS work as a whole. In Robins and Gillespie's words, there is a great danger of division between 'these territories that are "switched" into the network and those that are "unswitched" or even "unplugged"'. How to avoid this division? Solutions are complex and require that agencies involved in area development take seriously information, communications and technology policy, whilst bodies concerned with ICT policy-making must concern themselves with the geographical implications of their work.

Bibliography

Aglietta, M., 1989, *A Theory of Capitalist Regulation*, NLB, London.

Bell, D. 1973, *The Coming of Post-Industrial Society: a Venture in Social Forecasting*, Basic Books, New York.

Bell, D., 1989, 'The third technological revolution', *Dissent*, Spring, 164–76.

Boyer, R., 1986, *La théorie de la regulation: une analyse critique*, La Découverte, Paris.

Boyer, R., 1988, 'Technical change and the theory of "Régulation"', in G. Dosi *et al.* (eds), *Technical Change and Economic Theory*, Pinter, London, pp. 67–94.

Elam, M., 1990, 'Puzzling out the post-Fordist debate: technology, markets and institutions', *Economic and Industrial Democracy*, **11** (1), 9–37.

Finnegan, R., Salaman, G. and Thompson, K., 1988, *Information Technology: Social Issues*, Hodder & Stoughton/Open University Press, Sevenoaks.

Freeman, C. and Perez, C., 1988, 'Structural crises of adjustment, business cycles and investment behaviour', in G. Dosi *et al.* (eds), *Technical Change and Economic Theory*, Pinter, London, pp. 38–66.

Garnham, N., 1990, *Capitalism and Communication: Global Culture and the Economics of Information*, Sage, London.

Hirst, P. and Zeitlin, J. (eds), 1989a, *Reversing Industrial decline? Industrial Structure and Policy in Britain and her Competitors*, Berg, Oxford.

Hirst, P. and Zeitlin, J., 1989b, 'Flexible specialisation and the competitive failure of UK manufacturing', *Political Quarterly*, **60** (2), 164–78.

Hirst, P. and Zeitlin, J., 1991, 'Flexible specialisation versus post-Fordism: theory, evidence and policy implications', *Economy and Society*, **20** (1), 1–56.

ITAP, 1983, *Making a Business of Information: a Survey of New Opportunities*, HMSO, London.

Jessop, B., 1990, 'Regulation theories in retrospect and prospect', *Economy and Society*, **19** (2), 153–216.

Lipietz, A., 1987, *Mirages and Miracles*, Verso, London.

Mahon, R., 1987, 'From Fordism to ?: new technology, labor markets and unions', *Economic and Industrial Democracy*, **8**, 5–60.

Massey, D., 1984, 'Introduction: geography matters', in D. Massey and J. Allen (eds), *Geography Matters*, Cambridge University Press, Cambridge, pp. 1–11.

Moore, N. and Steele, J., 1991, *Information Intensive Britain: a Critical Analysis of the Policy Issues*, Policy Studies Institute, London.

Mosco, V., 1989, *The Pay- Per Society: Computers and Communication in the Information Age*, Garamond Press, Toronto.

Mosco, V., 1989, *The Pay-Per Society: Computers and Communication in the* University of Wisconsin Press, Madison.

Murray, R., 1991, *Local Space: Europe and the New Regionalism*, Centre for Local Economic Strategies, Manchester.

Naisbitt, J., 1983, *Megatrends*, Warner, New York.

Perez, C., 1983, 'Structural change and assimilation of new technologies in the economic and social system', *Futures*, **15** (5), 357–75.

Piore, M. and Sabel, C., 1984, *The Second Industrial Divide*, Basic Books, New York.

Porat, M.U., 1977, *The Information Economy: Sources and Methods for Measuring the Primary Information Sector*, US Department of Commerce, Office of Tele-communications, Washington, DC.

Roobeek, A., 1987, 'The crisis in Fordism and the rise of a new technological paradigm', *Futures*, **19** (2), 129–54.

Rustin, M., 1989, 'The politics of post-Fordism: or, the trouble with "new times"', *New Left Review*, (175), 54–77.

Sabel, C., 1989, 'Flexible specialisation and the re-emergence of regional economies', in P. Hirst and J. Zeitlin (eds), *Reversing Industrial Decline? Industrial Structure and Policy in Britain and her Competitors*, Berg, Oxford, pp. 17–70.

Schmitz, H., 1989, *Flexible Specialisation — a New Paradigm of Small-scale Industrialisation?* Institute for Development Studies, Brighton, Discussion Paper 261.

Slack, J. and Fejes, F. (eds), 1987, *The Ideology of the Information Age*, Ablex Publishing Corporation, Norwood, NJ.

Stearns, P., 1984, 'The idea of post-industrial society: some problems', *Journal of Social History*, **17**, 685–93.

Toffler, A., 1980, *The Third Wave*, Pan, London.

Weissman, R., 1987, 'Preface' in C. Bezold and R.L. Olson, *The Information Millennium*, Information Industry Association, Washington, DC.

Williams, K., Cutler, T., Williams, J. and Haslam, C., 1987, 'The end of mass production', *Economy and Society*, **16** (3), 405–39.

Zeitlin, J. (ed.), 1989, 'Local industrial strategies', special issue of *Economy and Society*, **18** (4).

Part I: The business of information*

---

*Chapters prepared by the Centre for Communication and Information Studies

2 The information business
Gareth Locksley

The information business has been with us for a long time. This is especially true of newspapers, books and journals. Smoke signals, pigeons, flashing mirrors and wire services have been in business for quite a while too. Now there are new forms of electronic business, information services and data broadcasting by satellite. Advertising is an important element of the business of information and 'junk mail' is a by-product of it. We can include the information/entertainment industries of radio, television, cinema, video and recorded music in the business of information. When the turnover of all the firms in these sectors are added together we are talking about big business.

The information business concerns the printed word, the moving image, electromagnetic waves and digital impulses. Often the business is just plain old speech, which remains the dominant form of communications. Frequently information is sold. For example, Reuters achieved a turnover in excess of £1 billion in 1988 from the sale of information. At other times, enterprises are paid to give information away. For example, the commercial television channels in the UK (the ITV network) received over £1.5 billion in advertising revenues in 1988. These advertisements were distributed free to viewers. British Telecom earns over £10 billion largely for conveying messages.

In some instances, information can command a price only if a very few people know the message, and at other times information has little value unless everyone gets the message. Often information is reassembled into a different form or structure to create new information. Examples might be an executive summary of a large report, the reworking of data from a survey, or Dire Straits' *Greatest Hits*. You cannot do this type of reassembly with an electric cooker or an Airbus 310.

Information can be carried on many media such as paper, vinyl, magnetic and video tape, compact, floppy and hard discs. It can be packaged and repackaged on any of these media and the business of packaging is substantial. There are massive industries related to collecting, handling and accessing information whose hardware products range from satellites and mainframe computers to humble telephones and personal radios. But the business of information is fundamentally different from the business of making the hardware of information.

These differences relate to the nature of information as a commodity. The consequences of these differences demand different strategies and practices for information businesses and users from those in more ordinary product markets. For example, a common contemporary London street cry is 'Three a tape, three for a fiver. Get yer top 40 tapes 'ere!' but one never hears the cry applied to Volvos, baked beans or Marks & Spencer pullovers. The tapes are of course unofficial copies and this 'bootleg' business is a form of theft which affects all information businesses and demands particular practices to protect the original 'author'. The photocopier, electronic eavesdropping devices and the copy utility on microcomputers place all information businesses at risk to this threat. There is misinformation which is deliberately generated to give its user a false trail. There are instances where a (hardware) firm had made imitations of competitors' products that fell to bits in a short time. These misproducts were designed to ruin the reputation of a competitor. Such practices are illegal and very rarely pursued. In any case, the purchaser can always test the (hardware) product for its genuineness. But it is not so easy for the consumer of information, particularly when he or she cannot test the information until it has been received and paid for. What is information and what is misinformation may be very difficult to discern.

The business of information is peculiar in comparison to traditional products like trucks or the market for lemons. This chapter examines these peculiarities and the issues, strategies and practices that ensue from them.

Characteristics of the information commodity

For analytical purposes the world can be divided into two types of products — information commodities and the traditional industrial products, termed here 'hardware'. We understand the economics of hardware businesses. These material goods normally have known production functions, that is, there is a 'recipe' of resources input to the production process which provides a predictable level of output. Here economies and diseconomies of scale are important. They encourage or discourage the expansion of output. Additionally, demand can be predicted with some degree of certainty. Market research and research and development provide both an estimate of the level of consumer demand and the precise characteristics of a product desired by the market. In this way the product can be adapted to assume these characteristics. Finally, hardware products are consumed in use, that is they are either destroyed in the act of consumption or depreciate through consumption.

Information commodities are very different. They are immaterial commodities whose physical existence is merely a set of signals on tape, paper or brain cells. Because they are often produced by a creative process their production function is frequently unknown and non-predictable. Con-

but often embodied in material things

sequently, a great deal of effort and resources may or may not produce usable output. It follows that costs exhibit a higher degree of unpredictability. Further, the production process is really reproduction of a 'first copy'.

It follows that cost structures consist of high first copy costs and low costs of reproduction. There is an incentive to saturate the market in these circumstances and where possible expand across geographic markets. Demand conditions are also problematic. Frequently the market is characterised by 'hits' and 'misses' where the former information commodity is very successful and the latter very unsuccessful. Usually it is difficult to predict which particular information commodity will be a hit. So it makes sense to produce a wide range of products in the expectation that at least one of them will cover the costs of all the others. This characteristic is particularly evident in the book and recorded music businesses.

Typically an information commodity can be repackaged and sold to several markets in largely unaltered form. We can term this process 'transproduction'. Information on a particular financial market might be sold at a high price, in a confidential report, before being repackaged for wider distribution. Later the same information will appear in a newspaper. This 'cascade' strategy, of differentiating the product by time, geographic location or medium, is also commonplace in the film, video and television sectors.

Finally, information is not destroyed by use, it can be reconsumed again and again. Some information is used in this way, for example scientific information. Other information has a very short shelf life, like evening newspapers. Reading the newspaper does not destroy its content but the passage of events destroys its usefulness.

These differences between the hardware and information sectors are determinate for the methods and dynamics of the business of information.

Information activities

For analytical purposes it is helpful to conceive of four separate information activities. (Asu Aksoy's chapter in this volume presents a much more sophisticated version of this model.) In an abstract sense these are quite discrete functions, though in business we frequently find that the separate activities are performed within the same enterprise. The quadrants of Figure 2.1 illustrate the concept of information activities.

The four quadrants comprise the chain of business activity for information. In its simplest form we can conceive of an individual author (quadrant 1) writing a book which a publisher edits and binds (quadrant 2). It is then sold to a book wholesaler and ends up on the shelves of W.H. Smith at Victoria Station (quadrant 3) where a commuter buys it and reads it on the journey home (quadrant 4). The flow through the chain is represented by the bold lines in Figure 2.1. However the business chain can be more complex.

Quadrant 1 is the activity of producing items of information. This is a creative process carried out by authors, computer programmers, journalists,

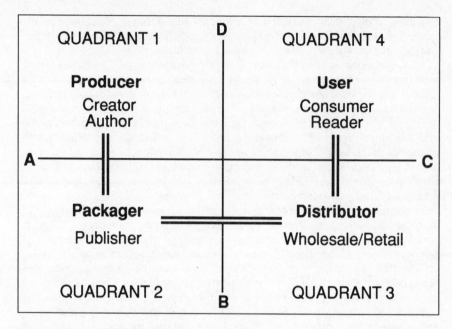

Figure 2.1 *Information activities by quadrant*

research workers or markets. In the latter case the interaction of supply and demand will produce information about prices and quantities as a by-product of realising an exchange. This information can then be captured. Rarely does the producer of information deal directly with the final user of information in quadrant 4, so very little crosses line D. Instead other activities intervene and the first of these is the activity of packaging information into usable bundles.

The Financial Times is such a packaged bundle of information drawn from a large number of information producers. The packaging process may involve storing the information on various media or reassembling information with other items old and new or simply binding and covering sheets of paper. In many cases the packagers and the producers of information work in the same enterprise (for example staff journalists) and at others the producers sell their output to the packagers (as in the case of free-lance journalists). In the latter case Line A represents a market relationship and commonly the interaction of the two activities will be subject to some form of regulation and control over copyright.

The next stage in the business chain, quadrant 3, is the activity of distributing packaged information. Again a firm in the information business may have in-house distribution facilities (like the *Evening Standard* vans) or hire the services of a specialist to get information to wholesalers and retailers (like the famed TNT trucks at Wapping). But there are more intricate relationships between packagers and distributors.

Access to distribution systems is vital to any business. Firms in the hardware businesses, such as computers, trucks and lemons, are usually faced with a plethora of distribution systems and always have the opportunity of setting up their own network. This is why we see the Ford, BP and Courage logos all over the landscape on controlled distribution outlets.

In contrast, distribution systems for information have developed in a centralised fashion. In the case of telecommunications and broadcasting for example, the government has regulated and limited distribution systems by controlling the number of competing networks and restricting the range of messages and services they can carry. The new distribution systems of cable and satellite are similarly subject to regulations on what they can carry or services they can offer. Even the distribution systems for books, newspapers, journals, films, videos and recorded music have developed concentrated forms. 'Indies' record labels need the distribution systems of 'major' labels. The same goes for independent film and TV programme makers. A big problem for publishers is to get their books on the shelves of W.H. Smith. The access issue is particularly intense where the capacity to distribute is less than the capacity to package so that some information cannot be distributed. This is not a matter that arises for the baked bean manufacturer in the age of the hypermarket.

A further twist to the issue arises where the distributor also happens to be an information producer and packager. If it now distributes another firm's information bundles it is helping a competitor potentially to its cost. If viewers are watching one channel they cannot watch another at the same time. In the hypermarket, 'own brand' baked beans are shelved next to the proprietary brands. So we can see that Line B in Figure 2.1 is of far more importance to the business of information than it is in other economic activities. This line forms the focus of regulation of the information business.

Distributors and retailers usually collect revenues from the final user of information as with most other businesses. Books, newspapers, journals and recorded music comply with these standard practices. But some information businesses do not, for example television stations which sell audiences to advertisers so the final consumer of television programmes does not pay directly.

The map of the information business can be used to examine several aspects of business strategy and behaviour. By tracking the activities of firms we trace their degree of integration (see Aksoy and Banks in this volume). So, for example, Reuters would appear in the first three quadrants. The company employs journalists and information gatherers. Their output is edited within the company in order to package it to meet customer needs. This is then distributed on Reuters' own telecommunications networks to dedicated equipment on the premises of customers. Equally the map could be used to trace the activities of Rupert Murdoch's information business which is both integrated by information market and exhibits a high degree of trans-production. In constructing these maps a spatial dimension can be introduced which examines the geography of the information business.

At a more abstract level it is possible to map the distribution of revenues and risk across the quadrants and use this to explain the dynamics of integration in different information sectors. Similarly, we can map the size distribution of firms across quadrants and measure the degree of concentration and the balance of market power at the intersection of the quadrants along lines A, B and C. Usually there are more information producers than packagers. Often the former tend to work in small units or in free-lance mode whilst the packagers are usually large economic units so that the balance of market power is unevenly distributed. On one side we find a dispersed atomistic structure and on the other side of the market an oligopolistic structure. Further, it is possible to map the distribution of regulation between the quadrants and use the distributions of revenues, risks and size, to help explain this state of affairs. Finally, the map can be used to analyse the impact of policy interventions on the business chain of information. If the government introduces rule X, restriction Y or tax Z on quadrant 2 what might be the outcome for the entire business chain?

Information behaviour

The strictly defined information business is concerned with two sets of participants in the information market — those who have information and those who want it. The interaction between these two sets in motion various modes of behaviour and influences the practices and strategies of actors. Figure 2.2 following Hirschleifer (1972) illustrates actions and responses on both sides of the information market.

The market for information, just like any other, involves those who possess a marketable commodity and those who are seeking it. The possessor can choose to keep the information for private use rather than selling it to the seeker. Here the information holder expects to gain more from the internal use of the information in consumption or production decisions than from selling it. We may find this type of decision in the hardware sector, for example, on whether to sell in-house components.

Possessor of information	Seeker of information
1 Private use	Production
2 Sale	Purchase
3 Gratuitous dissemination	Monitoring
4 Deception/authentication	Evaluation

Figure 2.2 *Modes of behaviour in information markets*

Equally, the seekers of information may decide to produce their own information by research or may attempt to 'pull' information into the market by offering a sufficiently attractive price. Note that it is quite possible for the possessor to sell information whilst still keeping a copy of it. However the purchaser of the information may wish to own it exclusively so that he or she can control its dissemination and the economic benefit derived from it. At the same time the purchaser of information may be able to resell the purchase whilst keeping a copy of it and undermining the prospects of the original possessor. In these circumstances control over copyright is decisive for the economic exploitation of information.

Clearly some information possessors prefer to give their information away through posters, television advertisements, flyers, classified advertisements, listings magazines, free sheets or by some electronic means like Oracle or Ceefax. Free information 'pushed' by its possessors is a material that oils our market systems though it is not without its detractors. Knowing that information is being disseminated freely seekers will engage in monitoring behaviour to locate the information that they need. That is, they will devote economic resources (their time) to collecting and assembling pushed information. Occasionally specialist businesses will perform this function, for a price, for information seekers and the seekers trade off their time for the fee they pay the intermediary. Travel agencies act in an analogous manner. Instead of the seekers of information on holidays ploughing through all the brochures, they can use the facilities of the travel agent who will key in the seekers' particulars (location, dates, price etc.) and extract a relevant selection from the holidays on offer.

Those who criticise free pushed information draw attention to its potential for deception through misinformation and some argue that since misinformation is cheaper to produce than valid information there is a lot of it about. Clearly information seekers will be aware of possible deceptions or will learn from experience. Consequently they will be involved in evaluating information. This could be a costly process at least in terms of seekers' time. Deception and evaluation introduce noise into the economic system which is damaging to the seeker and the valid possessor. For one it wastes time and for the other it threatens the viability of business operations. To solve this difficulty, respectable information providers attempt to authenticate their information. In the material goods sectors this is the function of guarantees. For the information business it is more difficult since it involves building up a reputation for honesty and accuracy. Companies providing information about themselves to potential investors use auditors to guarantee the authenticity of the information provided. There are also public bodies concerned to punish misinformation providers whilst trade associations are often formed with self-regulatory functions to oversee authentication of information. Of course, a similar problem exists in the hardware sector but there it is possible to 'test drive' products before purchase. When information is sold normally it is not revealed before it is purchased and when it is pushed there is no knowing its authenticity except by reference to the provider's reputation or the guarantees of associations and regulatory powers of the relevant authorities.

Information and communications technologies have been changing the shape of all of the information businesses. Through the application of these technologies information has increasingly become tradeable, that is it is either traded or it has the potential to be traded. More information could be for sale or is available at much lower resource costs than in the past. Information is increasingly entering formal markets and the ICTs are playing a key role in this process.

These are characteristics of the information economy and the information society. It follows that these developments mean there will be an expanding role for the information behaviour of research, pulling, pushing, monitoring deception/authentication and evaluation. In turn this implies regulatory intervention (especially for authentication and evaluation). Such a consideration runs counter to contemporary views on liberalised and deregulated information markets free of government intervention. The characteristics of information set in motion forms of information behaviour that are economic in nature and sometimes result in forms of business activities. A self-generating process of the business of information has thereby been established and this is a characteristic of the information economy.

Pricing information

In the hardware industries pricing is a relatively simple affair. The price of an article will reflect its cost of production and market conditions — what the market will take. Where competition prevails prices will not diverge for long from the costs of producing units (including some reasonable return which also reflects risks). Usually costs are measurable (at least on average) and the unit of production is easily defined. Prices and costs will guide the producer to a profitable level of output. A manufacturer can only push up the price of a product and restrict its output levels where it has a significant degree of market power. But usually for any given price a manufacturer in the material goods sectors will want to see as many items as possible. These clear-cut conditions do not prevail in the information business.

The price a firm has to pay to push information can be reasonably calculated. It will reflect the numbers of a defined target population a particular medium reaches. The 'demographics' of the intended audience are a major contributor to the price charged by the seller of audiences. These demographics have typically been defined in terms of socio-economic groups (A, B, C1, etc.) though now the targets may be defined in terms of 'life-style'. As a quantitative exercise there is a degree of imprecision in measuring both a medium's reach and its 'readership' of a particular target.

Hirschleifer (1972) recognises five attributes of information that influence its value to the user or producer and by implication the price it could fetch. The first of these is its certainty. This is a concept of information which perceives a distribution of the probability of an event occurring, where the probability of something occurring is 1 (or 100 per cent) then the information is certain and as its probability declines, say to 0.5, information is less certain and less valuable. Intuitively, we would be more willing to pay more for information on a 'dead cert' than for something that has 'a good chance'.

The diffusion of information also affects its value. For pushed information its value to the producer is maximised when the information gains maximum diffusion in the target population. For information that is sold the position is different. In some instances information has a high value only when it is narrowly diffused or when there is a monopoly over it. Through the use of the information the possessor or purchaser expects to gain a competitive advantage but this cannot be realised if the information is widely dispersed. For example, information of a particular technology may only command a high value when knowledge of it rests with one owner. In other cases information of a technology may be sold quite inexpensively because the possessor wants to build a 'standard' which can be developed profitably at a later date. Equally, someone wishing to sell a resource may sell fairly certain information about it cheaply because he or she fears that at auction the resource may not realise its full potential price.

Clearly two more factors have a direct bearing on the value of information and thereby its price. These are its applicability and its decision relevance. Some information may only be applicable to one economic agent so that the seller is faced by a monopsonist and the exchange may be unbalanced. Where the information is more generally applicable, that is there are more potential buyers, a wider market will develop for it.

Though information may be applicable to a particular economic enterprise it may not be relevant to current decisions and therefore only command a modest price. Conversely, it may be very relevant with obvious consequences for its value and price. Finally, the content of information will contribute to the determination of its price and value. Broadly, content can concern the environment of business (for example, appropriate regulations and their interpretation) which includes the strategies of other participants where the content forms market intelligence. Alternatively, the content of information may be classified according to the constituents of supply and demand functions. Here content can be constructed around notions of tastes, resources, technology, and the price and quantities of traded goods.

Clearly the price of information depends on the complex interaction of many factors and the process is made more complicated by the absence of any unit of measurement. We know what a kilo of coal, a litre of oil and a watt of electricity are. But what is a unit of information?

Business strategies and concerns

The characteristics of information as a commodity and the special nature of information markets demand that businesses operating in the sector adopt particular strategies and focus on certain concerns that are not so pressing for firms in the material goods sectors.

In normal circumstances material goods are literally consumed, durables lasting longer than perishables. The process of destruction occurs simultaneously with consumption and may lead to a form of instantaneous decay or to a long and gradual deterioration. However, it is common for material goods to be metaphorically reconsumed when in fact they have been destroyed. Each morning we consume the same breakfast cereal even though yesterday it was truly consumed. Equally, we demand the same services from motor cars, cookers and printers even though they are being worn out by use. In all of these cases the good in question is being reconsumed. These dynamics form the normal background to industrial businesses strategies.

Clearly the notion of reconsumption can apply to information. The user requires the computer-operating system and the sales ledger package to provide the same services whenever they are loaded. Equally we want the same information from a reference manual or timetable when we use it. However the act of consumption and reconsumption is not accompanied by the act of destruction. Information is not consumed in consumption or reconsumption. Of course, not all material goods and information are reconsumed or are only brought into use occasionally. Consequently there is a frequency of reconsumption dimension to the nature of goods. Newspapers are an extreme example of a product that is never reconsumed — who wants yesterday's paper? Television programming has a similar but more intense nature since who wants the previous programme? Consequently these businesses entail constant product renewal. Newspapers are reconstructed afresh on a daily basis and with the aid of new information technologies some attempts have been made to reconstruct them in much shorter time spans to provide 24-hour newspapers. Television programming is reconstructed on a real-time basis. Many databases are also reconstructed on a real-time basis, especially those dealing with financial information. Firms in these sectors wishing to remain viable will need to reach their markets continually because they cannot exist on a single product line. Consequently, each day these firms will have to re-establish their relationship with their customer base. Of course, marketing is important to producers in the material goods sector but for information it has an especially urgent status.

In these instances, formats of schedules and layout are used but the actual content of information is new. Strictly speaking, each newspaper edition or television transmission is a prototype. It has been researched but there is little development. This characteristic is in stark contrast to industrial goods where gradual product development and updating is used to improve the product and extend its life cycle.

Innovation and novelty are the dominating features of business operations whose information is continuously renewed. Running costs are of less importance given the condition of reproduction rather than production. But initial costs are more difficult to control in an environment where there is only a loose connection between inputs and outputs. A distinguishing feature of production in the information business is an emphasis on novelty and creativity, neither of which sit easily in strictly constructed production functions.

Some information products are not consumed in use yet are reused on a frequent basis. Here are the packaged products of the computer software industry — all those standard applications as well as all the operating systems — as well as standard works of reference. The customer will use the services of the software product regularly but will not destroy the product in this process so there will be no requirement for repeat purchases. For the producer of the computer software and reference works market demand is constrained by this characteristic.

To overcome this barrier to business expansion the producer can try constantly to enhance the software product and make previous versions of an application obsolete. Such a strategy may involve expanding or simplifying the functions performed within a given application or adding to the number of applications a package will perform to produce combined word processing, database and spread sheet packages. Given the ease of copying software, copyright and the licensing of copying becomes a central concern to business operations in the computer software business.

Many information products are used infrequently but are not consumed in use. Books, recorded music and sell-through video cassettes are all examples of information products that are bought and reconsumed at intervals. In these circumstances it would be an inappropriate business strategy to rely on a single product. Publishing one book or CD or even a limited range would not guarantee prolonged business success. Further, demand is particularly uncertain in these areas. Here width of product line is the dominating preoccupation. Typically, catalogues of individual products are marketed from which the consumer makes a choice. The catalogue represents the stock of available software to which new publications are added. At the same time some slow moving items are deleted so that the catalogue evolves over time.

This notion is not too different from the strategy pursued in many newspapers and magazines. These are constructed of many items not all of which appeal to all readers. The task for the newspaper or magazine is to present a sufficiently attractive bundle of items, some of which have no appeal, so that the reader will buy the entire product. The catalogue works in an analogous manner except that purchasers choose individual items from a catalogue that is marketed in its entirety.

The publishing sector has experienced successive waves of takeovers and mergers. This is partially explained by the desire to expand catalogues. A similar wave of mergers and acquisitions has occurred in the computer software sector with this same consideration as a contributory factor.

Width and length

Another feature of information publishing is the importance of economies of scope. Economies of scale refer to the length of production runs and are the dominating concern of material industrial goods production. Economies of scope refer to the advantages to be gained from the width of different product lines. Typically, many broadly defined information products are recycled in a largely unaltered state in different product markets. A film will become a video or a television programme and it may generate a record of its sound-track. The whole process may have started life as a book. Through exploiting essentially the same product, blueprint or idea in different media the copyright holders can maximise their returns. This strategy lies behind the success of Rupert Murdoch's companies, the Maxwell enterprises and firms like Bertelsmann. Economies of scope provide the incentive for acquisitions and mergers across the media with newspaper publishers buying into books and television.

Demand uncertainty

Market research is commonplace in business, especially in the industrial goods sector. Its purpose is to assess demand and use the results in the design of products. Though demand can never be precisely predicted, businesses in the material goods sector can expect some probablistic estimate of demand conditions which they can include in their planning processes. The Ford Edsel and Sinclair C5 are shining examples of products that went wrong. It is generally rare for such catastrophes to take place.

Conditions in the information business are very different. In any year a very large number of records are released, books published and films exhibited but only a small fraction of these attain the status of a 'hit'. Success in these sectors can lead to very substantial earnings given the condition of reproduction as opposed to production. Further, the income generated by hits covers the losses and low returns earned on the 'misses' and 'near hits'. However, it is extremely difficult to predict which particular offering will be a hit or to assume that there will be a string of hits emanating from a previous hit — the 'one hit wonder' phenomenon. Consequently, the information business experiences both uncertainty in initial costs and uncertainty of demand. This means that expenditure on product research and prototypes often relates imprecisely to the earnings from the product. Similar demand conditions characterise the computer software sector. For every Lotus 1-2-3 or Word-perfect success story there are dozens of Cabbage 7-8-9s or Ritespells that go unnoticed. In the book, record and audio-visual sectors, businesses pursue the strategy of exploiting economies of scope. A product may be a miss in one medium but it could generate some earnings in another. Even dud films can always get some return from the video rental and television markets.

Policy matters

Clearly, the information business is peculiar. It does not lend itself to analysis by the standard tool kit of an economist. Neither does it rest easily within the normal business strategy textbooks. The information business is far removed from traditional industries, like brewing, where both economics and business discplines can add to our understanding of the dynamics of the sector. But the business of information does not just challenge our modes of analysis. It also poses problems for policy-makers.

The matter of copyright policy deserves, and receives elsewhere, a thorough examination. It forms a central focus of debate at international fora such as the GATT Uruguay Round where the point at issue is the distribution of income. Generally, copyright over intellectual property raises matters of significant social and economic concern. These can be reduced to a potential for conflict between social and economic objectives.

In many circumstances the absence of enforceable property rights over information would act to discourage producers from producing information. Such an outcome would be detrimental to a wide constituency. But in other circumstances enforceable and exclusive property rights would grant their holders a valuable monopoly with which they could exploit a wide constituency. The problem for policy-makers is to draw a generally applicable copyright balance between these two conditions. Such a balance should both encourage the viable production and equitable diffusion of information. Here policy-makers are delineating the domains of the public and private spheres of activity.

Another important policy matter arises from the potential for conflict between sensible business strategies and the public interest. In the above description of the dynamics of the business of information two trends have been emphasised. These are the growing prevalence of both vertical integration and of repackaging products into different markets. When we add to these trends the increasing ease of moving across national frontiers we end up with integrated multi-media multi-national corporations. This in turn means oligopolistic structures in the supply of information. Taken to an extreme we could find that economic dynamics have produced the 'Pravda' model of information provision. (This matter is fully developed in Marian Banks' chapter in this volume.) Of course these structures are common in the material goods sectors. But information is peculiar.

It is its social and political status, summed up in the adage 'information is power', that firstly distinguishes information from other economic goods. And it is the extreme difficulty of validating information that further sets it apart from material goods. The problem of integrated multi-media multi-national oligopolies on the supply side is the political and social position they occupy. In controlling the supply of information they control the destiny of economies.

At a fundamental level the very laudable practices of businesses in the information sector may run counter to the public interest in democratic structures. All choices are based on information. But we do not always trust information, rather we judge it. We are best served by the clash of independent conflicting views, be these about the government's handling of the economy, the workability of a technology or the likely performance of a company. But the dynamics of the information business run contrary to these conditions. Again policy-makers are faced with the issue of defining the spheres of public interest and the domain of the private sector.

Such philosophical issues do not arise in brewing, car manufacturing or agriculture because information is funny (peculiar).

Bibliography

Hirschleifer, J., 1973, 'Where are we in the theory of information?', *American Economic Review*, **63** (2), 31–39.

3 Mapping the information business: integration for flexibility

Asu Aksoy

Introduction

At a time when the virtues of vertical integration and diversification strategies for conducting certain types of businesses are being questioned and corporations in various industries are shedding parts of their activities to concentrate on what is called the 'core' activity, firms operating in the information business are generally pursuing integration strategies for global expansion and growth. Robert Maxwell, for example, observed in his chairman's statement in the 1987 MCC report that 'the accomplishment of our strategic aim of becoming one of the top ten global media and communications businesses is underwritten by our vertical strategy for growth'. News Corporation owned by Murdoch which seeks to become a 'global communications company' already holds over 150 media properties on four continents, with interests in almost every segment of the information and communication business.

Since the late 1970s, new directions in corporate structure and strategy have been proposed and experimented with in a number of business sectors. Rapid technological change and shifting patterns of international trade and competition have introduced new pressures for both small and large firms. Competitive strategy increasingly addresses questions around organisation structure, management processes and locational issues. Partnerships and alliances between competing firms are increasingly becoming common in conjunction with the rapidity of technological change and growing competitiveness in global markets. Firms involved in various manufacturing activities like chemicals, steel, textiles and machine tools have been designing and implementing new processes such as computer integrated manufacturing, whereby product differentiation can be achieved at the capital goods level.

This means that they are trying and implementing new strategies based on customising products and offering differentiated goods alongside the standardised and mass-produced ones. The organisational structure of firms is continuously being revised leading to a sophisticated juggling act to keep certain activities in-house and dispense with others. Vertical disintegration strategies are being pursued more vehemently in some sectors with increasing reliance on subcontracting and networking arrangements between firms.

These trends in corporate strategy and structure are interpreted by some as indicative of a broader socio-economic change. Concepts like 'flexible specialisation' (Piore and Sabel, 1984), 'flexible regime of accumulation' (Scott, 1988), 'flexible accumulation' (Jessop *et al.*, 1987), despite their considerable differences, all point to the emergence of new forms of capital and labour organisation. The unifying theme in all these approaches is that the political economy of the advanced industrialised countries is undergoing a restructuring process. The flexible specialisation argument, for instance, states that the emerging trends, if understood and acted upon appropriately by the policy-forming bodies, can open up a new avenue for the restructuring of capitalist economies. This new avenue, it is argued, would be based on the appropriation of 'flexible specialisation' strategies which are markedly different from the mass-production strategies of the past (see Piore and Sabel, 1984).

Flexible specialisation strategies are seen to lead to a shift from mass production methods exploiting massive internal economies of scale, technical division of labour and standardisation of outputs to flexibly specialised production methods. Changes in production methods are followed by the changes in the management practices and firm organisation models. It is argued that there is a trend towards:

— the replacement of large and dedicated fixed capital by flexible, widely applicable and general purpose machinery;
— the replacement of a deskskilled and fragmented labour force by a flexible and multiskilled labour force;
— the replacement of the mass production line which necessitated large and integrated companies by a flexible, differentiated and customised product line that can accommodate small and flexibly specialised firms.

It is suggested that it is no longer necessary to integrate vertically in order to guarantee the supply of resources and sale of products. Networks of suppliers and subcontractors are said to be replacing vertically integrated structures (Antonelli, 1988). New management theories argue that big is frequently coming to mean a collection of smaller firms in new organisational combinations (Peters, 1989). Peter Drucker (1988) predicts that the typical large business in the future will be information-based with fewer than half the levels of management of its counterpart today, and its structure will resemble more a hospital or a symphony orchestra.

The degree to which these trends in corporate strategy and structure can become portents of a more fundamental change in the way capitalist production is organised and carried out is a contested issue. However, it is important to understand changes in the factors shaping and determining corporate strategies and structures. A crucial factor in the analysis of contemporary economic change and new trends in corporate strategy and structure is the emergence of powerful competitive nations, such as Japan, Korea and Taiwan. Faced with intensified competition on an increasingly global scale, corporations adopt new forms of production and labour management so as to overcome national boundaries, to capture and coordinate critical inputs and to achieve world-scale advantages. Globalisation of competition and the increasing vulnerability of national markets to competition underpins intensified rates of commercial, technological and organisational innovation. Companies are having to operate and compete in the world arena in terms of quality, efficiency, product variety and the close understanding of markets. Global corporations are increasingly involved in time-based competition. Globalisation leads to the emergence of new types of corporate strategies and organisational structures as a response to the growing need to sustain continuous product innovation and market share. Achieving flexibility is one of the ways of responding to changing and differential demand patterns for companies operating on a global scale across national boundaries and territories. Sourcing of inputs and producing of outputs globally on a flexible and just-in-time basis is becoming one of the major concerns of corporations.

These changes that are being witnessed — in production methods, organisational structures and corporate strategies — rather than being interpreted as pointers to a new regime of capitalist accumulation, might alternatively be seen as transitional responses to changing technology and market conditions. In these turbulent 'new times', large-scale producers like the semiconductor manufacturers or the international automobile industry are positioning themselves in order to achieve both economies of scope (through flexible specialisation) and scale economies (through mass production and globalisation) at the same time. It is important to place changes in corporate strategy and structures (flexible specialisation being one of the strategies) within the framework of businesses (small or large) facing turbulent times in terms of competitiveness, globalisation of markets, fast changes in technologies and labour skill requirements. Changes, certainly, are occurring in terms of the way firms adapt and adjust to new and dynamic conditions. Adjustment is the bread and butter of what firms in a market economy do in striving to acquire and defend their competitive positions. It can be argued that the magnitude of adjustment differs, in an uneven fashion, between industries, depending on the size, structure and management philosophy of the firms involved. However, as competitive pressures increase, the corporate emphasis becomes one of exploiting economies of scale and scope at the capital goods level and achieving time efficiencies at the levels of product innovation and organisational structure.

Corporate strategy and structure in the information business are shaped by similar market pressures and changes in the economic conjuncture. However, corporate responses in the information business are governed by the dynamics of the information business which display different characteristics compared to other types of activities. Firms involved in the information business are often engaged in conglomerate activities. Most of the big companies in the information business are highly integrated from production to distribution. Furthermore, these firms are integrating horizontally through mergers and acquisitions leading to the concentration of ownership. A rush of takeover bids is now taking place on an international level (as far as national regulations allow), as Marion Banks argues in the next chapter. Contrary to some arguments which suggest that the transition from Fordism to vertically-disintegrated flexible specialisation is the universal trend across different types of activities, corporate strategies in the information business point towards increasing concentration and integration.

Behind the strategies in the information business, characterised by integration, conglomeration and concentration, there lies the same business drive which is shared by firms in a variety of activities: to attain flexibility in a world economy characterised by volatility and global competition. In the following pages I shall attempt to develop a framework for the examination of the nature of corporate activity within the information business. I shall aim to demonstrate why and to what extent the information business is different, and to examine the underlying factors shaping strategies in the information business.

The information business map

The term 'business' covers all the stages that a consumption item has to go through, be it material or immaterial, in order to become a consumption good. The transformation process starts from the conception/innovation of the idea of the product and moves on to production, then to packaging and finally to distribution/dissemination. Therefore it cuts vertically through the economy which is conceptually organised into different sectors like the primary, secondary and the tertiary sectors.

In order to be able to address the question as to how strategies in the information business differ, it is helpful to conceptualise the information business as consisting of distinct stages through which the information product passes. These stages and their characteristics are captured in Figures 3.1 and 3.2.

Firms are located on the *Information Business Map* according to their main line of activities in the information production and servicing fields. Firms which are only involved in the production of information, communication and media technologies are not included in this framework. The information business map (which could be applied to any type of business) consists of four stages or quadrants (see Figure 3.1):

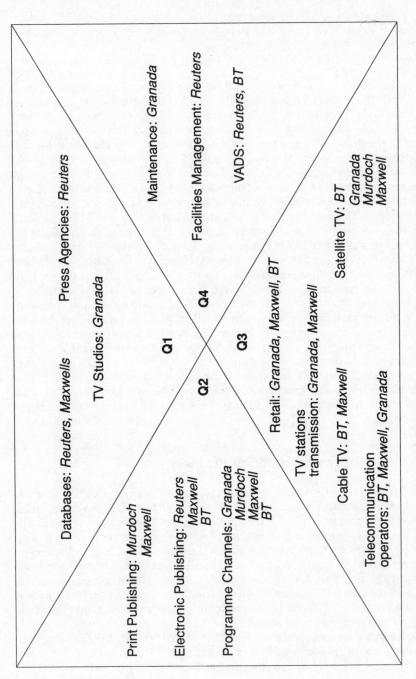

Databases: *Reuters, Maxwells*

Press Agencies: *Reuters*

Maintenance: *Granada*

TV Studios: *Granada*

Facilities Management: *Reuters*

VADS: *Reuters, BT*

Q1

Q4

Q2

Q3

Print Publishing: *Murdoch*
Maxwell

Electronic Publishing: *Reuters*
Maxwell
BT

Programme Channels: *Granada*
Murdoch
Maxwell
BT

Retail: *Granada, Maxwell, BT*

TV stations
transmission: *Granada, Maxwell*

Satellite TV: *BT*
Granada
Murdoch
Maxwell

Cable TV: *BT, Maxwell*

Telecommunication
operators: *BT, Maxwell, Granada*

Figure 3.1 *Map of major players in the UK information business: a case of vertical integration*

production/innovation/creation (Q1);
packaging/publishing/reproduction (Q2);
distribution/transmission/diffusion (Q3);
facilitation/integration/servicing (Q4).

The information business map distingushes between technologically and economically distinct stages through which the information product is commodified. It displays firms operating in this business according to their main line of activity. In the first quadrant — the production/innovation/creation quadrant — firms whose main activity consists of the production of information are included. In the second quadrant — the packaging/publishing/reproduction quadrant — firms whose main activity is to bring together and to reformat the existing information products and services are included. Packaging/publishing functions are very important in terms of enhancing the tradeability of information. The third quadrant — distribution, transmission and diffusion of information goods and services — consists of firms whose main source of revenue is through acting as the medium by which information is transmitted and distributed. Hence, the firms which would be classified under the third quadrant are telecommunications organisations and broadcasting transmission and relaying firms, such as satellite operators, wholesale and retail distributors of information products and post offices.[1]

The fourth quadrant comprises firms which perform service functions in order to enable the consumption and reconsumption of the finished product. These services might be relevant to the product itself, or they might act on the medium which provides the information product or service. Computer software services are a good example here. Without software most of the information products and services could not be provided. Marketing is another service which functions as an intermediary between the producer and the consumer.

The nature of the information business

Each stage in the information business is characterised by a different set of business concerns, market structures and technological make-up. The unifying characteristic of the information business, however, is that from the user's point of view, what matters is the information content of the product. The user is not very much concerned with the shape of the book, or the design of records and CDs. Information products are demanded for their *content* rather than for their format or conduit. Whilst a car manufacturer can enhance the demand for cars by introducing modifications such as changes of colour, number of doors, petrol consumption, in the information business, such incremental product innovations and improvements do not take place. Once a novel is written, or a news item is compiled, any further improvement or alternation to make it more user friendly or attractive will concern the packaging of the information product rather than the production of it.

In the information business, each and every product is unique and the processes for the production of information are less divisible than in the materials-processing industries such as car manufacturing. A novel can be written only once, and by a single author. This means that there is very little scope for process innovation at the production stage of information. Therefore, the pressure for firms in the information business is concentrated on being able to generate new products all the time, that is for continuous product innovation.

The information production process is a highly risky business as the main production input, that is human creativity, is transferable. Riskiness is also due to the fact that the information product is either totally destructible at the moment of consumption (like news items), or indestructible (like *Anna Karenina*). The riskiness of information production, and the fact that information production does not lend itself to process innovations, leads firms to concentrate on the packaging and distribution stages of the information business. A unique product, by virtue of its being easily transportable across different formats and conduits, is commodified in many ways and marketed to a multiplicity of audiences as widely as possible. The emphasis, in the information business, is more on exploiting the existing information in terms of reproducing it or repacking it. An important aspect of the information business lies, consequently, in the reproduction and distribution of the product. Once the master copy of an information product is available, constant product innovation is achieved at the packaging and reproduction stage. Therefore, the driving force in the information business, that is where income is generated and funding for new information products originates, is not the production quadrant but the packaging/publishing and distribution quadrants. Unlike many other businesses where the production activity itself is the main generator of income and corporate activity, in the information business it is the downstream activities like distribution and marketing which are the point of corporate focus.

The nature and the evolution of corporate strategies in the information business can be better understood by examining the distinguishing characteristics of the stages of the information business. Figure 3.2 draws an outline of these characteristics in terms of:

— number and size distribution of sellers and buyers;
— barriers to entry and exit;
— extent and character of product differentiation;
— international competition and tradeability;
— demand elasticity.

The production stage

The information production quadrant (Q1) is populated by large numbers of actors, who are usually not organised as business entities, but as authors,

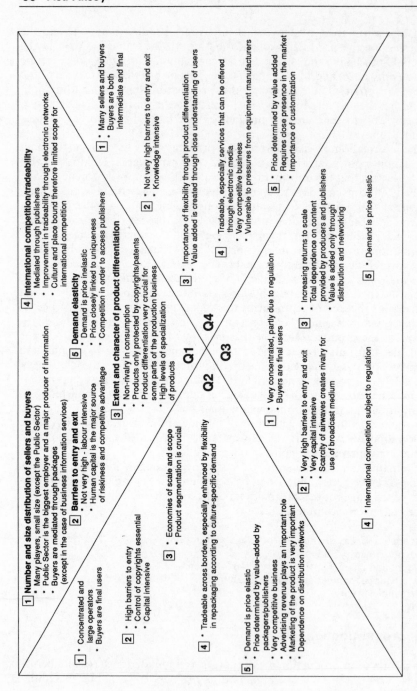

Figure 3.2 *Map of market structure of each stage of information business*

composers, scriptwriters, etc. Firms in this quadrant are usually small with the exception of the public sector. In so far as the public sector gets involved in commercial information production, its size makes it one of the largest in the information business.

Buyers of information products from the first quadrant are numerous as well, ranging from final consumers of books and newspapers to firms purchasing information for intermediate use, such as consultancy services. However, information producers usually do not come into contact directly with the consumers (except consultancies and management, search and coordination specialists).

Entry and exit barriers in the first quadrant are rather different from any other type of activity given that the central asset in the production stage is creativity. So long as firms can guarantee a constant flow of creative ideas they can enter the market-place. However, given that the essence of information production depends on the employment of creative human capital, this dependence introduces an element of risk in the short-term investment decisions in production. Creative human capital can be highly transportable and it might prove to be very difficult to appropriate the full value of the output of the creative labour because of the 'leaky' nature of information. This type of riskiness can discourage prospective producers from entering the market.

The lack of standardisability of the information product can also act as a barrier to entry. Information production is perhaps the only type of activity in which standardisation of product does not and cannot take place. Each time a new information product or service is produced it is novel and different, not exactly like what has been produced before. Not only the product itself but also the production process cannot easily be standardised. Lack of standardisation means that information producers cannot exploit economies of scale in the production of information. This means that competition in the information production stage is not based on prices and on bringing down costs through long-product runs, but is based on such factors as quality, timeliness and appropriateness. In connection with the lack of economies of scale and standardisation in the production process, learning costs involved in innovation for a new information product are very high. This is partially because each time the product has to be created from scratch, but more crucially it is to do with the nature of the information output as a cultural product whose consumption is determined by the cultural, aesthetic and information requirements of the consumers.

Competition among the information producers is directed at obtaining access to the packaging and distribution channels and not directed at increasing market share, as the producer is usually cut off from the final user and requires a mediator to gain access to markets. Authors and artists compete in terms of achieving the best deal from a publisher/packager and distributor. However, in some segments of the information production business — such as business consultancy, specialist information providers and databases — competition for market share takes place. In such cases, the competition for market share is not carried out in the form of price wars but rather through the ability to understand user requirements and produce a customised product. This is because of the price inelasticity of demand for certain types of information products, such as consultancy information, where what is critical for the consumer of information products is their timeliness, uniqueness and appropriateness, and not their price.

In cases where the role of the packager/publisher and distributor is minimal and where the information producer sells directly to the customer, the value added is appropriated by the producer at the instant the information product is sold to the customer. Therefore the protection of property rights and appropriability conditions does not matter much in such types of services and products. However, in other types of information products, where the information producer needs intermediaries to get to the customer, the conditions of appropriability are crucial. Unless information producers can claim property rights over their produce, they cannot guarantee their share of the value added. In most cases, the only way information producers can protect their product is through copyrights and patents. Copyrights and patents constitute the only ways through which revenue flows into the first quadrant of the information business can take place. Furthermore, these property rights are the sole means whereby an information producer can control the manner in which information products can be used and sold. They can, effectively, be used as entry barriers to publishers and distributors who have to acquire these rights.

The publishing and reproduction stage

The market structure in the packaging/publishing/reproduction quadrant (Q2) is very different. First of all, it is based on exploiting exclusive but wasting assets. It is a business of franchises and brand loyalty which can last for generations or can vanish in a very short period of time. The players in this area are few, each activity being concentrated in the hands of big publishing/reproduction houses. These players compete to get access to the information products produced in Q1, and the only way to do so is to own the rights to this material, that is either to own the copyrights or to own the talent itself.

The first step in turning a song, for example, into a revenue-earning asset is for a composer to sell the rights to the new composition for an advance and a share of the future royalties. The publisher then collects the royalty fees from the various entertainment media and, after deducting the composer's share, retains the remainder, known as the net publisher's share. Therefore, the way to raise the chances of commercial viability for a publishing business is to increase the range of copyright material in its portfolio and package the material in a way that is suitable for a variety of different distribution media. Thorn EMI, for instance, which has around 12 per cent of world music publishing revenues, rivalling Warner-Chappell, publishes the same material on record, CD, cassette, video, sheet music and film. The implied notion, here, is that of a cross-subsidy between individual products, between 'hits' and 'misses', and between the different channels of distribution.

Control of the copyright or patented material is a major entry barrier into the publishing business, and it is often cheaper to buy a company that has already built up these assets rather than start from scratch. This leads to concentration and increasing internationalisation of the publishing and reproduction activities. Apart from the increased economies of scope through a diversified portfolio, other powerful stimulants behind the merger moves in the publishing and reproduction quadrant are, first of all, to do with the possibility of benefiting from the economies of scale in marketing and distribution that a merger operation can give rise to, and, secondly, the need to guarantee advertising revenue. Given that advertisement revenues can be generated by a variety of mass media channels, such as newspapers and broadcasting, competition for advertisement revenue encourages cross-media ownership. A newspaper publisher, for instance, can maximise its advertisement revenue if it can own a competing TV station. Through merger strategies, which enable the control of the different media, companies can be put in a better position to enhance the segmentation of their product in terms of time, delivery system and geographic location. Segmentation means more revenues, whereby the exclusive copyright owner can repackage the same product in successive stages, first releasing it on film, then on video, then on TV and satellite channels.

In the publishing and reproduction business, the proximity to the end-user is crucial as the published material, whether on print, electronic or on celluloid, has to be targeted. Effective targeting requires access to a multiplicity of conduits, that is to the means of distribution. Consequently, one of the corporate strategies in this activity is to get favourable deals with the distributors, or actually to control the distribution business.

The distribution stage

Distribution on the whole is a very capital intensive business which is expensive to start and to run, and is characterised by increasing returns to scale. Distribution channels are regulated heavily in terms of the number of actors and in terms of what they can do and cannot do, which often leads to a regulated concentration of ownership. The reasons behind the regulation of different media are complex. In broadcasting the scarcity of radio waves has led to restricting entry. In telecommunications, the concern to guarantee universal service, and the fact that it is prohibitively expensive to build a telecommunication network, has led to a regulated monopoly of supply. As a result of the regulatory barriers and the prohibitive costs of entry to the distribution business, publishers and reproduction companies often find that they cannot enter the distribution market, that they cannot bypass it, and that they are price takers. Distribution operators, by means of actually controlling the distribution channels, play a very important role in terms of how information products are sold in markets, in terms of the geographical reach of services and quality and price of goods and services.

The increasing convergence between telecommunications and broadcasting carries considerable implications for the companies involved in the distribution business as well as for information publishers and reproducers. The convergence process is broadening the range of distribution media (thus cable TV networks can be used for interactive data services as well as for TV entertainment services, and telecommunication networks can transmit high quality pictures as well as telephone conversations). The long-standing distinctions between telecommunications and broadcasting are being eroded by technological change, and by the recent deregulatory moves in both telecommunication and broadcasting areas by various governments. If they can reposition themselves, this convergence represents significant opportunities for those information carriers and distributors that are already in this business.

Another implication of the convergence process is that the distribution companies no longer feel restricted only to the carriage of information, but target information production and publishing activities as new businesses to get into in order to derive maximum benefit out of the available carriage capacity. The capacity and the reach of the new carrier technologies, such as satellites, is such that the carrier companies are increasingly looking into the possibilities for vertically integrating into the production stage of the information business in order to guarantee the flow of information products. These integration strategies which are driven by a desire to benefit from economies of scale in distribution can take different forms, such as joint ventures, tie-in relations, or long-term contractual linkages. The existence of economies of scale in the distribution stage, economies of scope in the production and reproduction stages, and the convergence of the technological conduits — such as broadcasting and telecommunications for the delivery and diffusion of information goods and services — suggests the intensification of competition in the information business. In this competitive environment, the distribution companies, with their tentacles plugged into the consumption sphere, will play a substantial role.

The servicing stage

The fourth quadrant is where all services related to the information business are placed. They facilitate the production, packaging and distribution stages of the information business, and, like computer services, they function as the interface between the final users of information and the equipment necessary to support the handling of information. There are numerous players in the fourth quadrant as the barriers for entry and exit are not very high, and there are practically no regulations to limit the extent of activities. The services provided are always bespoke. They have to correspond to the specific requirement of the user. The achievement of flexibility, for this reason, is crucial for the service providers Flexibility in the service business can be enhanced by offering a variety of services and maximising economies of scope.

However, there is one major limitation for the service providers, and that is their dependence on hardware and therefore on hardware manufacturers. As hardware configurations change, the service provider has to adapt, and maybe acquire new expertise, to be able to stay in the market-place. For this reason, the service provider has to be flexible from the very start and avoid getting locked into a specific type of technological system. By being able to shift between different technological systems and a variety of user demands, the service provider can actually add more value to the product than the manufacturer.

The service provider acts as an interface between the user and the information goods, services and technologies producer. Therefore, the service provider has to be very close to the user in order to judge user requirements, and also close to the producer. This type of tension suggests that not many firms can survive in the services market-place. It is a very competitive market as services can be substituted by users' own internal service facilities, and additionally by the distribution operators and equipment manufacturers. Because of their established knowledge and capital base, equipment manufacturers and distributors can become formidable competitors if they choose to.

The service market is highly volatile. It is also dependent on the extent to which intermediary functions are required for the consumption of information products, technologies and services. The survival of the firms in the fourth quadrant is, therefore, based on strategies that emphasise the importance of adding value and achieving flexibility. By being very close to the users and producers, and by catering for their demands, service firms acquire specific learning which is difficult to transfer. This learning can become a very valuable source of comparative advantage, increasing the innovative potential of these firms.

Information hardware

An important dimension of the information business concerns to what extent and how the information hardware suppliers — such as VCR, television set, computing and telecommunication equipment manufacturers — position themselves to get involved in the different stages of the information business. Our information business map only covers firms whose primary output is information products and services and not technologies. Therefore IBM and Sony, for instance, are in the map in so far as they are involved, through joint ventures, mergers and acquisitions, in the production of information goods and services. Equipment manufacturers have always been involved in the provision of facilitating services which provide the interface between the user and the equipment. However, the drive for the manufacturers to get further into the information business has been increasing over the last years. As an analyst at Wertheim Scroder argues, 'if you are a manufacturer and can expand your marketshare a couple of percentage points by marketing Lawrence of Arabia along with your hardware, you will make a lot of money' (*Financial Times*, 28 September 1989).

Recent examples of hardware manufacturers entering into the information content provision market are numerous. The purchase of CBS Records (US) and Columbia Pictures (US), the world's largest music recording and film companies, by Sony of Japan constitutes a recent example of the corporate strategies in the information business that are centred around integrating on a global scale to be able to exploit synergies that emerge across media, and between software and hardware.

Corporate strategies in the information business

Vertical, horizontal and cross-media integration strategies are pursued vehemently in the information business, alongside the tendencies towards more use of subcontracting and towards new types of inter-corporate links. As in any other type of business, firms in the information business constantly revise their competitive strategies which involve 'make or buy' decisions and corporate links. Strategic choice also covers such issues as the extension of markets, investment for R&D and innovative ventures. However, because of the peculiarities of the information product — in terms of its appropriability conditions, technological make-up, labour intensity and differing dynamics of economies of scale and scope — corporate strategies in the information business are shaped by different concerns and factors from traditional industrial activities.

Firms in the first quadrant are constantly under takeover pressures from publishers and distributors. These pressures are shaped by short-term return considerations, where the publisher or the distributor is interested in investing in a creative idea on a short-term basis. Short-term transactions are preferred when the riskiness of the product is high. Given the high level of risk involved in information production and its R&D intensity, the production stage does not easily attract long-term investment for starting up new operations. The publishers and distributors prefer long-term binding contracts once the value of the product is proven. Therefore, the sustainability of continuous product innovation in the information business is very much dependent on the time span of contractual arrangements between the buyers and the sellers. The fact that the information production market-place is composed of a large number of small players can become a competitive weapon for the packaging and distribution companies to reduce prices and to use short-termism.

In the face of these pressures, one of the defensive strategies that the information producers follow involves organising into more powerful and bigger concerns. Information producer firms merge in order to achieve the advantages of size; to be able to gain access to markets by leveraging capital and management; and to stand firm against potential hostile takeover bids.

Apart from mergers and acquisitions, another way for the producer firms to achieve more bargaining power is to diversify into the other parts of the information business, such as publishing and reproduction. Diversification strategies might involve cross-media mergers, acquisitions and joint ventures. Or they might involve new types of inter-corporate arrangements between producers, publishers and distributors.

Within the publishing and reproduction stage, different types of strategies are exercised. Increasing concentration and internationalisation are the characteristics of this market-place. Comparative advantage in this segment of the information business is created through the exploitation of exclusive assets generated by the production sphere. Competitive strategies in the publishing and reproduction stage involve, on the one hand, ensuring continuous product innovation without committing huge resources, and, on the other, selling these products as widely as possible to mass and niche markets in order to benefit from economies of scale and scope in distribution. The need for a close understanding and the targeting of consumer markets leads these companies to emphasise downstream activities such as marketing and distribution. Flexibility in organising the distribution channels is increasingly perceived as being vital to maximise the revenues. Hence, cross-media deals and vertical integration strategies into the distribution media have become a central corporate response in the publishing and reproduction activities.

Another crucial aspect of the corporate strategies in the publishing and reproduction stage is the increasing concentration of the market-place through mergers. As the distribution companies increasingly seek to integrate their operations into the publishing and reproduction fields, firms in the publishing sphere join forces and assets through mergers.

The drive for vertical integration by the distribution companies into the information production, publishing and reproduction businesses is shaped by the need to guarantee the flow of inputs. This tendency is especially pronounced in distribution businesses, such as telecommunications and broadcasting, where the investment levels required to set up a distribution network, and consequently the need for utilising the distribution resources as flexibly and consistently as possible, are very high. An important restriction on distributors' attempts to diversify into the other segments of the information business arises from regulatory barriers. As regulatory barriers are relaxed, which is currently taking place in telecommunications, broadcasting and cable activities, firms involved in these activities are able to move to other segments of the information business.

The services quadrant is another area where there are many players and a wave of mergers. The UK computer services industry, for instance, has, over the last years been undergoing a major restructuring as a result of increasing mergers and acquisitions. The bidders can be equipment companies or other software houses. Firms which specialise in the provision of services are extremely vulnerable as they have to serve as intermediaries between hardware and software. They have to serve the users of information goods, services and technologies, as well as the producers of them. Hence, they are very much subjected to the strategies of the users and the producers. The service companies, then, have to search for means of attaining flexibility. This can be achieved by being able to offer a variety of services using the same basis of capital and labour investment. This is how they can avoid being locked into an unpredictable and uncertain relationship with hardware manufacturers, and how they can spread their customer base across different types of customised applications. The underlying emphasis in the service area is to be able to offer a variety of specialised services on a flexible basis according to demand patterns.

Conclusion

A tentative conclusion that can be drawn from the analysis so far suggests that there are very compelling reasons for firms in the downstream end of the information business to become involved in cross-media ownership and in vertical and horizontal integration. The corporate emphasis in the information business, which is characterised by economies of scale and scope in the distribution of information products rather than in the production of them, is on extending markets. The growth of market size, both geographically and in terms of customers, can be achieved through access to multi-media distribution channels and through close knowledge of customer demands. The two quadrants that add value to the information product in a significant way, that is the reproduction and the servicing quadrants (quadrants 2 and 4) come under heavy attack from the integration strategies of the distributors. The incentive and the driving force for the distributors towards vertical and horizontal integration is the need for them to utilise their capital intensive assets in a flexible way.

The way to attain flexibility in the information business is to integrate. This allows the firms to benefit from economies of size and economies of scope, and allows them to widen the possible channels of distribution in order to benefit from economies of scale. Competitive strategy in the information business is shaped by the need to achieve flexibility through integration. Integration in turn leads to concentration.

Information businesses are also highly vulnerable in terms of entry from all types of activities, especially the information technology producers and the capital intensive distribution companies. As technologies which handle, process and transmit information converge, the entry conditions for distribution and vertically integrated and strong media companies into new information markets becomes easier (see Figure 3.3 for the vertically integrated structure of the UK information business). Regulatory policies and frameworks can play an important role as a barrier mechanism for the excessive concentration and integration of the information business.

Sustainability is a particular problem for those segments of the information business which are characterised by high risks, high R&D intensity and a large

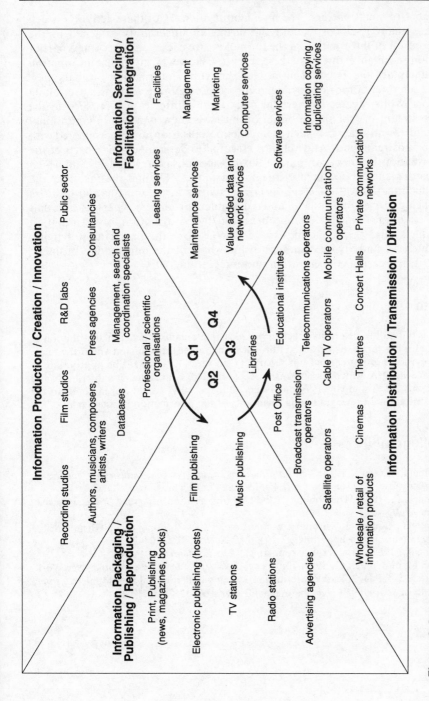

Figure 3.3 *Map of the information business*

number of small players. The high labour-intensity of these activities which makes them very costly, and the degree of uncertainty attached to the generation of information in the form of creative ideas, can become a barrier for long-term investments in these activities. However, given that information products are the essential inputs for the whole information business, new types of inter-corporate arrangements and corporate strategies are taking shape. Whilst aggressive vertical integration strategies are pursued in the downstream end of the information business, new types of organisational structures and strategies, such as flexible specialisation, are experimented with in the upstream end. And yet, it is essential to determine which parts of the information business can pursue flexible specialisation strategies and which parts are subject to intense integration moves. Despite the fact that the production/innovation/creation type activities in the information business are being carried out by small and independent producers, what is clear is that the scale of financial commitment for the distribution of information products, and the economies to be gained from the distribution activity, dictates the underlying dynamics of the whole of the information business: that is, increasing concentration and integration.

Note

1 It is difficult to determine whether broadcasting organisations fulfil distribution or publishing functions because in broadcasting, most transmission and programme provision are not carried out separately. In the UK, it would be appropriate to place the INA, which leases transmitters to the ITV companies, as a distributor and classify ITV companies as publishers. But the BBC would appear both in the distribution and programming quadrants of the information business map.

Bibliography

Antonelli, C. (ed.), 1988, *New Information Technology and Industrial Change: the Italian Case*, Kluwer Academic Publishers, Dordrecht.

Drucker, P., 1988, 'The coming of the new organisation', *Harvard Business Review*, Jan.–Feb.

Jessop, B., Bonnet, K., Bromley, S. and Ling, T., 1987, 'Popular capitalism, flexible accumulation and left strategy', *New Left Review*, 165, 104–22.

Peters, T., 1989, 'Tomorrow's companies', *The Economist*, 4 March.

Piore, M. and Sabel, C., 1984, *The Second Industrial Divide*, Basic Books, New York.

Scott, A.J., 1988, 'Flexible production systems and regional development', *International Journal of Urban and Regional Research*, **12** (2), 171–86.

4 Is more less? The dynamics of the information industry
Marion Banks

Introduction

The European information and communications industry is currently being restructured by the interaction of three key forces: technical change; the emergence of a political and economic philosophy which stresses the role of markets as an allocative mechanism; and business strategies which are increasingly 'transnational'. The combination of these forces is producing changes in the market structure of the European information industry, with multi-media, multi-national businesses becoming increasingly dominant.

Developments in both cable and satellite technology have created a vast increase in transmission capacity which has undermined the long-standing belief that a limitation on broadcasting existed as a result of spectrum scarcity. In the European countries which have developed cable infrastructures for television transmission, multi-channel access is now available in addition to the traditional terrestrial television service. Belgium, for instance, currently has access to dozens of TV channels, and many European countries will have extensive cable networks by the mid-1990s.

Developments in satellite technology have also alleviated pressure on the radio spectrum and have extended the possibility for information to be transmitted and broadcast, without hindrance, across regional and national boundaries. British channels will spill over into other European countries just as the signals of the proposed satellite broadcasting of France, for instance, may also reach Britain.

These technical developments have coincided with a political shift in Europe towards a more market-orientated economy. This has resulted in the privatisation and commercialisation of much of the European audio-visual industry (especially broadcasting) (see Bens *et al.*, 1987; McQuail and Siune, 1986). This represents a break from the past when the dominant model of broadcasting in Europe was a highly regulated public service system, embodying notions of social responsibility and universal service. This stood in sharp contrast to all other information provision. Newspapers, books, magazines and the film industry have been almost exclusively the domain of private business.

The advocates of market-based mechanisms for the allocation of broadcasting activities claim that competition can and will ensure the continuation of both diversity of programming and the maintenance of standards. Even if one accepts this proposition it is not axiomatic that privatisation creates competition: it is just as likely to lead to greater concentration. As can be seen in other sectors, concentrated industries are more prone instead to engage in product differentiation.

This chapter examines the dynamics of the information business in the free market and seeks to examine critically the view that the liberalisation of broadcasting in Europe will lead to greater consumer choice and diversity. On the contrary, it is argued that the long-term horizontal integration of business strategies will lead to greater concentration which will in turn subvert the 'disciplines' of an atomistic 'free' market. This will lead towards the replacement of publicly owned and regulated monopolies by privately owned oligopolies.

It is argued that the information and communications businesses are characterised by an economic and operational structure which engenders business strategies which lead to:

— the concentration of ownership in specific markets, thereby undermining the business pluralism concept of diversity;
— the development of multi-media businesses which challenge the notion that the existence of different media produces business pluralism and hence diversity;
— the repackaging and reselling of the information product in new formats; this suggests that an increase in the number of media does not of itself increase product diversity;
— the expansion of audiences, both nationally and internationally, through transnational operations based on greater uniformity of programme content. (This can potentially reduce the ability of local stations to serve the diverse interests of their local and regional publics);
— the fusion of small entities (businesses, regions, countries) with larger players, as well as joint venture agreements, in order to spread risks or reach a larger market. The price of survival in the market-place for the small country or region may be the compulsion to create products for an international audience at the expense of its service to its immediate, local audience.

The rationale for 'privatisation' in general fails to recognise the distinction between product diversification and product differentiation. Deregulation and privatisation are predicated on the belief that more output is equivalent to more choice. However, the issue is not the expansion of output *per se* but of content — hence the distinction between product diversification and product differentiation. For broadcasting, product differentiation can be defined as more variations on a particular programming theme whilst diversification can be defined as widening the range of programming, so as to satisfy more specific or minority interests, which might include regional or small nation interests. [Diversification/differentiation might be better terms than, say, 'high' and 'low' culture, since the former rests on notions of 'audience reach' whilst the latter relates to 'programme content'.] One can contrast the difference between, say, the strategy for radio deregulation in the UK where the emphasis appears to be on expansion through diversification as opposed to the case of television, for which examples are cited in this chapter, of expansion through differentiation.

Wider issues and problems arise from the increase in business ownership of information relating to freedom of expression, accountability and the importance of viewers as citizens not just as consumers. For instance, in these circumstances, freedom of expression might well become the prerogative of business, whilst that of the individual remains dependent on the patronage of business. Equally, in these circumstances we can question whether an information business which is predominantly financed by advertising will be responsive to sectors of the population whose economic position means that they are not important as consumers.

These are important areas of study but are not dealt with here. This chapter questions aspects of the dominant view that diversity and choice in the provision of information may be increased by, for instance, liberalisation of broadcasting or expansion in the number of information media. On the contrary, it is posited, the information business operating in the 'market-place' contains within it a logic and rationale which suggests the opposite may occur.

Concentration of ownership

There is a tendency towards concentration of ownership in the information business which occurs in specific markets selling similar products and is rooted in the specific economics of information. The most important of these are high first copy (prototype) and low reproduction costs. The latter range from nil, to distribute an extra unit in broadcasting, to negligible, to reproduce a video copy, to relatively low for newspapers (*Royal Commission on the Press*, 1962; Bagdikian, 1983). For example, the costs to a broadcasting channel of producing a programme are the same if its audience is 3 million or 30 million. By utilising modern satellite transmissions it costs no more to transmit a programme to the population of almost one third of the globe (if they own direct reception equipment) than to a small highland community in Scotland.

There is, given the points outlined above, an exceptionally strong incentive to seek the highest sales penetration possible in order to reduce unit costs, as well as maximise revenue from sales. Ultimately, this produces a trend towards concentration in a specific information market. According to Bagdikian, lower unit costs can give the largest business a powerful advantage, since smaller businesses have to leave the market on account of their relatively higher cost base.

Concentration occurs in specific markets selling similar products and aiming at a specific audience (Bens *et al.*, 1987): the characteristics of this specificity could be regional, national, or others such as purchasing power etc., as for example *The Financial Times*, which does not have a UK competitor for its market segment.

The allocation of advertising revenue reinforces this trend. As Bagdikian (1983) noted in his study of US newspapers, the need of advertisers for the largest newspapers circulation or audience share has created a tendency to 'unwittingly eliminate second place' and has led to a monopoly in almost every metropolitan newspaper in the United States.[1] The cycle of lower unit costs, together with the advertiser's requirement for access to the largest number of potential consumers, inexorably leads to advertisers turning to the dominant operator, in publishing or broadcasting, who can deliver the highest penetration.

This also acts as an incentive to the business to increase its circulation or audience, since it justifies higher marginal revenue from advertisers in the form of higher advertising rates. Whilst advertisers in the long run do not desire a monopoly, and indeed complain that monopolies in many areas lead to their being charged 'monopoly' prices, this is the inadvertent consequence of their rational business decisions as advertisers. The logic of economic and business decisions by owners and advertisers at this microlevel of a specific market embodies an internal tendency towards concentration of ownership of the information business.

Moreover, once a business monopoly or semi-monopoly has been established in a given market, this can act as a barrier to entry for new or potential entrants, given that advertisers will only transfer to the new entrant when access to the desired consumers has been established.[2] This in turn can take some years to establish: examples include *Today*, *USA Today* and the many still loss-making European satellite channels. According to *The Financial Times* (19 September 1987), *USA Today* lost $500m during the five years of 1982–7 before breaking even. This suggests that the newcomer needs to be able to sustain many years of considerable losses.

The costs of entry in the form of high initial costs and negative returns in the early years are punitive for many small entities, but they provide opportunities for the transnational multi-media operator with the capacity to absorb high short-term losses from revenues from other media or countries, in anticipation of high profits later. (*The Financial Times* (19 September 1987) made this point concerning *USA Today* and its owner Mr Gannett: 'Gannett plundered the ability to get staff and capital from other newspapers . . . 5 years of losses . . . would have crippled a news organisation weaker than Gannett'.) Furthermore, large firms which are vertically, as well as horizontally, integrated, may be in a better position to absorb short-term losses by reducing their costs of operation. Rupert Murdoch's reliance on *Times* journalists (in a studio at Wapping) for his Sky Channel is an example of this phenomenon.

This tendency towards concentration of ownership in a given market undermines the very pluralism which is cited as the guarantee of diversity in information provision (i.e. the notion that diversity and alternative views are guaranteed by competing information selling businesses). This tendency occurs in a given market selling similar products and aiming at a specific set of consumers.

Diversification of interests — the tendency towards multi-media ownership

The thesis that diversity of sources of information is available through different competing media is challenged by the tendency towards multi-media ownership. Hitherto discrete and separate sectors now complement one another in various ways. The motive behind the multi-media character of current information business operations include:

— the defensive motive — investing in a sector which represents potential competition for one's share either of the media market or, more importantly, of advertising revenue, in order to protect that share;
— the cost motive — the spreading of high first copy costs by repackaging and recycling the product in new forms;
— the scope motive — exploiting multi-media 'tie-ins' or releases.

A key reason for newspaper publishers investing in other media is competition for the media market (readership, audience etc.), but more important is the threat posed to advertising revenue by new commercialised media (Bunce, 1976; Bens *et al.*, 1987). This motive lies behind the pattern of newspaper publishers in the UK owning regional newspapers and consumer magazines or having stakes in radio stations, commercial television and the new media. It is in part a defensive action. It is a reflexive action to the perceived potential threat posed by new entrants or other media to its advertising revenue. Ironically, rather than the print media (newspapers, etc.) being made obsolete by newer information media, they have been able to accommodate and exploit them as opportunities for new sources of profit.

For example, Bickel (1930), Levin (1960) and Bunce (1976) have outlined in detail the involvement of the press in the early development of radio in the USA, including the conflicts with, and involvement of, US regulatory bodies such as the FCC or later Congress. By 1927 48 radio stations in the USA were owned by newspapers; 69 sponsored programmes and 97 gave news programmes by airwaves.[3] Bunce noted that by 1950 US newspapers owned 85 per cent of local television stations: this percentage fell to 46 per cent (1974) as television itself became a national medium, coinciding with its dependence on national as distinct from local advertising:

Economic integration of broadcasting and the daily printed press assures some control and protection against intermedia competition for advertising and audiences ... In the early days of radio, publisher-broadcasters were more conspicuous in their efforts to shape the new medium along lines that prevented threats to printed press stability... It is surely more than co-incidental that today daily newspapers receive most of their revenue from local advertising,[4] while national advertising comprises the bulk of television revenue; that the daily press is still primarily a news organ, while TV is essentially an entertainment medium; that the daily papers rely heavily on local news, while television does very little programming whatsoever (Bunce, 1976, p. 62).

Privatisation of the audio-visual industry in Europe is acting as a stimulus for further multi-media ownership of the information business because all the major publishers have become involved in the newly privatised or privatising audio-visual channels. This is a consequence of the perceived threat to their advertising revenue base in national and regional markets: 'The printed press, and especially magazines, would be unable to stop the drain of advertisements for certain specific products (food, cosmetics, detergents, etc.), towards the audiovisual media...' (Bens *et al.*, 1987, p. 24). Further, Bens notes there is a pattern of increased linkages (multi-media and multi-national) between businesses through 'various risk sharing fusions' such as joint ventures and co-production deals.

For instance, Williams (1985) showed that the major actors in the private channels in Germany are that country's four major players in the existing media, in particular newspaper and magazine publishers. Further, these concerns are all involved in multi-media/multi-national linkages/fusions/interlocks. Sassoon (1985) and Bens *et al.* (1987) highlighted similar patterns for Italy and France respectively following deregulation of broadcasting.[5] My discussions with Alvarez[6] on the most recent developments in Spain suggest a similar long-term pattern. She pointed out that the proposals for private channels are currently being re-discussed in parliament and there is 'complete confusion': this is 'an expensive adventure': we are getting 'new groups with involvement by the international press' because we do not 'have the expertise or finance' for these ventures.

What then are the implications of this development for diversity and choice in information provision? Given that press involvement is logically going to be in those areas where its specific type or segment of advertising revenue is threatened, it follows that particular segments of 'consumers' or citizens could receive much of their information, albeit via different media, from the same owner. This may occur in a segment defined by geographic region or characteristics such as purchasing power. This suggests that increasing the number of advertising sponsored media or magazines aimed at a particular market does not necessarily increase business pluralism but rather the opposite. Again, diversity of sources of information may be reduced[7] and its effects disguised by a 'spurious' diversity represented by the way in which the information is presented.

Old wine in new bottles: the new media

A further reason for the trend towards multi-media ownership is rooted in the high first copy costs of information and the relative inelasticity of 'creation' costs. Business strategy will logically attempt to spread/reduce this element by recycling and repackaging the product to be resold in a different media (Miège et al., 1986; Bens et al., 1987). For example, the presale of rights by the film industry utilises each medium and includes a time-lag between each stage: (1) Theatrical release; (2) Pay cable; (3) Network television; (4) Video; (5) Television syndication (to off-network stations); (6) Other cable.

Traditional newspapers and journals/magazines can also resell their product. Given the economics of information already mentioned, i.e. high creation and first copy costs, the newspaper or magazine publisher can increase revenue by selling this information in alternative forms: 'The economic specificity of information must be taken into account . . . Press companies are forced to look for ways of increasing their rate of return on information already being produced and collected. Their strategy involves diversifying into new formats' (Miège et al., 1986, p. 278). Miège et al. show this to have occurred in the magazine industry in France during the past twenty years 'but the strategy is above all aimed at the new media' (Miège et al, 1986, p. 278). There is a similar pattern for videotex in the United States where newspaper publishers own the major operators, and Bens et al. (1987) study of videotex in Europe also highlighted this pattern. Recent examples in the UK are the value-added telephone services of newspapers, e.g. Guardian 'Cricketline' or Financial Times 'Shareline'.

This development undermines the notion that a profusion or increase in the number of terminals, outlets or media will automatically increase diversity: as noted earlier diversity in 'forms' or 'formats' cannot be taken to constitute diversity in choice of information.

The multi-media product: the drive to maximise exposure

There are also operational reasons for multi-media conglomeration (Flichy, 1980; Kilborn, 1986). As Flichy noted:

> These different forms of horizontal concentration between media . . . do not only correspond to the financial logic inherent in conglomerate structure. The objective is also to launch multi-media operations, as is exemplified in the simultaneous release of a film, a book, or a record entitled Star Wars. These products, spin-offs of a film or a broadcast, often receive huge audiences as they benefit from the success of the first product.

An example of this phenomenon is the 1987 low budget musical Dirty Dancing made by Nestion Inc. RCA Records US spent only $200,000 on songs, a combination of new songs and some '60s hits. The sound-track was popular and became a hit, as did the film and later a video cassette. This 'hit' 'spawned' a series of related entertainment including a 'touring stage show' of the singers from the sound-trace and a TV series based on the film shown on CBS. The *Dirty Dancing* sound-track was the third most popular album in the USA, and RCA hope to repeat the success with another album of '60s hits, called — *More Dirty Dancing*.

In total the multi-media release of *Dirty Dancing* grossed $350 million by August 1988. RCA alone, in the period to June 1988, earned $105 million, representing 25 per cent of its total US revenue. This multi-media release potential of the 'winning formula' has led to record companies buying studios and vice versa (*Business Week International*, 15 August 1988). Multi-media release also involves book publishing. For instance, Flichy notes that the book of *The Holocaust* rapidly sold 1.5 million copies after the broadcast.

This phenomenon, however, could adversely affect product diversity. Cultural industries such as the music industry have generally been characterised as as oligopolies which relied on a large number of small independents to provide the innovation and creativity. However, if the 'hits' are brought in from other branches of the multi-media business, then this smaller creative and innovative sector may suffer. As a consequence, there might be an overall reduction in diversity and innovation.

As Flichy (1980) noted: 'Most of the economists that have studied the cultural industries have noticed that these industries were based on a complex dual structure, which associated large oligopolistic groups and small firms. Whereas the former could possibly smother the latter, they did not do so because the small firms were insuring the continuity of the whole communication branch. The arrival of large multi-media groups put an end to this equilibrium'. The multi-media release/tie-in phenomenon, whilst making 'business sense', contains the potential to reduce diversity, both by increasing the financial vulnerability of small businesses which provided diversity and served particular publics and by a reduction in overall 'variety' of product.

There is, however, a trend which could be a countervailing force to this phenomenon: the trend towards subcontracting production to small businesses in audio-visual, for instance. This trend, which both cuts costs and shifts the risk of innovation onto small companies suggests the market in total needs an oligopoly and smaller businesses. However, the degree to which these businesses will have 'power' to decide what is produced remains to be seen.

Expansion and the 'transnational' product

The high first copy costs of information production already outlined, coupled with the potential to increase and/or maximise revenue from advertising, provides a powerful incentive for broadcasting businesses to expand across regional and national boundaries. However, this expansion may have implications for the information product of the transborder broadcaster and for the small broadcaster of the receiving region or country. The evidence suggests that a secondary effect of expansion (e.g. from local to national or international) is that the product itself becomes more uniform or trans-national.

Writers such as Bens *et al*. (1987) show an increasing trend in Europe to expand the market share of the local audio-visual medium for the business reasons outlined above: 'the evolution towards the prototype of a commercial station aiming at increasing its market share and trying to penetrate on the national and even international market.' (Bens *et al*., 1987).

Herein lies the significance of developments in transmission. Satellite transmission costs are both distance and volume insensitive: the cost of reaching each extra 'consumer' is nil, which implies rapidly falling average costs. Added to this is that greater consumer penetration means advertisers can be charged more. Hence the business rationale for the drive to expand markets: cost minimisation coupled with revenue maximisation. For instance, if Thames Television were transmitted by a satellite whose footprint covered the whole of the UK and direct reception were possible, the cost of distribution to Thames would not increase but its revenues from advertising could.

Bens explains this type of temptation in Europe: for instance, if TDF-1 in France, or German television, is distributed by satellite, there will be pressure to cross national boundaries, for the above reasons, and to transmit to the neighbouring countries within its footprint. These countries already receive some overspill from German terrestrial broadcasters.

The question is: can the product which is appropriate for transregional and/or transnational audiences serve the interests or needs of a local community? Is a process set in motion whereby the original aim of decentralisation and of producing local content is lost? The evidence cited in this chapter suggests that the product (e.g. programme) itself undergoes a significant change which militates against the interests and/or information needs of local communities, who want or need specific, tailor-made pro-grammes rather than variants of a transnational product.

Bunce's (1976) study showed that the shift from local broadcasting to national in the USA changed the product to a more uniform, and entertainment-led, product. Further, the expansion of US broadcasters internationally increased this shift from local content. That is to say, the diverse information interests/needs of the American people may not be served by that country's undoubted economic strength in traded information products. For instance, if Scottish TV were transmitted to the whole of the UK, much of its local programming may not be appropriate or relevant to national audiences (e.g. informational programmes only salient to local groups). Therefore a consequence of the tendency to expand markets is to create what has been called the transnational product — one designed to maximise viewing and, because of its relative homogeneity, to reduce average programming costs.

Thus the very *raison d'être* of decentralisation, a commitment to serve diverse local needs/interests, could be lost by the tendency to expand. That is, a development which makes sense from a business perspective (such as to increase revenue from advertising by increasing the audience or access to potential consumers, or from the macro-economic needs of a country, such as to increase its balance of trade) may result in the loss of product diversity for its own population.

The response of small entities

A similar consequence for the product as that outlined above may result from the way small entities, be they a business, region or country, respond to, or compete with, the lower unit costs of the larger players in the market-place. For instance, how does the small broadcaster in Belgium contest overspill or expansion from the broadcasters of its larger neighbours? Can they survive without entering into joint ventures or co-production deals? Could this lead to a small entity (e.g. broadcaster of a small country) attempting, as a way of competing, to concentrate on creating information products for an export market? Can the product which will sell in external markets also serve the diverse information needs of its own society?

The evidence suggests (Bens *et al.*, 1987) that the response of small entities is to form 'far-reaching fusions' with other players as the only way to survive: joint ventures and/or co-production deals, including attempts to export. Studies such as that of Bens highlight the high degree of interlock of European information businesses, such as multi-media and multi-national linkages and spanning national and international markets. These linkages suggest less than perfect business competition and even offer the scope for oligopolistic collusion. However the point I want to highlight here is that the product of, for instance, a co-production agreement will tend to be tailored for the larger audience or market rather than that of the smaller 'partner'.

For instance, the Irish broadcasting organisation, RTE, is a small entity which has some, as yet small, experience of the strategy of co-productions and of the consequent change to product when there is 'one eye on the US market'. Sheehan (1987) argued that a disproportionately high amount of the resources of this small broadcaster was put into 'expensive' co-productions with players from other countries which thereby reduced the range of product available to serve a local public. Rockett *et al.* (1988) also noted a similar pattern in the early development of Irish film: 'chiefly directed at an Irish-American audience', rather than its home market.

There is therefore a general problem when we refer to tradeable information products. Whilst information exchange between countries is desirable, if a small entity primarily produces for an external or export market the plurality of information needs of the groups of its own society could suffer. Put another way, a trade surplus in information products may have macro-economic benefits but could have secondary drawbacks for the people of a given country. It has been suggested that these developments have some similarities with the economic situation of poorer countries producing cash crops for the markets of the richer countries. Conceivably, therefore, the route for the small entity to survive in the market-place, given the economics of information outlined at the outset, will ultimately yield the same product as the larger player. In effect, the small entity survives by servicing the large player, almost as a 'subcontractor'.

Conclusion

The consequences of exposing the information business to the full effect of market forces will tend, in the long term, to engender concentration of ownership. Although short-term opportunities exist for new entrants, the economics of the industry militate against their long-term survival. In effect, new entrants become quick leavers. Technological change has made possible the profusion of channels. However, this in itself does not constitute a vast increase in choice and diversity. Rather, a shift to advertising as the source of finance is resulting in increased multi-media ownership coupled with a reduction in product diversity due to the tendency to repackage and resell information in different forms or formats. These tendencies challenge the business pluralism basis of information diversity. Further, the pressure to maximise revenue from advertising through expansion could result in broadcasters creating and tailoring a product for multi-markets hence neglecting the specific information requirement of some or all of its own citizens.

In sum, the information business, operating in the market-place, contains within it an internal tendency/bias against diversity and choice in information sources for citizens. Thus privatisation could encourage these tendencies, and the consequences of the deregulating policies could be the exact opposite of the policy objectives.

Notes

1 According to *The Observer*, 98 per cent of US metropolitan newspapers have no newspaper competition; see also *Euromonitor* (1988) report on UK national newspapers which argues that when the current phase of increasing revenue from cost cutting restructuring is complete (about two more years) increased revenue will only be possible through competing for market share within each newspaper market segment, i.e. popular, middle market and quality. This analysis suggests that we may get further ownership concentration in each segment of the UK newspaper industry.

2 Currently, there is a wider argument on this so called 'chicken and egg' situation of 'no audience, no advertising revenue'. Financial analysts now talk also of the 'brand loyalty' which an existing medium enjoys, whilst the new entry can take time to establish its 'brand'. In turn this perspective argues that advertisers find 'brand loyalty' useful in that it enables accurate targeting of advertising, i.e. the purchasing power etc. of a given audience, or newspaper readership. This in turn acts as a further barrier to entry for newcomers.

3 The initial impetus for the spread of radio in the US came from the manufacturers of

the equipment: a 'cartel' which included General Electric, Westinghouse and American Telephone & Telegraph. That is (in a form of vertical integration) the manufacturers of radio receivers 'operated radio stations for the purpose of stimulating the sale of home receiving that they . . . would manufacture' (Bagdikian, 1983, p. 141). However, the press became involved when it realised that broadcasting could also become a medium for the transmission of commercial and other information which hitherto had been perceived to pose a threat to the 'form' of the printed medium (which in turn would threaten its revenue base).

4 We can also discern this pattern in Britain, e.g. the ownership by quality newspapers of regional newspapers (both are more dependent on 'classified' advertising as distinct from display advertising), of 'independent' local radio, and, increasingly, of free newspapers both of which are perceived to be competitors of regional newspapers.

5 I might add at this point that it is very difficult to gather information on the situation in Italy from the UK. The usual journals such as *Cable and Satellite Europe* whilst widely recording the activities of Berlusconi (a/the major player in the Italian media) in other European countries give very little information on Italy itself.

6 My thanks to M.C. Alvarez, Basque University, for information on developments in Spain.

7 Moreover, the multi-owner in a given market can offer reduced advertising rates and thereby increase the barriers to entry. Rupert Murdoch's News Corporation has concluded an agreement with Gillette for both the multi-media and the global advertising of its product; whilst business analysts assume this is at special rates the details of this contract have not been revealed.

Bibliography

Bagdikian, B., 1983, *The Media Monopoly*, Beacon Press, Boston.

Baistow, T., 1985, *Fourth Rate Estate*, Comedia, London.

Bens, E. *et al.*, 1987, *Impact of New Communications Technologies on the Media Industry in the EC-Countries*, FAST Report No. 160.

Bickell, K.A., 1930, *New Empires: The Newspaper and the Radio*, Lippincott, Philadelphia.

Brants, H., 1985, 'Broadcasting and politics in the Netherlands' in R. Kuhn (ed.), *Broadcasting and Politics in Western Europe*, Cass, London.

Bunce, W., 1976, *Television in the Corporate Interest*, Praeger, New York.

Euromonitor Report on Newspapers, 1988, Euromonitor, London.

Flichy, P., 1980, *Les industries de l'imaginaire*, Presses Universitaires de Grenoble, Grenoble.

Garnham, N., 1991, 'Public service versus the market', in *Capitalism and Communications*, Sage, London, 115–35.

Head, S., 1985, 'Economics of broadcasting', *World Broadcasting Systems*.

Kilborn, 1986, *Multi-Media Melting Pot*, Comedia, London.

Kuhn, R., (ed.), 1985, *Broadcasting and Politics in Western Europe*, Cass, London.

Levin, H.J., 1960, *Broadcasting Regulation and Joint Ownership of Media*, New York University Press, New York.

McQuail, D. and Siune, K., (eds), 1986, *New Media Politics – Comparative Perspectives in Western Europe*, Sage, London.

Mattelart, A., Delcourt, X. and Mattelart, M., 1984, *International Image Markets*. Comedia, London.
Miège, B. *et al.*, 1986, *L'industrialisation de l'audiovisuel*, Aubier-Montaigne, Paris.
Rockett *et al.*, 1987, *Cinema and Ireland*, Routledge, London.
Royal Commission on the Press, 1962, HMSO, London, Cmnd. 1811.
Sassoon, D., 1985, 'Political and market forces in Italian broadcasting' in R. Kuhn (ed.), *Broadcasting and Politics in Western Europe*, Cass, London.
Williams, A., 1985, 'Pluralism in the West German media: the press broadcasting and cable' in R. Kuhn (ed.), *Broadcasting and Politics in Western Europe*, Cass, London.

5 The online database service sector: development and directions

Harry East, Ian Rowlands and Vicki Forrest

One of the more important phenomena of the last twenty years of the 'information industry' has been the development of techniques for handling textual and numeric information in machine-readable form. 'Electronic publishing', a term coined to embrace these new methods, describes a complex mix of technologies: some producing conventional printed products, others making possible the exploitation of previously untapped markets. New markets have been opened up through technical innovations in software, hardware and telecommunications — technologies converging to offer new means for producing and distributing information. Of the many new business opportunities created by electronic publishing, the most mature sector for many is that represented by machine-readable databases, particularly online services.

Problems of scope and definition

Any definition of what is meant precisely by 'online services' must, for reasons outlined below, be provisional. The difficulties of defining the scope of the sector are considerable, and cloud the interpretation of many measures which are used to estimate the dimensions of the industry.

A broad view of online services could easily embrace electronic messaging services (such as Telecom Gold), teletext, viewdata, cable services, banking services (such as cashpoint machines — ATMs — and home banking), teleconferencing and voicetex — as well as online databases and databanks. The latter typically share the following characteristics:

—*content services* with high added-value;
—*interactive access* in real-time;
—*batch updating*;
—*public domain;*
—*one-to-many communication.*

No other electronic medium shares this particular mix of essential features: teletex is non-interactive; messaging and conference services offer one-to-one or one-to-few communication only; home banking services have low value-added content.

Collier, in examining the indicators currently used to analyse the size and growth of the online sector (and their lack of reliability), has formed a relatively narrow view of 'electronic information services' and recognises six basic types (Collier, 1988):

1. *text and bibliographic systems* e.g. DIALOG, Datastar;
2. *data and transactional systems* e.g. Reuters Monitor;
3. *industry-group systems* e.g. SITA (inter-airline), Istel (travel agents), American Express;
4. *intra-organisational systems* such as those found in large organisations like ICI and the police force;
5. *public-access services* such as Prestel;
6. *in-house online services* e.g. newspaper publishers.

This chapter is mainly concerned with Collier's classes 1 and 2 — those services most obviously in the public domain. The remainder are either private or closed/limited access systems, albeit often large and commercially important ones. This chapter broadly defines online services as those which offer their users the ability to search and retrieve specific information held on *remote* computers — by gaining access, via telecommunications networks to structured files of textual or numeric data (databases). It also highlights UK issues and initiatives in a wider international context. In the area of online services, the distinction between UK and wider European developments is an important one. Despite efforts at the level of the European Commission, which are often considerable, the UK market inevitably resembles that of the United States rather than Europe at large.

Emergence of the online sector

The origins of the online service industry can be traced to the 1960s, when providers of printed abstracting and indexing services began to computerise their data handling procedures with the advent of computer-assisted type-setting techniques. A by-product of these printing activities was magnetic tape copies — essentially the first databases. But it was not until the 1970s that electronic databases could be searched interactively, and at a distance, as they are today. In order to 'host' extensive databases on large time-sharing computers and offer the sophisticated file organisation and search software needed for online access, substantial investment was required. Much of the R&D investment which led to the first host services becoming operational came, either directly or indirectly, from US Federal funds. One of the largest services — DIALOG — arose out of Lockheed's contractual activities for NASA; another — ORBIT — was developed by the Systems Development Corporation and found its first application at the Wright-Patterson base of the US Air Force.

Initially accessible only to select groups of users, online services became available commercially by the mid-1970s: in 1974, 18 DIALOG files were on offer to the public (this number had grown to approximately 300 in 1989). The majority of early databases had been produced by government and non-profit organisations but from the mid-1970s private companies began to enter the market-place in increasing numbers.

The number of databases grew rapidly, and the services offered became more diverse. The first databases offered bibliographic information almost exclusively, largely in the fields of science and technology. Later an increasing number of numeric and full-text files became available. The user population grew accordingly, leading to fiercer competition between service suppliers.

Market development

The development of a viable online industry, servicing an international market, was stimulated by technical progress in a number of key 'enabling' areas, favouring both consumers and vendors:

— the development of *time-share systems*, where one computer could be used simultaneously by a number of operators performing different tasks;
— increasing density and decreasing costs of *storage media*, allowing for more economic storage of large databases;
— *wider availability* of cheap and reliable 'intelligent' terminals or microcomputers, offering convenient access to remote systems;
— faster and cheaper telecommunications services, especially *packet-switched services*, with tariffs related to volume of traffic rather than distance;
— larger volumes of information produced in electronically-stored form as part of more *integrated electronic publishing* operations;
— the development of *sophisticated communications software* making online access increasingly transparent to users;
— the availability of software packages allowing for the *local storage and manipulation* ('downloading') of online data and their incorporation into in-house databases.

But, while much has been made of the role of technology, it is clear that technology-push alone cannot sustain this new industry. In the context of information technology as a whole, Smith has argued that the current revolution is as much one of *investment* as of technical innovation: 'of transformation of scale more than of technological horizon' (Smith, 1982).

Similarly, de Sola Pool, in his studies of a technological breakthrough from the nineteenth century, *Forecasting the Telephone*, observes that:

> what actually emerged was determined by what could be effectively marketed, for what activities capital could be raised, and what arrangements would allow for efficient billing — in short by economic considerations ... one needs to bring to bear a technical-economic analysis that explores the investment and marketing possibilities of each technical alternative ... some of the very best forecasts were made by people like Graham Bell and Theodore Vail, who not only understood the technology well but also had to face up to hard market facts on which their success depended (de Sola Pool, 1983).

This view is echoed by Dunn and Boyle: 'for the past ten years the online industry has emphasized search techniques, data-base content, and mechanics. Suppliers and vendors alike emphasized what could be delivered, not what customers wanted' (Dunn and Boyle, 1984).

Some of the more successful services have been those which responded to the specific needs of a limited clientele, such as those requiring access to real-time financial information services or to the full-texts of case law. Once the existence of substantially greater potential demand was recognised and — most importantly — costs had fallen sufficiently to permit its exploitation, the industry began to make the transition to become more market-led. As a recent industry report neatly summarises: 'initially expertise in technological design was of primary importance, but as the industry matured companies had to become more market driven' (CSP International, 1986).

Certainly, the nature of the industry at present supports such a model. Market considerations and, in particular, strategies for increasing end-use, underpin many new developments in technological and marketing strategies, for example:

— *experiments with pricing policies* (for example, off-peak discounts);
— introduction of *value-added network services (VANs)*;
— development of *software for data manipulation*;
— *search language enhancements* increasingly geared towards the needs of the end-user rather than specialised intermediaries.

Moreover, as competition intensifies, the industry has begun to undergo structural changes, associated with vertical and horizontal integration and cooperation — illustrated, for example, by the development and spread of gateways which interconnect host services and rationalise access points for users.

Such a characterisation does, none the less, run the risk of under-emphasising the continuing importance of technology, in constant two-way *interaction* with the market. As Rowlands has noted: 'the new technological developments which emerge almost daily, enable new actors to participate in the market, often undercutting traditional producers and delivery systems' (Rowlands, 1988). The recent entry of several new players into the market for

CD-ROM products testifies to the importance of the role of technology. Indeed, in attempting to model past market development in the online sector, Cullen assumes that electronic information services remain essentially technology-driven; innovation favours those suppliers — and newcomers — who are best able to exploit the new market opportunities which result (Cullen, 1986).

Online market indicators

The emergence of an identifiable, if ill-defined, 'information industry' has not, unfortunately, been accompanied by the collection and publication of regular, standardised industry statistics. There are few reliable indicators of the size and growth of the online sector in the UK, or elsewhere. Those who could most easily provide the relevant data — the service suppliers — are under no legal obligation to do so, and remain reluctant to divulge this commercially sensitive information. It has been suggested that the main reason for this reticence is that most European hosts are not in fact operating at a profit (Link, 1988). Most independent industry surveys have suffered from supply-side secrecy; some have been described as 'appalling catalogues of errors and omissions' (White, 1988).

Some researchers have turned to consumers as an alternative source of data (Turpie et al., 1987). Whilst the prospects for these surveys of national demand might appear brighter, it remains a fact that any attempt to collect data on the online industry faces considerable problems. In the first instance, online databases are accessible internationally — through an increasingly complex world-wide system of host computers, gateways and data communications networks — making it virtually impossible to produce figures for one national industry in isolation.

In the second instance, measuring the online industry presents many problems of definition and classification and nowhere is this more apparent than in relation to indicators of online 'use', a concept difficult to define and quantify. In discussing various measures of the market for online services, Schwuchow concludes that the best is that based on revenues in that: 'it is the only indicator, which reduces the size of the market for online database services as well as the size of the market for real-time online services to a common denominator' (Schwuchow, 1988) — a factor of considerable significance, as these two types of service are very different in many ways.

While obtaining reliable estimates of national revenues appears to present intractable problems, information on consumer expenditure seems to be more attainable. In the United States, such data are regularly published as a result of the Information Market Indicators survey (Williams, 1985). These data are obtained from the analysis of invoices sent by service suppliers to representative samples of user organisations in different sectors of the online-using community. This method enables figures to be produced for spending, within each sector, on individual hosts *and* databases. The technique has been adopted by the authors at the Centre for Communication and Information Studies to monitor continuously the expenditure of selected groups of online users (East and Forrest, 1988).

The above centre has also surveyed UK database producers in an attempt to disaggregate their online revenues from other sources of income (Rowlands and Vogel, 1989). It is an indication of the powerful position of the host-distributors that, although they supply database producers with royalty payments based on the volume of use of their products, they do not usually reveal to them the actual sources of these revenues.

At the European level, the European Commission has recently created an 'Information Market Observatory' to stimulate the provision of fuller statistics, relating to Community countries, in this area.

Despite all the above qualifications, the following sections attempt to present an overview of the current state of the market, based on available information.

World markets for online information

In 1979/80, the first issue of the *Directory of Online Databases* catalogued 400 online databases and 59 international host services. The latest issue (January 1989) reveals a tenfold increase over this period and lists a total of 3,699 databases and 555 host services (see Table 5.1).

If these figures are regarded as being indicative of market demand, then the United States clearly enjoys an overwhelming strategic advantage — both in terms of the number of databases and services and their diversity. This dominance may largely be attributed to three characteristics particular to the American industry:

— its *long lead time* in market development;
— its *economies of scale* in the home market;
— its *economies of scope* through a few major 'information supermarkets' (e.g. DIALOG).

Table 5.1 World-wide databases and hosts, 1989

	Number of databases	Number of services
United States	2,434	327
United Kingdom	266	40
France	168	32
West Germany	141	17
Rest of the World	690	139
Total	3,699	555

Source: Director of Online Databases, January 1988, Cuadra/Elsevier, New York

Table 5.2 Estimates of online market size, 1986

	$USm
United States	4,500
United Kingdom	640
Switzerland	220
France	186
Germany	123
Other European	131

Source: European Electronic Information Industry 1986–1991, 1988, Link Resources Corporation, London

Table 5.3 Breakdown of European online market by sector.

	$USm
Financial services	800
Econometric services	100
Text and bibliographic	400

Source: European Electronic Information Industry 1986–1991, 1988, Link Resources Corporation, London

In contrast, European services entered the online arena comparatively recently and their domestic markets offer fewer opportunities for economies of scale, tending not only to be very much smaller but also fragmented by cultural and linguistic barriers. A significant level of state subsidy in some European countries (though not in the UK) introduces a degree of market distortion which the industry itself (and the European Commission increasingly) regards as inimicable to commercial development.

Attempts have been made to estimate the overall value of the international market for online services. Market researchers Frost & Sullivan Inc. (1983) projected the value of the total world market (1987) for online services to be of the order of US$8,158m. A conflicting estimate (Collier, 1988) (which excludes the financial services sector) values the total European text and bibliographic services at only US$49m (with a North American market worth US$380m). 1986 estimates by Link Resources for the US and European markets are presented in Table 5.2.

According to Link, the total European market is therefore estimated to be worth around US$1,300m, with the UK generating almost 50 per cent of revenues — largely due to its role as a financial centre. The relative importance of equity trading and foreign exchange services (such as Reuters) in the European context is clearly shown in Table 5.3.

Link anticipates that the European market will sustain annual growth rates of 30 per cent, resulting in business worth US$1,860m by 1990. The North American market is expected to attain a degree of 'levelling off' over this period — as might be expected from an industry in the early stages of maturity.

Trade in online services

As well as its strategic advantages of scale and maturity, the United States dominates world trade in online information. A survey of international trade in electronic specialised information services conducted by CSP International (1986) found that EC countries spent ECU 113m on text database services (either imported or produced in the internal market) in 1985. The combined external trade deficit of the EC countries was estimated at ECU 32m — contrasting with a US surplus of ECU 45m. Community imports (ECU 48m) stood at a level of three times exports — mostly in favour of the United States. While European producers have found important niche markets for financial, scientific and patents information, a negative trade gap with the USA is likely to be a predominant feature of trade relations for some time to come.

East and Forrest (1989) have estimated that 79 per cent of the UK expenditure on online bibliographic and reference services is exported to foreign hosts and database producers, some 58 per cent to the United States.

The UK market for online information

One estimate, by Electronic Publishing Services, currently values the UK market at about US$980m, equivalent to a 52 per cent share of the European market (Young, 1988). This figure reflects the success of UK equity trading and foreign exchange services which contribute around 45 per cent of total UK online revenues.

Financial performance in the UK online arena is highly variable; as Table 5.4 reveals, a few companies, such as Reuters, are retaining very high profits (ICC, 1988). Unfortunately, it is not possible to disaggregate revenues attributable to electronic forms of delivery from these figures.

Table 5.4 Financial performance (1986) of leading UK online suppliers

Company	Sales (£000s)	Pre-Tax (£000s)	P/E per cent
Butterworth	1,176	−415	−35.3
CCN Systems	25,195	5,775	22.9
Datasolve	32,996	2,310	7.0
Datastream	21,914	6,786	31.0
Dun & Bradstreet	31,370	7,417	23.6
Extel	5,978	1,181	19.8
Finsbury Data Services*	2,063	−734	−35.6
FT Business Information	19,555	2,993	15.3
ICC Information Group	6,478	188	2.9
Jordan & Sons	6,106	506	8.3
McCarthy Information	1,124	60	5.3
Pergamon Infoline	2,454	−2,247	−91.6
Reuters	620,900	130,100	21.0

Note: *interim half-year results

Source: The UK Information Industry: a Financial Survey, 1987, Jordan & Sons, London

With the exception of a few large producers (e.g. Derwent, INSPEC), the database production industry is characterised by a large number of small players — with a ratio of databases to producers of less than two. The databases offered commercially tend, on the whole, to be small as well. Of 266 UK databases analysed in 1988, 171 'small' databases (64.3 per cent) contained fewer than 75,000 records. A further 62 'medium' databases (23.3 per cent) contained fewer than a quarter of a million records.

A recent survey by the Centre for Communication and Information Studies indicates that online information is now the single most important source of income for database publishers, accounting for approximately 62 per cent of all their information product sales. Moreover, on average 38 per cent of database publishers' turnover derived from computer-based information comes from overseas markets (Rowlands and Vogel, 1989).

In terms of subject coverage, the dominant areas in the UK online market are in business and finance, science, technology and medicine (see Table 5.5). The social sciences, humanities, law and government are less favourably represented, perhaps less attractive areas to the profit-seeking organisations now dominating the market. In science, technology and medicine, the pattern of database ownership tends to reflect the existence of conventional print-based services before the advent of electronic delivery. Most of the services in these areas come from the non-commercial sector.

Table 5.5 UK databases by subject coverage, 1988

	Number of databases	%
Business and industry	116	43.6
Science, technology	62	23.3
Medical, biological sciences	25	9.4
Current affairs	17	6.4
Legal, government	16	6.0
Social sciences, humanities	15	5.6
Other	15	5.6

Prospects for future market development

Many commentators believe that the next two or three years represent a potential watershed for electronic publishers. Significant steps forward in the marketing of new services are anticipated, not least in the area of databases offered on optical media — most analysts now expect a significant market for CD-ROM hardware and software to emerge by the early 1990s (Gurnsey and White, 1988).

Many information producers are accepting the need for electronic products to find a place of their own in the market, and as competition becomes more acute, rationalisation of products and services is likely to continue at an accelerated pace.

The key to a financially viable online database sector hinges on the potential for far greater economies of scale which high volumes of service use by individual end-users would realise. A commonly held scenario has been that: 'a network marketplace will result from the establishment of low cost computer-communications networks. These networks will provide the transport system for information products and services so that a mass production, mass distribution, mass marketing and mass consumption information processing industry can develop, much like other important advances in transport' (Dordick *et al.*, 1981). As yet, there is little sign of anything approaching this level of critical mass demand for online services.

To date, the most successful online services have been those of a transactional nature (e.g. for share dealing and inter-airline reservations) — which are characterised by serving communities of end-users who require specific facts related to an urgent need. In environments such as futures trading, online services have become an indispensable tool of the trade. In contrast, the market for text and bibliographic systems remains considerably less buoyant (in terms of take-up relative to the potential number of consumers). To a large extent, and despite some effort on the part of service vendors, text-based services have failed to attract a sufficient volume of end-use and still tend, on the whole, to be accessed through trained information specialists acting as intermediaries.

In those few small pockets of the text and reference sector where end-use is prevalent, service vendors have only found a ready market where special factors have provided them with a comparative advantage, enabling them to overcome widespread consumer resistance — often based on perceptions of the high price and 'unfriendliness' of many online systems. Significant levels of end-use have become established in areas of business, commerce and industry where there are manifest needs for:

— extremely current information on financial markets such as stocks, bonds and commodities markets;
— rapid and comprehensive searches of large volumes of full text, as in the case of law firms and newspapers;
— highly specific scientific, technical and patents information to support R&D activities;
— access to credit ratings, company performance and marketing data in the course of making commercial decisions.

A clearer understanding of the factors, including user sensitisation, investment in training and the psychology of man-machine interaction is needed on both the demand and the supply sides of the market if the latter is to attain its full potential.

The online industry has clearly been moving away from an almost exclusive emphasis on the library sector into the more lucrative business and commercial fields. However, as the online business tries to break into new markets, there is a distinct need for both hosts and database producers to identify and segment new demand for their services. Market development lies in the ability of producers and service vendors to allow end-user need to 'drive' their business.

Competitive adjustment

The costs and high levels of investment associated with running large-scale online databases and servicing users are large. With a few notable exceptions, database producers and service operators are failing to realise attractive returns on investment — particularly in the text and bibliographic sector. DIALOG, the largest online host in this sector, returned net profits of only $9.7m on sales of $98.1m for the 1987 financial year (contrasted with Reuters' revenues of $1,639m for the same period). The number of new entrants to the text/bibliographic arena continues to expand, while at the same time the sector as a whole is gradually losing overall market share to financial real-time services. In response to increasingly fierce competition, and continuing technological advances, a number of industry trends and adjustments are becoming evident.

New emphasis on marketing

A survey conducted in 1985 did little to dispel the general impression that marketing was not being given sufficient priority by many UK database producers (Bibby and East, 1986). Many of the smaller players tended to be product, rather than market oriented, under-capitalised and directed towards local markets. However, there are recent signs which suggest that service operators are becoming more receptive to the 'climate of opportunity'. More emphasis is being placed on promotional activities and on improving training, help desk facilities and documentation.

New pricing mechanisms

Partly in response to decreasing unit costs for telecommunications and falling hardware and software prices, online tariffs are showing a disproportionately slow increase — far below the general rate of inflation. From this point of view, the use of online services is becoming relatively inexpensive — a trend hastened by reaction to stiffer competition within the industry. New pricing mechanisms reflect a greater emphasis on volume rather than time charging — faster telecommunication rates and more efficient hardware and software are eroding the traditional pricing mechanisms based on connect hour usage. The challenge of finding optimal pricing mechanisms which are equitable to users, producers and service operators alike is redefining traditional relationships and is likely to reshape parts of the industry. For example, Chemical Abstracts Service (CAS) has unilaterally acted to protect its own interests as a database producer — by demanding complete control over pricing of those hosts who offer its data. To gain further control, CAS has integrated vertically and now self-hosts its products — in direct competition with its own products mounted on other host services.

Gateways and system integration

The vast proliferation and diversification of databases and host services over the last few years has been one of the most remarkable aspects of the online industry. This explosive pattern of growth is illustrated by data from the *Directory of Online Databases* (see Table 5.6).

Table 5.6 World-wide growth of online services

	1980/81	1984/85	1989 (January)
Numbers of:			
Databases	600	2,453	4,062
Database Producers	340	1,189	1,813
Hosts	93	362	600
Gateways	0	0	75

Source: Directory of Online Databases, January 1988, Cuadra/Elsevier, New York

Responding to this proliferation, there has been a significant shift within the industry to rationalise the multitude of access points to online services by means of 'gateways' — essentially technical devices for interconnecting networks. For the sake of clarity, it is useful to distinguish three kinds of gateway service:

— *public front-end to public host* (e.g. EasyNet, a highly intelligent front-end system which routes users to hosts and databases which are judged most appropriate to a particular query);
— *private host to public host* (e.g. a connection between a company-owned system or network and a public host);
— *interconnection of two public hosts* (e.g. transparent access to a number of online services from electronic mail services such as Telecom Gold).

The implications of gateway connections are complex in strategic and business terms. The question of why a service operator would want to allow its users to switch (transparently) through to another host can be answered in terms of user convenience, extra revenue generation and competitive positioning. Inward gateways offer hosts the possibility of addressing a new and relevant user audience at little cost — the prospect of large numbers of light users accessing via a gateway is commercially very attractive. And by offering gateway access to *complementary* data held on another system, hosts can realise effects of synergy if their users perceive the benefits of 'one-stop shopping'.

However, by their very nature, gateway interfaces create potential conflicts of interests: both between hosts and between database producers and gateway operators. The US National Federation of Abstracting & Indexing Services (NFAIS) has proposed a voluntary public Code of Practice in an attempt to regulate abuses (such as access to unlicensed databases) and resolve conflicting interests. The traditional close working relationship between database producers and hosts may become eroded by the gateway phenomenon, and compound the difficulties of targeting their users effectively.

System enhancements

New facilities are constantly being developed by host services, complementing and extending their classical searching facilities, in an attempt to maintain competitive edge and hopefully forge a closer link between product design and market acceptance. As well as making improvements in the ease of use of their systems, hosts are rapidly introducing many innovative features into their software, including:

— *multifile searching*: a facility to concatenate and interrogate several related databases simultaneously in a single search;
— *mapping*: using the results of one search to provide input automatically for another search in a related database;
— *formatting and downloading*: more and better facilities for sorting and defining the layout of search results and for integrating them with in-house databases;
— *statistical analysis* of search results (e.g. Pergamon Orbit InfoLine's GET command and ZOOM from ESA-IRS);
— *graphic manipulation* of numerical data (e.g. graphical viewdata displays of company performance metrics on ICC);
— *online document ordering*: facilities for ordering photocopies of original documents direct from the database producer.

Structural change

In the 1970s, when electronic publishing was still very much in its infancy, the whole phenomenon was largely regarded as a displacement technology. Prognostications that the 1980s would see the printed book begin a slow slide into oblivion can now be seen to be hopelessly misplaced. A similar argument now revolves around the potential of optical media to displace dial-up access to online services. With the experience of two decades, it now seems far more likely that multi-media information products will continue to co-exist, often with the same producer or publisher targeting different markets through different media. New hybrid services are emerging which conveniently repackage existing data for new markets. One example, the database

Biobusiness, brings together subsets of *BIOSIS* and *ABI/Inform* (databases covering the biological and management sciences respectively), to offer an information service to those concerned with planning and managing R&D programmes in biotechnology.

A process of vertical integration is becoming apparent at many levels across the online industry and is redefining traditional relationships:

> In the last few years the information industry has grown increasingly restive ... this restlessness, combined with the development of new methods of accessing, storing and distributing information, has made the relationship between the different participants much more fluid than it has been for some time. Or, if these relationships are not yet fluid, a desire to make them so has been evidenced (Aitchison, 1988).

Many database producers are becoming self-hosting — an increasingly attractive option as more and more gateway services become operational. Others are bypassing hosts by publishing their data on optical media (CD-ROMs). Online hosts are offering press and wire services and thereby acting as primitive newspapers (without interpretation or editorial bias) or are becoming directly involved in database production. But overall, there is a tendency towards consolidation, with large producers becoming even larger, and an increase in acquisitions and producer-vendor mergers.

Compared with the linguistic and cultural fragmentation of other European entrants into a world market dominated by the USA, the UK has benefited from the accessibility of its services. Other European countries continue to be more reliant on home markets, supported by direct or indirect public subsidy. Given the relatively small dimensions of the European market, where more than 50 per cent of revenues fall to US vendors, it is possible that one or two major European hosts will emerge from an over-supplied bibliographic/full-text market to capture a high level of market share. Indeed, while the Pergamon InfoLine service remained an essentially UK-based operation, its market share was low. Acquisition and merger with the US-based Orbit and BRS services has not only increased the repertoire of the enlarged service, but also captured an established share in the US market.

The impact of the implementation of a single European market on the database service industry is not easy to predict. Benefits may arise more through economies of scope rather than of scale. Enhanced availability of capital will strengthen the trend towards greater concentration — in the recent past major players in the European market (e.g. Pergamon) have tended to look to the American market for acquisitions. A unified, and possibly rationalised industry, is essential if a commercially viable European online services industry is to confront the established pattern of US dominance.

Bibliography

Aitchison, T.M., 1988, 'The database producer in the information chain', *Journal of Information Science*, **16** (6), 319–27.

Bibby, L. and East, H., 1986, 'Marketing of databases produced in the United Kingdom', *Journal of Information Science*, **12** (1), 23–30.

Collier, H.R., 1988, 'What actually is the online universe?' in *Proceedings of the 12th International Online Information Meeting*, London, 6–8 December 1988, Learned Information, Oxford, 723–32.

CSP International, 1986, *International Trade in Electronic Specialised Information Services*, CSP International, London.

Cullen, A., 1986, 'Electronic information services: an emerging market opportunity?', *Telecommunications Policy*, **10** (4), 299–312.

de Sola Pool, I., 1983, *Forecasting the Telephone: a Retrospective Technology Assessment of the Telephone*, Ablex Publishing Corporation, Norwood, New Jersey.

Dordick, H., Nanus, B. and Bradley, H., 1981, *The Emerging Network Marketplace*, Ablex Publishing Corporation, Norwood, New Jersey.

Dunn, R.G. and Boyle, H.F., 1984, 'Online searching: an analysis of marketing issues', *Information Services & Use*, **4**, 147–54.

East, H. and Forrest, V., 1988, 'Indicators of online use' in *Proceedings of the 12th International Online Information Meeting*, London, 6–8 December 1988, Learned Information, Oxford, 91–102.

East, H. and Forrest, V., 1989, 'Transborder flows of online service revenues', in *Proceedings of the 13th International Online Information Meeting*, London, 12–14 December 1989.

Frost & Sullivan Inc., 1983, *Database Services in Western Europe*, Frost & Sullivan Inc., New York.

Gurnsey, J. and White, M., 1988, 'Electronic publishing: a reprise', *Information Media & Technology*, **21** (4), 170–3.

ICC, 1988, *ICC Financial Surveys: Business Information Providers, Advisers and Consultants*, Inter-Company Comparisons, London.

Link Resources Corporation, 1988, *European Electronic Information Industry 1986–1991*, Link Resources Corporation, London.

Rowlands, D.G., 1988, 'Towards an information market model', *Aslib Proceedings*, **40** (1), 27–30.

Rowlands, I. and Vogel, S., 1989, 'Online database production in the UK: a supply-side study', in *Proceedings of the 13th International Online Information Meeting*, London, 12–14 December 1989.

Schwuchow, W., 1988, 'The development of the international market for online information services', in *Proceedings of the 14th FID Conference*, Helsinki, 28 August–1 September 1988, 166–78.

Smith, A., 1982, 'Information technology and the myth of abundance', *Daedalus*, **111** (4), 1–16.

Turpie, G., Sippings, G. and Ramsden, H., 1987, *The Use of Information Technology by Information Centres: the Aslib Information Technology Survey 1987*, Aslib, London.

White, M., 1988, 'Don't you know or have you something to hide?', *Information World Review*, March 1988, 16.

Williams, M.E., 1985, 'Usage and revenue data for the online database industry', *Online Review*, **9** (3), 205–10.

Young, K., 1988, 'UK database service is worth £546m', *Financial Times*, 12 December 1988, 12.

Part II: The technology of information*

---

*Chapters prepared by the Centre for Information and Communication Technology

6 Information technology and the information economy

Ian Miles and Mark Matthews

Introduction

Everyone, it seems, agrees that the 'information economy' is an important fact of life; but, like certain other facts of life, there may be more talk about it than action, and a great deal of this talk is discreetly silent about the details involved. How far, and in what respects, we consider the information economy to be something new, and how far it is simply a continuation of well-established trends, has considerable bearing on what research we undertake, and what practical actions and policies are implied.

This chapter outlines an approach to the 'information economy' which relates it to the application of new Information Technology (IT) throughout the economy — not just to IT-producing sectors (like electronics and software), nor just to information sectors (like broadcasting and databases). We explore implications of this argument for empirical appraisals of the 'information economy'; there are many reasons why we require better empirical analysis of IT-related developments. Sweeping claims are made as to the changes that are under way, but we have limited material with which to evaluate these claims. Even basic issues of the performance of different sectors and economies in terms of the production, uptake and use of IT likewise remain largely unclear, although government policies have striven to promote various areas of IT development and diffusion.

Current statistics do, as we shall show, allow for some limited examination of many key issues. But they are limited. While in the long run new types of statistics will probably have to be produced, at present IT is a fairly recent phenomenon, which our accounting systems have yet to fully accommodate; and a rapidly evolving one, making it hard to establish enduring classificatory schemata in many areas. Many IT-related products and activities pose additional problems because of their service components (such as software products and telecommunications services), and the trend from 'stand-alone' discrete applications to systems integration and network activities. Finally, many IT applications are taking place in areas of the economy and society that are poorly covered in existing statistics — notably in service sectors of the economy (many of which, furthermore, are small enterprises). Nevertheless, we can use existing data for some purposes, and this chapter explores an approach to using available data to study developments in the 'information economy'. We develop an Information Technology Accounting Framework (ITAF), illustrations of which are provided using UK data.

What is the information economy?

The aggregative approach

The introduction to this volume makes two things clear. First, it is now argued across a broad span of opinion that Western industrial societies have entered a new stage of development: that they are being (or have already been) transformed into 'information economies' (or some related term) — although some commentators are entirely sceptical of the notion. Second, this agreement masks considerable divergence in concepts of the information economy — to the point that some people using the term are probably in greater agreement with those rejecting it than with many other users![1]

The wide use of terms such as 'information economy' and 'information society' is relatively recent: earlier accounts tended to use the term 'post-industrial society'. The theorists of post-industrial society asserted that the service sector(s) and service occupations were inexorably growing in importance in advanced industrial societies due to shifts in final demand toward services, and that this would mean a weakening of economic power based on the ownership of material capital.[2] In very similar ways, many information economy theorists talk of the rise of an information sector, of the growth of information occupations, of information products as 'superior goods' (in the economists' sense), and of knowledge displacing wealth as the basis of power. Information has always been important for economic affairs, but, the argument goes, the expansion of information sectors and information occupations — so that these are now numerically important, and in some cases dominant, parts of industrial economies — means a change in economic affairs worthy of the title 'information economy'.

This 'information economy approach' proposes new classifications of sectors and occupations, so as to identify information activities. Following the pioneering work of Machlup (1962) and especially Porat (1977), considerable effort has gone into reclassifying national data so as to chart their development. Following on Porat's approach, reports from the prestigious OECD (1981, 1986 — the latter is entitled *Trends in the Information Economy*) have depicted increases in employment and economic output in information categories in the main Western countries; the approach has even been applied to developing countries like China and Korea.[3]

The approach has been valuable in drawing attention to the role of information activities in industrial societies. The role of information in economic life had received surprisingly little attention, outside a rather narrow 'economics of information' literature.[4] But there are problems with the definitions of information activities used in the approach, and questions as to its appropriateness for tackling the policy and research problems associated with the information economy.

First, consider the question of *defining information activities*: How are we to define what constitutes information employment and information products? All human labour involves information processing, and all commodities embody and provide information. In other words, are not all occupations and products to some extent information occupations and products?

A second and related challenge to the approach is its *aggregative* nature. The information economy approach does try to overcome a major weakness of the post-industrialists: their treatment of 'services' as effectively homogeneous.[5] As what economists term the 'service sector' has grown to exceed, in employment and output terms, manufacturing and primary activities in Western societies, it has become increasingly evident that a great range of diverse activities has been lumped together into this category. By distinguishing an 'information sector' from other services, the information economy approach goes some way toward acknowledging this. The approach also allows the possibility of making distinctions within the information sector — for instance the OECD studies refer to primary and secondary information sectors. These studies show the information sector growing in the way that all services were described as doing in the post-industrial account — while the remainder of (non-information) services shows a more faltering development path.

But this still involves aggregating very heterogeneous activities together. Thus the OECD information occupations range from 'information machine workers' (e.g. bookbinders, to take what may be a non-obvious example) to 'process control and supervisory workers' (e.g. sales supervisors), from 'communication workers' (e.g. stage directors) to 'scientific and technical workers' (e.g. metallurgists). These occupations involve different skills, different functions (e.g. some are more a matter of organising other people, some a matter of controlling technical systems, some involve processing data or knowledge), and different products (media products, face-to-face contacts, etc.). Other than in very abstract terms, there is hardly likely to be a common factor underlying the expansion of these diverse occupations (if indeed they do all expand). It is at best unhelpful arm-waving to attribute trends in these occupations in common to growing demand for information (or for information products and communication services).

Indeed, quite a different argument is made by some critics of the 'information economy' viewpoint, often inspired by Braverman's (1974) evaluation of trends in the *division of labour*. They stress that information occupations have often been created by transferring some informational components of other jobs to specialised staff, such as supervisors and managers. Many other jobs have been 'de-skilled' as elements of planning and design have been removed, rendering the work more routine. Information tasks become more visible when made the province of a particular set of workers, rather than forming an unremarked feature of non-information jobs. This does not necessarily mean that it is more important — though it may be subject to more planning and rationalisation. There might be less information work going on, if specialised workers are accomplishing it more efficiently!

We do not believe that the increased division of labour is the only factor at work here, but the point that incautious use of statistics can suggest growth in activities, when all that is involved is a redistribution of activities among statistical categories, is a valid one. And this leads on to a third point. The recognition that all jobs involve information-processing has considerable relevance for the employment dimensions of technological change. The 'information occupations' are not necessarily the jobs that are most affected by new information technologies: robots, for instance, are more liable to displace production-line workers than scientists. Indeed, if information jobs were most vulnerable to new technologies, the statistical trends in the 'information economy' could well be reversed.

A fourth, and final, point, concerns the ambiguity of the term 'information economy'. Often the term is used not to describe *part* of the economy, but to label a new *phase* of activity. This implies qualitative change — not merely the development of quantitative trends, such as the steady growth of information activities. The approach we have been criticising here actually deals with such long-term trends, rather than discontinuities. Its grand claims as to providing a view of a new era are thus decidedly shaky. We will argue below that there are more convincing ways of discussing qualitative change, which actually complement the aggregative approach's analysis of long-term trends.

Techno-economic change

The term 'information economy' has actually become prominent not just because of a steady growth of information workers or sectors, but also because of the emergence of *new* Information Technology (IT). An alternative approach to the 'information economy', thus, relates it to the transformation in economic affairs associated with the development and diffusion of new IT. The 'information economy' is then a term that describes the whole economy. It does not refer to 'information sectors' alone, nor to an economy that is dominated by these sectors. Nor does it refer to IT-producing sectors alone. *All* sectors are potentially IT-using sectors, whose activities may be re-orientated more or less gradually around the potentials of the new technology. Personal computers are already widely used in all branches of extractive, construction, manufacturing and service industries. New telecommunications facilities — mobile communications, value-added network services, etc. — are becoming commonplace.[6]

This wide-ranging diffusion of IT, and the remarkable development of hosts of new applications of the technological potential, can be interpreted as a 'technological revolution'.[7] As in other technological revolutions, across wide swathes of the economy managers, research workers, professionals and other decision-makers are taking advantage of tremendous increases in the power, and decreases in the price, of 'heartland technologies'. Explaining what we mean here will mean explaining what is new about new IT.

Heartland technologies offer increases in efficiency and effectiveness in carrying out functions common to an extremely wide range of production processes and embodied in an extremely wide range of products. In the past, for instance, these functions have often involved the use of energy (steam and electric power are the technical basis of earlier technological revolutions). In the present instance, the wide scope for application of microelectronics reflects (a) reduced price and increased power made possible for many forms of information processing (data storage, data manipulation, data communication, etc.) and (b) the (often unremarked) centrality of information processing of one sort or another in all economic activities. IT can thus be a pervasive technology, used across the economy.

Radical change in the cost of information-processing in production processes enables new economies in the use of energy, materials and labour. New economic opportunities are created — for instance, information resources may themselves be sold as commodities; new markets may be addressed; new products, new product quality control, or new economies of scope may be achieved. Thus, the structure of costs and markets appears in a new light as the practicability of applying the new heartland technology is recognised. Economic actors may seek these opportunities proactively; but also, they may face challenges as new competitors may appear, and the strategy of familiar competitors — and collaborators too — may change. Whether or not, and how, to use IT is a matter of social choice, of course, but these choices are very much conditioned by the choices that others are making. Innovators will seek to seize favourable opportunities so as to achieve their goals, by effecting change in production processes and in products and markets.

Our IT approach has implications for the aggregative information economy analysis. IT innovations, after all, do process information: they will usually be associated with different patterns of information use. Often IT innovations may be associated with the production of new types of information — especially as experience with new technologies grows, and it becomes recognised that they allow for new types of activity in addition to the rationalisation of established practices. Much of the new use of information — for instance, the flow of electronically encoded data among workstations in a flexible manufacturing system — goes well beyond the activities of the 'information sector' as conventionally understood.

It is widely forecast that much more of the information that is generated in social and economic activities will be processed using IT; and that this will lead to the data being used in new ways, adding new capabilities to production, distribution and consumption. This will be paralleled by developments in the 'information sector', such as the emergence and

expansion of electronic publishing, online databases, management information systems, and the like. The development of the information economy,
then, is likely to see transformations of all sorts of information and
intelligence functions in firms and public agencies, and the emergence of new
activities and actors.

The research implications of this approach to the information economy
include developing instruments and methods to study this proliferation and
diffusion of IT-based activities — rather than focusing on indicators of the
scale of information activities as in the aggregative approach. We thus seek to
develop an IT Accounting Framework (ITAF). But we still need to clear away
some of the confusion surrounding new IT.

What is IT?

In thinking about technological revolutions, we stressed 'new' IT based on
microelectronic technology. But the class of *all* information and communications technologies is huge — it includes books and printing presses, LP
records and record players, typewriters, and even erasers, talking drums and
fires used to produce smoke signals! New IT is often thrown together with
traditional information and communications technologies in statistical
series — and social scientists interested in cultural dimensions of communications media may also fail to see the significance of the distinction for
their purposes. Such social scientists will often be dubious as to whether to
include information-processing systems whose activity is not designed to
contribute to an information product: for example, a computer that controls
the production process of tinned food or motor cars, or a microprocessor
control system for household energy management or security.

We would argue that *new* IT is distinct in key respects from earlier
technologies. The cheapness and power of microelectronics means that
information can be coded and processed electronically in a wide range of
devices, and to transform the information in a virtually limitless number of
ways. One of the characteristic features of microelectronic-based systems is
their *programmability*, the possibility of instructing them to handle data in
different ways; another is their *reflexivity*, the capacity not only to perform a
task, but also to store or transmit information on how they have performed it.[8]
Traditional information and communications technologies offer much less
flexibility in these respects. The programmability of IT creates requirements,
of course, for programs: the development of software activities is dealt with in
Tim Brady's chapter in this volume.

It was in practice possible to reprogramme earlier valve-based computers —
contemporary free-standing software programs were developed after the
'hard-wiring' of the early electronic computers, but the principles were
already recognised by Babbage and Lovelace in their unrealised plans for
mechanical computers in the nineteenth century. Microelectronics has
rendered this programmability available in the form of *cheap, small and*

powerful devices. Microprocessors may be programmable by users, or (as in many consumer devices and other 'dedicated' applications) they may be produced with dedicated programming capabilities built into them in line with anticipated user requirements. In either case, the possibility of considerable feats of information manipulation is realised.

In contrast, most traditional information and communications technologies involve limited information-processing. They are mostly media, receptacles that store or transmit data, processing it only to the extent that a translation between media is required. (Until the development at least of electronics, much of this translation work was done by human operatives — the readers and writers of texts, telegraph operators, and so on.) New IT supports flexible and powerful capabilities for all types of information processing: production, storage/retrieval, transmission/reception and manipulation of information. To date this rests on microelectronics, although complementary technologies (such as optoelectronics) contribute to the application of microelectronics, and in the future alternatives to the silicon 'chip' (e.g. Gallium Arsenide systems, optical chips, biochips) may well rise to greater prominence.

The evolution of microelectronics is the outcome of a long trajectory of development of semiconductor technology, from transistors to Integrated Circuits (ICs) and progressively higher levels of integration (e.g. Very Large Scale Integration, VLSI, representing the equivalent of tens of thousands of transistors per chip). Along with these increases in computing power and decreases in size, there have been marked cost reductions, of the order of $c.28$ per cent per annum, in ICs, with an estimated reduction of 35 per cent per annum in the cost of each bit of information processed.[9]

In consequence, it has been possible to incorporate ICs economically into an ever-widening range of products and processses. Microprocessors have accordingly diffused from the arena of Data Processing — large-scale administrative number-crunching for scientific calculations — into industrial control (e.g. regulating process operations, allowing for programmable machine tools), into new types of computer application (such as word processing) and communications, and into consumer products such as Compact Disc systems and video games.

IT is both pervasive across the whole economy and pervasive across a wide range of applications. It is not just that computers are used for office work, or mobile communications for coordinating sales staff, in many sectors; IT is being applied to process control, information systems, electronic funds transfer and many other applications in sector after sector. Both sector-specific and general IT applications are rapidly proliferating and diffusing. The 'convergence' of computing and communications, and the digitalisation of data of all kinds, makes it easier to transport information from one device and/or process to another. These developments offer scope for the sorts of change in economic (and social) activity that warrant the application of the term 'information economy'.

New IT has been discussed in terms of semiconductor-based technology; these are currently central, but the semicondutor or microprocessor does not have a complete monopoly of IT developments. Analogue machines and hybrid machines are still produced; electronic valves have even made a small come-back in military uses, due to their resistance to the effects of electromagnetic pulse; and in the future, we may use optical computers and biochips. Statistical studies may need to distinguish between the functional characteristics of the technology and the particular technologies used to provide these characteristics, since in the future new types of IT may emerge which premature definitional closure might end up overlooking either by exclusion or by absorption.

Let us elaborate on the *information-processing function of IT*. Information-processing technologies involve (often simultaneously) a number of distinct components:

— the automatic production of information in forms suitable for automatic processing;
— the automatic storage/retrieval of such information;
— the automatic transmission/reception of such information; and the actual manipulation of such information by automatic means.

Production is the creation of coded data about events (environmental changes, physical stimuli, etc.) by devices such as sensors and timers. *Data input* devices may be used to handle information created by human beings (e.g. keyboards, voice inputs, 'mice', although this is more suitably seen as the IT system transforming data from one medium (keypresses) to another (electronic signals); where the inputs are not the deliberate choice of human agents (e.g. where blood pressure is measured by a medical system, or movement in a room by a security system), then the IT system is more clearly involved in data production.

Storage/retrieval is the representation of data in a more or less permanent form on a medium (so that the data are retained in that 'carrier', which typically remains in one location, although, of course, software may be reproduced and distributed to different locations by physically transporting floppy discs); whereas in *transmission/reception* we refer to the passage of data through a medium (within which it generally rests for a brief period of time only). These two types of information-processing are in many respects similar, although the media involved are different ones: one involves transmission of data through time (storage), the other through space (transmission). But in both cases, some translation of the data into new formats may be required to convert to and from forms suitable for storage and transmission.

Translation of data from one format to another is one form of *manipulation* of information, but in the case of storage and transmission activities there is not usually any intention to add to or reduce the data involved (except in limited, technical features). Other forms of information manipulation *may* also be reversible, so that the original information content can be reproduced; but they may also change the data irretrievably, as when, for example, the output of a routine is to solve an equation or abstract an article, to extract a specific combination of items from a database, or provide an answer to a question posed by an expert system. Information that has been manipulated may be presented to users via an *output system* of some sort; and it may be used to *actuate* (control) devices such as robots, automobile engines, etc.

Microelectronics has provided cheap and efficient programmable devices which are able to manipulate information — especially information coded in digital electronic form — and, in turn, this increases the scope for data storage/retrieval and data transmission/reception devices. Speedy manipulation of large volumes of uncoded input data facilitates rapid improvements of sensor technology (optoelectronic and chematronic as well as more traditional mechanical sensors).

Current achievements in information manipulation depend upon the programmability of microelectronics; and upon these achievements depend in large part the improvements in information-processing functions more generally. The core information technologies of computers and telecommunications are critically dependent on these functions, since their main functions are information-processing. Other products may also have these as key functions, and many other products will make some use of these functions to further their main (non-information-processing) ends.

IT production and use

Producing and using sectors

The information economy involves the transformation of a very wide range of economic activities, as IT is applied within effectively all sectors and a vast number of production and distribution processes. It thus makes sense to think not only of *whether or not* IT is being used, but of the *extent* of IT use, the 'degree of informatisation' of different sectors, products or national economies.

We distinguish between sectors that produce IT hardware products — semiconductors, computers, telecommunications equipment — for trade as their primary activities, and the sectors that make use of these IT products. Brady's chapter shows that, where software is concerned, such a distinction becomes rather imprecise: some of the heavier users of IT produce in-house software to a high extent. Whereas computer producers are responsible for much general-purpose and systems software development, users are responsible for much industry-specific applications software — along with the software sector itself.

A complete definition of IT-producing sectors will go beyond those branches responsible for the manufacture of microelectronics. Just studying these would exclude many firms, sectors and products that provide information-processing functionality — such as microcomputers, whose manufacturers generally buy in the chips around which their models are built. And it would exclude the related software and service industries and producers of essential 'complementary technologies' (such as optical fibres for telecommunications).

The production of chips and related semiconductor-based materials can be interpreted as the 'IT heartland sector'; around and including this heart there lies an 'IT core sector'. This comprises a set of related industries which are also producing, in large part, multipurpose IT hardware and service products (rather than IT-using products for specific applications). The telecommunications and computer equipment industries are parts of the core IT sector, whose overall product ranges are not targeted to a narrow spectrum of users. (In contrast the machine tool industries or the consumer electronics industries are not producing such core IT products, and are more focused in terms of markets.)

The sectors that produce Integrated Circuit semiconductor technology are supplying programmability. (Programmability may be supplied through other heartland technologies, but at present microelectronics is integral to the rapid diffusion of new IT, and thus to the development of the information economy.) The computer industry embodies this programmability to provide general-purpose information manipulation IT. The telecommunications equipment industry embodies this programmability to provide general-purpose information transmission/reception IT. Data storage/retrieval systems are produced in these sectors (especially the former), as are sensor technologies; and they are also produced in other engineering industries: it is hard to distinguish these IT-producing industries in the available data. The software sector (which is also hard to distinguish statistically in the series we examine below) allows the programmability to be realised, by supplying the programs themselves. The IT-producing sector as discussed here thus contains several distinct industries which, while interrelated, to some extent have their own dynamics — whatever broad 'convergence' tendencies exist. (Simply contrasting the fortunes of national computer and telecommunications firms across OECD countries makes this clear.)

In hardware terms, at least, few sectors of the economy will be IT-producing, and most simply IT-using sectors (in practice by now there are no sectors in which there is not some use of IT, even if it is only a simple office computer). Most sectors utilise programs and programmability, or the manipulation, storage/retrieval, and transmission/reception capabilities which they empower, to accomplish their own ends. These ends may involve the processing of raw materials or goods; they may involve the 'processing' of people (as in health or education services). They may even involve the supply of information products (e.g. the media industries), or the processing of mainly symbolic material (e.g. the financial sectors, which process symbols of value and of property rights). But we can describe these as IT-using, as embodying IT in their processes (and even their products), rather than as IT-producing.

One source of UK official statistics tells us about which sectors of the economy are purchasing ICs (or other active components) for incorporation into their products. This is the (1984) *Purchases Inquiry* published by the Business Statistics Office as a special edition of *Business Monitor*, which details the purchases for current consumption made by different manufacturing sectors. Very few sectors are recorded as purchasing ICs to an extent worth recording. When considered as a proportion of all purchases, our two core IT-producing sectors, telecommunications equipment and EDP (electronic data processing — i.e. computers) manufacturing stand out dramatically as leading users. Each has more than 20 per cent of their expenditure going to these items — more than twice the proportion displayed by any other sector. This validates our treating these as core IT-producers: they are heavily dependent on IT heartland technology in a relatively 'unpackaged' form. (Only four other sectors are recorded as making IC and related purchases: radio and electronic capital goods; electronic instruments and controls; alarms and signalling; and the highest, consumer electronics. These industries might be included in a wider definition of IT-producing sectors.)

Services, ignored in the *Purchases Inquiry*, should also be considered. Computer and telecommunications services are closely tied to the DP and telecommunications equipment industries, respectively. Computer services include software production and maintenance, and also hardware main-tenance and (in British official statistics at any rate) VANS and professional services (such as training and consultancy for computer use). Telecommunica-tions services include basic telephony, cellular and related communications systems, and some data communication services. (VANS seem logically to fit within this service group; the current classification reflects some VANS having originated in online computer services leasing time on remote mainframes for company data processing.) While these services are (pre-sumably) not themselves *direct* consumers of ICs to any extent, their activities are centred around the microelectronics-based hardware supplied by their associated manufacturing sectors. And the services do more than add value to the hardware: they are *necessities* for the hardware to be applied, they are intrinsic components of new IT (which corresponds to the interpretation of technology as not merely material artefacts, but also as involving knowledge and skills). Thus we should treat them as part of the IT-producing sector rather than merely as IT-users. In practice, this is easier said than done: data on such services are often comparatively weak.

IT-intensity

Measuring the degree to which sectors are high or low users — more or less IT-intensive — poses some problems. Value measures (expenditure on IT as compared to other products) are liable to be misleading due to the rapid decreases in IT costs. Most physical measures (microcomputers per employee, for example), will also fail to reflect the substantial quantitative and qualitative differences between distinct generations of IT.

The increased performance and decreased cost of IT need to be borne in mind when interpreting data on IT-intensity. A simple totalling-up of items of equipment of different vintages may be misleading, especially given the emergence of new applications using more powerful equipment. In many surveys of IT equipment, distinctions are made between different classes of equipment: microcomputer, minicomputer, mainframe computer, etc. In some surveys items are graded in terms of current price bands. Very few researchers have sought to document trends in IT power — e.g. amount of RAM available, level of information flow in bits/second, etc. — although there have been some efforts in this direction. Efforts to address the distinct generations of IT systems are also uncommon, although there are specialised surveys of specific generations of equipment or services (for example, studies of the diffusion of fourth-generation languages). Equally important are qualitative changes, those associated with 'convergence' in particular. As computer and communications systems become linked, a computer is not a computer is not a computer... because it is part of a network! While commentators have drawn attention to the growing role of systems integration in IT products, and a number of surveys document that this trend does indeed exist, few statistical studies have touched on this development.[10]

Thus, although we use value data below, readers should be cautious about reading it too literally, for these reasons: counting up money spent on IT devices is like counting up expenditure on apples and oranges — and on fruit juice and vitamin pills! We could conceive of numerous indicators of IT-intensity related to different classes of IT product. For sectors these might involve, for instance, consumption of computers, of software, of tele-communications equipment, of communications services; for products we could similarly consider the embodiment of IT hardware, of lines of software code, etc. In practice, the selection of IT-intensity indicators that will be available is generally limited, and we are lucky to be able to experiment with more than one! The heterogeneity of IT products is better viewed as indicative of issues to explore in research, than as a regrettable obstacle to analysis. For instance, we can imagine examining patterns of emphasis in the consumption of different classes of IT product across sectors of the economy, which should be a fruitful way of examining both the actuality of 'convergence' in practice and the factors leading to distinctive applications of IT.

We shall focus on sectors in the statistical analyses below. It is, however, possible to consider occupations (IT-producing occupations like electronic engineering and systems analysis, IT-using occupations like keyboarding) and products (core IT products and IT-using products like industrial robots and microwave ovens) in similar ways. IT-using jobs and products can also be thought of in terms of their IT-intensity: but data for addressing these topics are even more limited.

To explain briefly our approach to products, we consider IT products to be those whose function is centrally a matter of programmable information-processing (computers, calculators, telecommunications systems, etc.). Other technologies may be IT-using ones, products in which IT is embodied so as to enhance the primary functions of the product with the functionality of new IT. IT-intensity (e.g. the cost of chips as a proportion of the products total costs) may be misleading, since the ICs may play a very significant role for very little extra cost. Research into IT embodiment might try to use price deflator-based indicators in order to deal with these price reductions of ICs and other components. This will probably require close work on the *Purchase Enquiry* and on other data sources, in order to be able to pick out these effects in more detail.

The simple fact that IT is embodied to some extent in the product — e.g. it incorporates microelectronic controls — may sometimes be the key issue. (Microelectronic controls that are only a small fraction of an industrial machine's production costs may be crucial for networking the machine to others so as to incorporate it in a flexible manufacturing system, etc. Equally, however, the low price of microelectronics means that relatively frivolous embodiments of IT are made in products, adding little to their functionality — e.g. the digital clocks incorporated in many electronics devices, at least in those cases where the clock is not capable of controlling when the device turns on and off. Even sophisticated systems at present frequently use dedicated microprocessors in such a way as to rule out the chances of reprogramming them or networking them to other devices.)

This approach to IT embodiment results in classifications that may not correspond to those in much of the literature. For instance, it will mean classifying some products that many other commentators would term 'information technology' as IT-using but not as IT products themselves (for example industrial robots); and we will be classifying these, along with others, such as motor cars, that such commentators would not regard as 'information technology'. Both instances are products which have acquired microcomputer controls and even communications facilities so as to *enhance* their core functionality (e.g. handling materials, transporting people); but the information-processing is not the core function as it is for computers or telecommunication systems.

Statistical analysis of the information economy

An IT Accounting Framework

Our discussion above suggests that understanding the information economy requires attention to the interrelationships between differentiated IT activities and other economic activities — rather than trying to develop a single measure of the informatisation of an economy at the outset. This informs our approach to an IT Accounting Framework (ITAF).

This approach has two components. There is a *conceptual* component, involving debate over the analytical categories into which data (and proposals for new data) are placed: *what* 'empty boxes' we would like to have filled. And there is an *operational* component, debate over available, and potential, data sources: *how* such boxes are to be filled. There is at present insufficient clarity in both these areas — a more structured debate is essential if significant progress is to be made.

We try to avoid premature closure of this debate by adopting what should be seen as a flexible analytical approach to the ITAF, within which different definitions can be experimented with. At present it seems that this can be facilitated through the use of widely available spreadsheet software, transforming official data into the core ITAF categories. These transformed data can then be used by researchers to construct their own 'customised' measures appropriate to the questions being investigated based upon the core ITAF concepts.

An ITAF involves a rather more formal approach to the topics discussed earlier. We shall represent the information-processing function as IT, and follow this function with the specific technology used in brackets. Thus IT(SEMI) is this function performed by semiconductor technology. As a first definition of the IT(SEMI) activity, we suggest: 'The provision of general-purpose programmable information-processing functions (manipulation and/ or transmission of electronically encoded information) utilising semi-conductor technology'. In what follows we will focus upon IT(SEMI), which, as noted earlier, is the dominant IT at present.

We earlier discussed various facets of information-processing, most notably contrasting the transformation of information (computation) with the transmission of information (telecommunication, to achieve which manipulation is necessary, of course). The former can be conceived of as adding value by logical manipulation, the latter as adding value by relocation. We can define IT(SEMI)COMP as the processing function, and IT(SEMI) TRAN as the transmission function. A piece of equipment able to accomplish both functions can be designated as IT(SEMI)C&C.

The ITAF analysis of *software* poses special problems, due, particularly, to the paucity of data on the subject. Clearly, unless special surveys are used or undertaken, as in Brady's study, much will rest upon the eventual treatment of traded software in national accounts statistics. The 'commodity composition of output' tables (the 'make matrix'), which give estimates of each industry's principal product and non-principal product output, should feature a traded software commodity vector and corresponding industry vector. In the following discussion we are forced to focus on hardware.

IT *components* play an important role in both end-use and embodied categories. We designate these as IT(SEMI)CPT. The ITAF can use IT(SEMI)CPT flows derived from the intermediate output commodity flow matrices — data similar to the *Purchases Enquiry* statistics cited above — as a means of determining IT(SEMI) embodiment in consumer and capital goods. However, in this chapter we shall only consider fixed capital formation, the purchase of IT as investment goods (e.g. computers to control processes). IT(SEMI)CPT will not figure directly here — the ICs will be built into machine tools, computers, etc. purchased from other sectors. Components are likely to feature strongly in analyses of trade flows and the IT(SEMI) import composition of goods, and may contribute to the analysis of IT process applications. Nevertheless, here we shall be dealing with IT(SEMI)INV, i.e. semiconductor-based new IT investment goods, and examining their purchase across the economy.

Data on the diffusion of IT

The main official source relevant to IT diffusion and IT-intensity is the *Input-Output Tables*. Input-output analysis brings data on the interchanges between different industries together into a common table; this arrangement of data allows for versatile analysis. For IT Accounting purposes, there are evident possibilities for assessing the purchases from IT-related sectors by other parts of the economy, to calculate the contribution of these IT sectors to the final output of other sectors, and so on. How far can input-output tables be used to assess IT-related purchases by the various sectors of the economy? Five relevant branches of industry are distinguished:

— office machinery and computer equipment;
— telecommunications etc. equipment, electronic capital goods;
— electronic components and sub-assemblies;
— instrument engineering;
— telecommunications services.

In the present development of the ITAF, we focus on the first two of these sectors as IT-producing sectors, following on our arguments earlier in this chapter.

Input-output data have been used to address questions concerning IT in some previous work. In particular, Roach's (1987) analysis of the US capital stock provides useful estimates of the IT component of the capital stock by broad sector. Roach bases his estimates upon the industry-commodity capital stock matrices provided by the US Department of Commerce. These data allow the capital stock (i.e. stock of investment goods) of each industry defined to be disaggregated by its commodity composition. Thus it is possible, if the commodity classes allow (as they do for the US data), to calculate the IT component of each industry's capital stock. Roach shows, for example, that non-manufacturing branches held over 80 per cent of the IT capital stock in 1985. This suggests that the IT capital stock is highly concentrated in (service) industries dealing primarily with information. (Precisely these sectors where fewest data are available!)

Some problems with input-output data

Classification schemata Industries and sectors are defined in several ways; for present purposes the most relevant are (1) the UK standard industrial classification (SIC) in both its 1968 and 1980 versions; and (2) two levels of aggregation used in input-output classifications. The latter schemes are still based upon SIC codes, but the precise mapping of data from one classification to another (its 'reconciliation') varies across different input-output tables. To avoid confusion arising from industrial headings appearing to be the same when the actual sectoral definition differs, we will use a shorthand formulation to refer to the classification type, its version and the code for the sector concerned (in that order). Apologies to readers for the proliferation of abbreviations that ensues!

SIC sectors are labelled 'SIC' and qualified by the year in which they were introduced. Two such schemes are relevant to the following discussion: SIC(68) and SIC(80). This classification type and 'vintage' is then followed by the 2, 3 or 4-digit (for SIC(80) only) code and title for the unit of analysis concerned. Thus we have SIC(year)<code>:<title>. *Input-output sectors* are labelled 'IO', and are prefixed by 'F' if they are the full (published) classification, or 'A' if they are the more aggregate system (corresponding to a classification used in the National Accounts 'Blue Book'). Otherwise they follow the same format as the SIC system above, i.e. <F or A>IO(year) <code>:<title>. It should be noted that there are some differences according to whether we are referring to sales or purchases; but these concern rows or columns inserted in the IO tables for specific accounting reasons (such as taxes), so this does not affect the references to 'real' sectors.

Sectoral coverage   The input-output categories for services are far less disaggregated than those for manufacturing. In the 1979 tables, of 100 branches of the economy, only eleven (or twelve if we add 'public administration etc., domestic service, ownership of dwellings') are services. And of these, transport is disaggregated into four varieties while importantly different activities are made into bedfellows ('post and telecommunications', 'banking, finance, insurance, professional and business services, hiring'). The 1984 tables, fortunately, do distinguish post from telecommunications, along with other improvements which give us some fourteen services. This severely limits the usefulness of the input-output tables as a basis for comparing services in detail to other sectors.

Fluctuations in investment   Input-output data are not published annually for the UK, and only appear after some delay. (1984 tables were only published in 1988; the previous tables concerned 1979.) We are provided with snapshots of the UK economy as it was a while ago, rather than more dynamic and up-to-date data. This is not believed to be too much of a problem for studies of intermediate output flows, because the structure of these flows changes little over time. With respect to gross fixed capital formation, however, it does pose serious problems.

Since fixed capital investment fluctuates fairly heavily around business cycles, comparisons of IT investment across sectors may confound enduring sectoral differences with year-on-year fluctuations. We can expect bunched investments in IT(SEMI) and perhaps a more general structural relationship between IT(SEMI)INV and other forms of plant and machinery investment. This problem requires further research, drawing both upon appropriate time-series plant and machinery investment data (such as is contained in the UK Census of Production), and generating primary research where necessary in order to relate IT(SEMI)INV patterns (which are as yet poorly understood) to general plant and machinery investment patterns.

Leasing In the 1979 tables, equipment purchased to be leased out was included under AIO(79)33: 'Financial & misc. services'. However, the 1984 tables distinguish leased equipment as a separate sector (AIO(84)36: 'Banking leased'), allowing us to explore the importance of leasing in IT investment.

From the 1984 Input-Output data (Table 10) we find that just under 20 per cent of FIO(84)43: 'office machinery and computer equipment' investment, is destined to be leased out, while a negligible proportion of AIO(84)47: 'telecommunication etc.' equipment is leased out. (This suggests that the 'telecommunications services' category may conceal some leasing.) Office and computer equipment constitutes some 13 per cent of total fixed capital investment destined for leasing. Office and computer equipment leasing share is not especially high as a share of all office and computer machinery investment, but it does constitute the third largest share of the total value of leased equipment, second only to motor vehicles and wooden furniture.

These data illustrate the importance of leasing in aggregate, but do not tell us where leased equipment ends up being used. We must therefore draw upon other sources of information to estimate the sectoral distribution of leased equipment — or simply assume that it is distributed in line with IT investment purchases, something that we are rather dubious about.

IT sectors and products In the first instance we are interested in devices whose primary (end-use) characteristic is based upon the IT(SEMI) function as defined above. Three FIO(84) commodity classes conform to this *restrictive* definition:

FIO(84)43: Office machinery and computer equipment
FIO(84)47: Telecommunication etc. equipment, electronic capital goods
FIO(84)48: Electronic components and sub-assemblies

We will refer to these as the IT(SEMI)DEF1 commodity types. But the actual output of a sector may not be reflected in its title, so we need to look at three and four-digit level data given in the Census of Production reports. We cannot give full details of this part of the study here, but the main points are summarised below.

First, the FIO(84)43 sector largely produces computer equipment: these are around 90 per cent of the sales, the rest being office machinery. Second, FIO(84)48, consists of two subgroups: SIC(80)3444 (components other than active components, mainly for electronic equipment), SIC(80)3453 (active components and sub-assembles and components mainly for electronic consumer goods); the sales of these subgroups are roughly of equal magnitude, and neither appears to present any problems as an operationalisation of IT(SEMI)CPT.

The third case — FIO(84)47 — is more complex. This sector consists of three components: SIC(80)3441 (telegraph and telephone apparatus and equipment), SIC(80)3442 (electrical instruments and control systems) and SIC(80)3443 (radio and electronic capital goods), contributing roughly 30 per cent, 20 per cent and 50 per cent of its output; we are as yet uncertain as to the latter two groups' relevance to the ITAF IT(SEMI)TRAN category. However, it remains to be established how far this is a real problem: for example, SIC(80)3443 may contain microwave and other technology, and SIC(80)3442 network test and control devices, which can be classed as a telecommunication activity.

IT-intensity indicators

We conclude this section with some preliminary estimates of IT(SEMI)INV patterns, to illustrate the type of descriptive statistics the ITAF provides. The material discussed relates only to patterns of fixed capital investment in general (specific estimates of plant and machinery investment are also available). They are rough 'first cuts' at the sort of results we are attempting to produce via the development of an ITAF. Given the problems of investment fluctuations and leasing problems, the industry level estimates may be of limited reliability as longitudinal or cross-sectional generalisations. Many other types of statistic can be constructed from the input-output source material; and these data may be related, further, to data from other sources (e.g. employment data).

The gross fixed capital formation matrix, and its component plant and machinery investment matrix, consist of a set of (commodity defined) column vectors. Each vector tells us the commodity composition of investment by purchasing industry, and our IT investment estimates are derived from these.

Several features of the results are of interest. For one thing, they give a very similar picture to Roach's (1987) for the USA — around 80 per cent of IT investment comes from services sectors of the economy, for instance. Likewise, the IT share of plant and machinery investment (around 25 per cent) is very similar to that cited for the USA in 1985 by the Office of Technology Assessment (1988).

Table 6.1 displays IT(SEMI) investment by investing industry. AIO(84)36, which is the 'Banking leased' category, is shown in bold (in order to emphasise the potential importance of the leasing adjustment which should be made for more precision). Table 6.2 goes on to present ITAF measures aggregated into 'grand sectors' of the all-inclusive type we earlier criticised!). As well as the share of each sector's investment in IT, we present two 'Comparative IT investment intensity ratios'. A ratio less than one means that an industry accounts for a smaller share of IT spend than its share of total fixed capital investment expenditure. A ratio greater than one means it accounts for a greater share of IT spend than its share of total fixed capital investment. These provide useful insights into where IT is being applied most heavily.

These results confirm the importance of service sectors as IT-using sectors. Not only are they dominant users: a greater proportion of their investment is IT investment. The 'IT revolution' appears to be especially a transformation of the service sectors. The data indicate that some services are being 'industrialised' in the information economy — and suggest that the in-

Table 6.1 IT (SEMI) DEF1 investment intensity by industry, 1984

AIO(84)		£m IT(DEF1)	£m Total	Percent It
1	Agriculture	5.30	1,092.50	0.49
2	Forestry	1.60	103.60	1.54
3	Fishing	1.60	11.10	14.41
4	Coal & Coke	5.20	339.80	1.53
5	Extracts of oil & gas	76.90	3,068.10	2.51
6	Oil processing	22.30	186.70	11.94
7	Electric etc.	100.60	2,015.60	4.99
8	Gas supply	130.70	628.80	20.79
9	Water supply	3.80	413.10	0.92
10	Metals	21.10	381.60	5.53
11	Oth mins & prods	28.70	497.60	5.77
12	Chemical & fibres	29.60	1,003.30	2.95
13	Metal goods nes	20.10	320.40	6.27
14	Mechanical engineering	24.20	618.10	3.92
15	Electric & instruments	269.80	950.40	28.39
16	Vehicles & parts	45.80	622.90	7.35
17	Other trans equip	25.80	283.90	9.09
18	Food	49.80	921.60	5.40
19	Drink & tobacco	28.50	343.90	8.29
20	Textiles	0	208.60	0
21	Clothing & footwear	11.00	148.50	7.41
22	Timber	5.40	170.20	3.17
23	Paper	24.50	706.70	3.47
24	Rubber	10.90	330.50	3.30
25	Other manuf	2.70	59.60	4.53
26	Construction	10.20	545.20	1.87
27	Wholesale	260.90	1,470.40	17.74
28	Retail & repair	407.10	2,498.40	16.29
29	Hotels & catering	13.40	761.70	1.76
30	Railways	2.40	281.40	0.85
31	Other inland transport	62.20	1,118.40	5.56
32	Sea transport	8.00	577.00	1.39
33	Air transport	6.80	419.50	1.62
34	Other transport	24.90	560.90	4.44
35	Communications	1,126.80	1,825.10	61.74
36	**Banking leased**	**490.60**	**3,719.80**	**13.19**
37	Banking other	601.00	2,401.10	25.03
38	Business services	400.50	3,062.40	13.08
39	Public administration	63.10	1,325.50	4.76
40	Roads	5.20	1,504.00	0.35
41	Education	39.60	952.20	4.16
42	Health services	23.80	1,112.70	2.14
43	Sanitary services	1.10	641.40	0.17
44	Misc. services	231.00	1,543.30	14.97
45	Dwellings	0	11,036.00	0
46	Transfer costs	0	2,604.00	0
47	Total	4,724.50	55,387.50	8.53

Source: Calculated from *Input-Output Data*, 1984

Table 6.2 Comparative IT investment intensity ratios, 1984

Sectors: AIO(84)		Indicators: PCINVCOM	PCINVTEL	CITIIRCOM	CITIRTEL
1–3	Agriculture, forestry, fishing	0.6	0.1	0.13	0.02
4–11	Extractive sector	1.7	3.5	0.37	0.87
12–25	Manufacturing	4.1	4.0	0.92	1.00
26	Construction	0.5	1.4	0.10	0.35
27–45	(less 36) Services (excluding leasing)	5.7	4.6	1.26	1.15
27–45	(less 36 and 37) Services other than telecommunications	5.8	1.8	1.28	0.45

Definitions:
PCINVCOM = % of sectoral investment in computers
PCINVTEL = % of sectoral investment in telecomms equipment
CITIIRCOM = comparative IT investment intensity ratio for computers
CITIRTEL = comparative IT investment intensity ratio for telecommunica-
= tions equipment
Source: Calculated from *Input-Output Data*, 1984

formation economy involves very heterogeneous patterns of development in different areas.

Conclusions

Research on the information economy can move beyond stressing the importance of information to economic affairs. It can examine the specific uses of specific classes of information, and the role of technical change in these processes. This means shifting focus from the 'information sector' to information activities in all sectors, and extending it to processes other than those yielding 'information products' or employment of 'information workers'.

IT Accounting does not pretend to provide answers to all questions about the socio-economic implications of IT. But it does provide a systematic framework for analysis of some of the most useful existing data. This means that we can engage in informed discussion about both definitional and substantive issues; and at the same time generate statistical results (and identify limitations in the data!).

The term 'information economy' can be usefully applied to the transformations associated with the application of new IT to such activities. The lack of empirical analysis of the diffusion of IT and the diversity of IT applications is remarkable. One obvious conclusion of this study is that more attention should be devoted to establishing just what data are available for analysis, and to overcoming their major shortcomings. Among these shortcomings, most notably, are the lack of data on IT services, and on IT use in services. Our analysis here has demonstrated the importance of IT in overall investment, and the importance of services as a source of IT investment.

Increasingly it becomes inappropriate to consider manufacturing and services as contrasting sectors: they are becoming more alike and they are becoming more integrated. From 'manufacturing *versus* services' and 'manufacturing *or* services', attention needs to shift to 'manufacturing *and* services'. Debates as to whether we are deindustrialising or moving to a post-industrial society are misleading: the question is, what combinations of manufacturing and service activities are crucial in the information economy? The integration of sectors is likely to be the key element is quantitative and qualitative growth in the future.

Notes

1. For critical approaches — not without some recuperation of the term — see Slack and Fejes, 1987.
2. The prime exponent of this viewpoint is Bell, 1974; a good early critique is Kleinberg, 1973.
3. These are largely statistical exercises, but there are more historically rich accounts: see, for example, Beniger, 1986.
4. For an introduction, see Monk, 1989.
5. Gershuny and Miles, 1983; Miles and Gershuny, 1987.
6. See Miles, Rush, Turner and Bessant, 1988.
7. See, for example, Freeman and Soete, 1987, who are unusually painstaking in their attempt to show why the much-touted 'IT Revolution' really warrants the label 'revolution'.
8. See Beniger, 1986, for a provocative discussion of programmability; Zuboff, 1988, deals with the implications of reflexivity.
9. See Braun and Macdonald, 1982, for a concise account; useful material is gathered in Forester, 1981, 1985.
10. See Miles *et al.*, 1989.

Bibliography

Bell, D., 1973, *The Coming of Post-Industrial Society*, Basic Books, New York.
Beniger, J.R., 1986, *The Control Revolution*, MIT Press, Cambridge.

Braun, E. and Macdonald, S. 1982, *Revolution in Miniature*, Cambridge University Press, Cambridge, 2nd edn.

Braverman, H., 1974, *Labour and Monopoly Capital*, Monthly Review Press, New York.

David, P.A., 1976, *Technical Choice, Innovation and Economic Growth*, Cambridge University Press, Cambridge.

Dostal, W., 1981, 'The contribution of information and related technologies to productivity growth' in OECD, *Microelectronics, Productivity and Employment*, OECD (ICCP series), Paris.

Forester, T., (ed.), 1981, *The Microelectronics Revolution*, Basil Blackwell, Oxford.

Forester, T. (ed.), 1985, *The Information Technology Revolution*, Basil Blackwell, Oxford.

Freeman, C., Clark, J. and Soete, L., 1982, *Technical Change and Unemployment*, Frances Pinter, London.

Freeman, C. and Soete, L. (eds), 1987, *Technical Change and Full Employment*, Basil Blackwell, Oxford.

Gershuny, J. and Miles, I., 1983, *The New Service Economy*, Frances Pinter, London.

Kleinberg, B., 1973, *American Society in the Post-Industrial Age*, Charles E. Merril, Columbus, Ohio.

Kobayashi, K., 1986, *Computers and Communications*, John Wiley, Boston.

Machlup, F., 1962, *The Production and Distribution of Knowledge in the United States*, Princeton University Press, Princeton.

Marchand, D.A. and Horton, F.W., 1986, *Infotrends: Profiting from your Information Resources*, John Wiley, New York.

Miles, I. and Gershuny, J., 1987, 'The social economics of information technology' in R. Finnegan, G. Salaman and K. Thompson, (eds), *Information Technology: Social Issues*, Hodder & Stoughton, London.

Miles, I., Rush, H., Turner, K. and Bessant, J., 1988, *Information Horizons*, Edward Elgar, Aldershot.

Miles, I. *et al.*, 1989, *Mapping and Measuring the Information Economy*, British Library R&D Department, London.

Monk, P., 1989, *Technological Change in the Information Economy*, Frances Pinter, London.

OECD, 1981, *Information Activities, Electronics and Telecommunications Technologies, vol. 1*, OECD (ICCP series), Paris.

OECD, 1986, *Trends in the Information Economy*, OECD (ICCP series), Paris.

OECD, 1987, *Information Technology and Economic Prospects*, OECD (ICCP series), Paris.

Office of Technology Assessment, 1988, *Technology and the American Economic Transition*, US Government Printing Office, Washington, DC.

Porat, M., 1977, *The Information Economy*, US Department of Commerce, Washington, DC.

Roach, S.S., 1987, *America's Technology Dilemma: a Profile of the Information Economy*, Special Economic Study, Morgan Stanley & Co, New York.

Slack, J.D. and Fejes, F. (eds), 1987, *The Ideology of the Information Age*, Ablex Publishing Corporation, Norwood, New Jersey.

Soete, L., 1987, 'The newly emerging information technology sector' in C. Freeman and L. Soete (eds), *Technical Change and Full Employment*, Basil Blackwell, Oxford.

Zuboff, S., 1988, *In the Age of the Smart Machine*, Basic Books, New York.

7 Software activities in the UK: who does what?

Tim Brady

Introduction

As has been noted in other chapters in this volume (see for example Ian Miles and Mark Matthews) new Information Technology (IT) is being applied widely across the economy. It is being applied to change many production processes (for example, computer-controlled machine tools are displacing conventional equipment, word processors are displacing typewriters), and it involves new products as well. Some new products — the machine tool and dedicated word processor — are devices that may be identified as hardware; even these devices require some software to operate them, although the software may be physically built into them on a special 'chip'. But new IT services and software are also products in their own right, sometimes being sold, sometimes produced within organisations for their own use.

While there are numerous studies about the use of IT hardware in UK industry there have been few dealing with software and services as part of industrial processes. Software activities have received attention as far as the computer services sector is concerned, but software is produced by IT professionals in many other sectors in the economy. This chapter presents a perspective on the role of software in the information economy, and from this outlines issues for empirical research, illustrating these with results from a survey of software activities in the UK.

What is software?

Any computer system consists of both hardware and software — they are interdependent, neither will work in isolation. In simple terms, software can be thought of as an *informational* component of a computer system — the set of instructions which determines and controls the operation of the computer hardware, whilst the hardware can be defined as the physical components of a computer system — including central processing units, disk drives, tape drives, printers, etc. Mark Matthews and Ian Miles discussed how the programmability of microelectronics provides the basis for the application of new IT to a wide range of information-processing tasks: software supplies the programmes whereby this feature can be realised.

Most modern computers, whether they are mainframes or micros, consist of the same basic components following the original design developed by John von Neumann in the 1940s. Computers work by storing and manipulating information. Items of information are stored in the memory locations in a computer and are manipulated by what is known as the central processing unit (CPU).

There are generally two types of memory location — read only memory (ROM) and random access memory (RAM). ROM locations contain information which is placed into memory when the computer is assembled. As the name suggests, the computer is able to 'read' information in a ROM location but is not able to 'write' new information into ROM or replace the existing information stored there. The information in ROM is permanent. In contrast, the RAM locations can accept new information each time the computer is used. This may come from input from the keyboard or from files stored on disk, tape or other media. The information in RAM is only temporarily stored there. It will stay in RAM as long as the computer is turned on and as long as it is not deleted.

Information is called up from a memory location and stored temporarily in a 'register'. Other pieces of information are also called up and placed in other registers within the CPU. Once all the necessary pieces of information have been called from the memory into the CPU registers, the arithmetic/logic unit in the CPU processes them in some way — e.g. adding together or subtracting the contents of two registers. Once the manipulation of the data is complete, the result is sent back to the memory locations where it is 'written' into part of the RAM (random access memory). The control/timing unit in the CPU directs the movement of information between the memory location and the arithmetic/logic unit. Software determines what information is stored in the memory locations and what manipulations will be carried out in the CPU.

Software languages

There are several different classes of software, which shall be defined later, but all programs have to be written in such a way that the computer hardware can subsequently understand the instructions contained in the program. A special subset of software, software languages, has evolved to facilitate this. In order to understand this better it is necessary to dip briefly into the history of computing.

It is generally accepted that there have been five generations of computers. The first generation were developed in the 1940s and were based on vacuum tubes. The second generation evolved during the 1950s based on transistors. The mid-1960s saw the third generation with the development of integrated circuit chips. The fourth generation computers first evolved in the mid-1970s, coinciding with the development of large-scale integrated circuits and has continued to the present day with the development of very large-scale integrated circuits. These four generations are all based on the von Neumann architecture (as described above). Latterly, a fifth generation of computers utilising parallel processing architectures has been developed, although such developments have only just begun to be commercialised.

Generations of software languages have been created, too, more or less corresponding to the hardware generations, building upon the opportunities offered by more powerful computers. But whereas old hardware generations tend to die out, software languages tend to live on from one generation to the next. When a new computer is replaced by an old one, the user may want to continue to use familiar software. But let us consider the generations of software languages. (See Baron, 1988, for a readable general account.)

In the early days of computing in the 1940s, there was no such thing as software as a separate product. The early electrical computers, such as ENIAC, were programmed by the users physically setting switches to allow the computer to perform a specific set of calculations. In order to perform a different set of calculations the switches had to be physically reset. The first software languages were developed to emulate the actions of these switches. These *machine codes* consist of sequences of binary numbers (0s and 1s) which are used to turn on and off switches in the computer hardware.

Machine code was the first of the low-level languages, so-called because they were far removed from natural language. Later, in the early 1950s, *assembly languages* were developed which used codes which were slightly more like natural languages, using mnemonic in place of binary sequences: a line of assembly language thus corresponds directly to a sequence of machine code. These languages can be thought of as the first generation of software.

By the late 1950s and early 1960s transistors were being produced cheaply enough to be used in computers: this led to significant improvements in size, speed and reliability. This period also coincided with the development of the first higher-level software languages — such as Fortran and Cobol — so called because they incorporated modern syntactic conventions. Fortran was developed for solving scientific problems while Cobol was developed to address problems for business and commercial applications of computers.

Through the 1960s, new languages, such as PL/1 and Algol, incorporating more sophisticated syntactic conventions were developed. At the same time, the early Fortran and Cobol languages were revised to take on board these new conventions (this is an example of how software languages may 'evolve', rather than 'dying out'); together with the other new languages they came to be called *third generation languages*. What distinguishes this generation from the previous one is that they could (in principle) be generally applicable to problem solving, in contrast to the second generation which were designed for specialised functions. Today languages developed more recently, such as Ada,

Pascal and C, are still regarded as third generation languages. All such languages are generally referred to as high-level languages.

Fourth generation languages emerged during the 1980s, and include modern business-oriented languages which allow users with no formal training in computer programming to access data from large databases. Such languages are called non-procedural or descriptive, since they allow people to specify the problem to be solved rather than how the computer should solve the problem. Other more general languages such as Prolog and Smalltalk also use this non-procedural approach.

Classes of software

In addition to software languages, other classes of software have been designed to solve particular problems. The two main classes are systems software and applications software, but within these are many subclasses.

Systems software includes the operating system (OS),[1] compilers/assemblers, communications monitors, translators and 'utilities'. The actual configuration of the systems software will differ from machine to machine — it is possible to have different operating systems on the same piece of hardware — and there will be differences in systems software in mainframe, mini and microcomputers. Alongside systems software there is a range of tools which allow end-users to retrieve and organise, manage and manipulate data and databases and to develop programs.[2]

The second main category of software, applications (or applications solutions, because it is designed to solve specific problems) software can be split into two categories: general application software (including such applications as payroll, accounts, human resources management, office software, word processing, electronic mail, etc.) which is usable across many industry sectors; and industry-specific application software, which as the name suggests, usually applies to particular sectors only (e.g. banking/financial software, manufacturing software, retailing software, housing benefit administration, etc.).

Software may also be supplied in different modes and stored on a variety of media. The different modes of software include standard packages (i.e. a piece of software sold 'off the shelf' for generalised use); modified packages (i.e. a standard package tailored to the requirements of a particular customer); and bespoke or customised software (i.e. written from scratch specifically for an individual customer). The media on which software is stored include floppy disc, tape, cartridge, or firmware (this is a special example of software whereby a program is stored on electronic circuits within the hardware — ROM chips, referred to above in the description of the von Neumann architecture, are an example of firmware).

Stages in software development

Irrespective of the application area, project size or complexity of the system, the development of a piece of software can be divided into a number of different stages.

The most commonly accepted representation of the software life cycle is the 'waterfall model' through which are represented the successive stages in the software development process:

— requirements analysis — when a general definition of the requirements is established, feasibility studies are undertaken, a development plan is defined and cost/benefit analysis is undertaken;

— systems specification — when a description of the system is developed including functional and data requirements;

— design — when the system architecture is defined and the basic algorithms are established;

— implementation — when the programming, i.e. the task of writing code, takes place;

— testing — when pieces of code are tested and integrated with other (tested) pieces of code; and

— maintenance — which takes place after the system is being used and involves making changes in the software to correct problems as they reveal themselves or to provide additional functionality.

Macro and Buxton (1987) note that if maintenance is left aside, then generally about 15 per cent of the effort is spent on specification, 35 per cent on design, 15 per cent on coding and 35 per cent on testing. The actual percentages vary depending on the end application for which the software is being developed. For instance, safety critical software (e.g. that operating a power station) will require a lot more testing and validation, and a greater proportion of effort would be devoted to that part of the process than for other applications.

Software maintenance is often neglected in studies of the software production process, but nevertheless it is an important phase estimated to account for between 50 per cent and 80 per cent of the costs of a software system over its lifetime. There are several categories of maintenance — corrective, adaptive and perfective. Only the first category is comparable to the kind of repair activity generally associated with the term maintenance. The other two are really more like on-going development: adaptive to take account of changes in data inputs and files, and to hardware or systems software; perfective to allow for enhancements for users, improvements in program documentation and recoding for efficiency in computation.

Who produces software?

Historically, software was developed within user organisations or supplied free by hardware manufacturers when they delivered a computer system. A large proportion of the software in use today still comes from these two sources. But since the late 1960s software has become a 'tradeable' commodity and we have witnessed the emergence of the software industry to market this 'tradeable' element of software. The 'industry' consists of software houses, systems houses (firms who buy in hardware and add software to provide complete systems), hardware manufacturers, distributors and dealers and sometimes subsidiaries of user organisations who 'spin-off' software products originally developed for their own in-house consumption.

In the early days of computing (i.e. during the late 1940s and early 1950s) computers were mainly used for scientific problem solving. There was no body of expertise available — the computer industry was in its infancy, there was no software industry — so the scientists, in addition to being the users, were forced to act as programmers and even hardware engineers. Hardware suppliers were exactly that — they supplied hardware to the customers who then had to program the machines themselves.

At the time, most computers were in government agencies — General Electric became the first private company to install a computer in 1954. Operating systems did not exist. The first operating systems were developed by users as a means of increasing productivity of the computer operations department by automating the process of executing programs. They were machine specific but, as operating systems became more complex, pressure from user groups forced manufacturers to take on development work in this area. The various manufacturers took different approaches to the problems associated with operating systems and this led to proprietary systems software being developed.

As demand for computers in business rose, both computer manufacturers and early business users looked to secure their own programming resources to write applications software. For hardware manufacturers it was the practice for software to be 'bundled' in with the cost of the hardware. This included both systems and applications software. In June 1969 IBM announced that it was going to charge separately for software. The 'unbundling' of software contributed to the creation of what is now called the independent software industry. Software houses had already started to appear, but IBM's decision accelerated the process. Software itself became a tradeable commodity.

The unbundling met with mixed reactions from the users — the large ones which already had teams of programmers developing applications were in favour, whilst smaller users, who relied on hardware manufacturers to supply their software, were faced with increased computing costs. If they stayed with manufacturers' software they would have to pay extra, if they decided to produce in-house they would have to recruit in-house programmers at considerable expense, if they went to the emerging software houses they would also have to pay extra. The 'make or buy' dilemma exists for users to this day.

Today, then, software is developed by people in a number of locations — hardware and systems manufacturers, software and systems houses, end-users' data processing departments, consultants. There are also dealers and distributors who do not develop software as such but who may supply and support software developed by others. Hardware manufacturers, software and systems houses and consultants may also supply and support software developed by others in this way.

There is a shortage of good data about software activities in many of these locations. There have been several studies in recent years examining the 'software industry' (e.g. ACARD, 1986; Coopers and Lybrand, 1987; Grindley, 1988). These studies have been mainly concerned with examining the relative competitiveness of the UK computer services sector. All the studies emphasise the difficulty of defining the software industry. As we have noted above, there are several different types of software, several modes of software, numerous languages and there are also important distinctions between the hardware for which the software is written. This means that rather than there being a single homogeneous market for software there are in reality a multiplicity of markets.

These studies provide a useful analysis of the computer services sector and the relative position of the UK 'software industry' in what is increasingly becoming an international market. They note that the UK market overall accounts for around 4–5 per cent of the world market but that the estimated share of the world market attributed to UK suppliers is only 2–3 per cent. The vast majority of these sales are to the UK domestic market (where UK suppliers hold about half the market) with sales to the rest of the world accounting for only 0.5 per cent of the world market.

The studies point out some specific weaknesses of UK computer services firms: poor marketing; deficiencies in management skills; a poor image inhibiting sales of home-produced products. They note that UK firms are particularly weak in markets closely associated with hardware — much of the UK software market is made up of the systems and utilities software packages supplied by the American hardware vendors.

Why is software important?

The discussion above shows the interdependence of software and hardware. Other chapters have noted the phenomenal growth of the IT sector and the widespread diffusion of IT into virtually every area of industry and commerce. As IT continues to diffuse, software may become as generic to production (of service products as well as manufactured goods) in the future as the shaping, machining and joining of materials are to manufacturing now. Increasingly, organisations are utilising IT in their products, production processes and the provision of services to provide them with some competitive advantage. Software is already recognised as the major cost associated with IT applications (OECD, 1985). As organisations come to realise the strategic importance of IT, software too will become an increasingly important factor in realising competitive advantage. But there are a number of concerns about software which have raised doubts about the ability of organisations to exploit IT fully in order to achieve these gains in competitiveness. Collectively these concerns have become referred to as the *software crisis*.

The software crisis is characterised by an emerging gap between the promise of what can be delivered by the increased performance of the hardware and the reality of what the software allows. There appear to be two strands to the gap — the first relates to the inadequacy of software in relation to hardware; and the second to the inadequacy of software in relation to the needs, wants and expectations of IT users.

Throughout the successive generations there have been substantial decreases in the price and phenomenal improvements in performance of hardware. For example, a 1987 state-of-the-art personal computer has twenty times the processing power, twenty times the main memory and five hundred times the disk storage capacity as a 1977 state-of-the-art personal computer, but costs far less (Forrester, 1987, p. 2). At the same time, hardware has become more compact and more reliable. Furthermore the pace of innovation has been maintained with a constant stream of new developments.

Whilst there have been some significant advances in software — for example, many of the software packages developed for personal computers during the 1980s exhibit staggering advances over previous software produced for mainframes and minicomputers — the performance and cost improvements have not equalled those observed for hardware. There is a perception that overall developments in software production have lagged behind those in hardware developments. At the same time, as IT has rapidly diffused throughout all sectors of the economy and to more parts of the organisation, user expectations have risen and the demand for high performance, easy-to-use software has increased.

There have been long delays in the release of new software products and updates in existing products from software firms. In user firms, backlogs in implementing new applications have become the norm in many organisations. Projects have often overrun, both in terms of time and budget. There have been problems with quality, reliability and maintainability of software and with productivity. A recent study carried out for the UK government indicates that £500 million is wasted each year due to lack of quality control during software design and development. Low productivity in software suppliers is estimated to waste £50 million per annum; project overruns waste £25 million for suppliers plus a further £25 million for user organisations; errors in software waste an estimated £130 million in suppliers plus a further £20 million in users; and maintenance wastes £270 million of user resources (Price Waterhouse, 1988b).

Skill shortages have become widespread. A survey conducted by the National Computing Centre (NCC) suggested a shortfall of at least 4,000 and possibly as many as 7,000 in the user community alone (Buckroyd and Cornford, 1988). Another survey of IT skills shortages concluded that shortages of experienced staff were likely to remain over the period to 1990. They also concluded that, as economic, technological and organisational factors would vary in the future, the changing balance of supply and demand of IT skills should be further monitored to allow training policies to be modified (Connor and Pearson, 1986).

Surveying software activities

The concerns described above have been addressed in research in two main ways — via detailed reviews of the computer services sector and by specialised studies of the pattern of skills shortages. In our own research we have been trying to go beyond these starting-points so as to get a broader picture of the pattern of software activities in the UK today. We argued earlier that some software activities are now common in many IT users; this will presumably be most intensive in major users, and fortunately several lists of large computer installations are in existence. We circulated some 6,000 establishments drawn from one of these registers, with the aim of gathering a sample of these large users spanning the main sectors of UK industry and services: the responses covered some 1,352 sites, from whom information was provided on 636 mainframes, 4,326 minis and 25,103 microcomputers, and on over 19,000 items of software.

The survey study was complemented by detailed interview-based case study research in a sample of the respondents, which provides us with more insight about the dynamics of change, and the strategies pursued by organisations, than the snapshot provided by the survey can do. However, we shall here briefly focus on a few highlights of the survey analysis.

One of the main concerns of this study was the structure of software activities: how is software of various kinds obtained? We are able to relate different items of software to different sources of supply: thus 34 per cent of listed items of software were obtained from hardware suppliers, 23 per cent from software houses, 11 per cent from dealers and 1 per cent from consultants: around 20 per cent were produced in-house by users. (Another 10 per cent are of unknown origin — figures have been rounded up, so they may not total to 100 per cent). Hardware suppliers and software houses were, not surprisingly, the main source of systems software and utilities, and also for applications tools: these very basic forms of software, which are required to develop and apply software to final uses, are relatively rarely produced by users themselves. In contrast, in-house teams are used most often as a source for industry-specific applications software (followed by software houses): here the understanding of precise user requirements seems to predominate.

The survey data are extremely rich, and enable us to go further, and examine sources of different types of software for different types of computer. Across all types of software, dealers are a more important source for microcomputers than for other computers — i.e. standard packages are more likely to be in use (perhaps because the large number of microcomputers makes it possible for software writers to achieve sufficient economies of scale to produce tradeable products). As Table 7.1 shows, 24 per cent of systems software items for microcomputers were obtained from dealers — as compared to less than 5 per cent for other computers — and 36 per cent of utilities, 39 per cent of application tools, 40 per cent of general applications solutions and 11 per cent of industry-specific applications (compared, respectively, to less than 10 per cent for the first two classes, less than 3 per cent for the second two).

Table 7.1 Sourcing of software by types of hardware

| | Source of software (%) | | | | |
	In-house staff	Hardware manuf.	Software house	Consult-ants	Dealers
Systems Software					
Hardware					
Microcomputers	9	59	15	2	24
Minicomputers	12	72	15	1	4
Mainframes	9	89	14	0	2
Utilities Software					
Hardware					
Microcomputers	11	41	21	0	36
Minicomputers	8	67	25	1	6
Mainframes	13	72	42	1	2
Applications Tools					
Hardware					
Microcomputers	13	28	31	2	39
Minicomputers	12	44	36	1	8
Mainframes	14	63	44	2	3
General Applications					
Hardware					
Microcomputers	25	18	34	5	40
Minicomputers	53	27	54	4	3
Mainframes	62	23	59	1	0
Industry-Specific					
Hardware					
Microcomputers	45	15	31	5	11
Minicomputers	58	11	31	5	1
Mainframes	61	26	33	2	0

Note: Figures may not add to 100% due to rounding, and since any site may use more than one source

The pattern of production of software across sectors and regions is complex, reflecting their historical experience with IT in specific applications. However, various generalisations are possible: for instance, that larger firms are more likely to produce software in-house than small firms (although our survey did turn up various firms involved in computer services, and producing software products for trade, themselves). Firms that were early users of IT are more likely to produce their own software — but the survey demonstrates the important role of packaged solutions, and our interview studies suggest that there is a shift toward the use of packages, where possible, on a wide front.

This shift to the use of packages reflects the software crisis, and is an effort to find a solution to it. Software staff are in short supply: where an organisation has (and can retain!) in-house competence, the growing use of IT is liable to mean increasing demand on these resources. Packaged solutions may not provide precisely the functionality that is required, but sometimes a product that can do most of the job immediately is better than one which promises to do the whole job in an indefinite future. (Problems with, and delays from, software houses are widely reported: in-house development schemes have often been crippled by a leakage of key staff.) Packages are often modified slightly to cope with particular needs: we found this most common for general applications (20 per cent modified packages, 42 per cent standard packages) and industry-specific applications (16 per cent and 24 per cent respectively).

But there is also some evidence that software capabilities are being treated as strategic resources with companies increasingly giving IT management a senior role. IT systems that are deemed to be essential to the company's business are much more likely to be developed in-house than others. But as new competences are being demanded, skill shortages and bottle-necks persist, and new training practices may be required.

Conclusions

Software is an increasingly important part of the information economy: with the diffusion of IT, software becomes a vital enabling technology. The problems that this creates for accounting practices and statistical monitoring of industrial activity (e.g. is software to be counted as an investment? is software development R&D?), for firm strategies (make or buy? how to maintain? base systems on hardware or software requirements?) and for policy (who should support what training and retraining?) are substantial.

The development of software activities is a major determinant of the shape of the information economy, for the decisions made in setting software strategies will help determine what sorts of IT applications we see, and how rapidly they are developed and applied. Discussions of the software crisis tend to assume that the issue is merely the rate of diffusion of IT, but the way in which IT is implemented depends to a great extent on software strategy.

Notes

1. The hardware's operating system (OS) supervises the control functions associated with the hardware and which involve the management of resources, such as scheduling of the central processing unit's time, allocation of memory, supervision of input/output operations to and from the system resources and peripherals. Compilers/asemblers transform programs from one language into another which is machine readable. Performance measurement/system resource management

software monitors and evaluates system resource utilisation and increases system performance and efficiency by optimising system resources allocation. Communications software provides terminal access and monitoring functions to handle data entry and delivery in an on-line environment, as well as enabling the various parts of the system to communicate with each other.

The OS also oversees the provision of utilities such as translators and cross/assemblers (which also translate programs from one language to another machine-readable language), program support software (which controls user access and maintains and protects data), sort/merge software (which enables files to be arranged in logical sequences or to be combined) and job accounting software (found in mainframes) which monitors machine usage by individual users/units and bills systems users.

2. There are numerous sub-categories here which can be grouped into four main classes: data access/retrieval software (including report generators, on-line query software and graphics software); data management software (including database management systems (DBMS), data/file managers, data dictionaries and non-procedural DBMS); data manipulation software (which includes modelling/simulation, analysis, spreadsheet and decision support systems); and program design/development software (which includes program pre-precessors and optimisers, data/program generators, program documentation generators, program editors and debuggers, and subroutines and procedures common to a majority of programs).

Bibliography

ACARD (Advisory Council for Applied Research and Development), 1986, *Software: a Vital Key to UK Competitiveness*, HMSO, London.

Baron, N.S., 1988, *Computer Languages: a Guide for the Perplexed*, Harmondsworth, Penguin.

Buckroyd, B. and Cornford, D., 1988, *The IT Skills Crisis: the Way Ahead*, NCC Publications, London.

Connor, H. and Pearson, R., 1986, *Information Technology into the 1990s*, Institute of Manpower Studies, Brighton.

Coopers and Lybrand, 1987, *Computing Services Industry 1986–1996 — a Decade of Opportunity*, Department of Trade and Industry, London.

Forester, T. (ed.), 1985, *High-tech Society*, Basil Blackwell, Oxford.

Grindley, K., 1988, *The UK Software Industry: a Survey of the Industry and Evaluation of Policy*, London Business School, London.

Macro, A. and Buxton, J., 1987, *The Craft of Software Engineering*, Addison-Wesley, Wokingham.

OECD, 1985, *Software: an Emerging Industry*, OECD, Paris.

Price Waterhouse, 1988a, *Information Technology Review 1988/89*, Price Waterhouse, London.

Price Waterhouse, 1988b, *Software Quality Standards: the Costs and Benefits*, Price Waterhouse, London.

8 The composition of the defence IT sector

Bernard Harbor and William Walker

Introduction

No discussion of the 'information economy' is realistic without an analysis of the role of military research and development (R&D) and procurement. This is not only because these activities were central to the early development of computing and microelectronics. In recent years, the Ministry of Defence (MoD) has accounted for around one-third of the British electronics industry's domestic sales and has provided a similar proportion of its R&D expenditure. Moreover, MoD provides over 90 per cent of total government funded R&D in the electronics sector (Walker, 1988). Britain is also a substantial exporter of defence electronics equipment which remains one of the few areas of IT in which there is a trade surplus. The British electronics industry is thus unusual in its strong orientation towards defence markets.

The development of civilian capabilities has therefore been strongly influenced by electronics firms' substantial involvement in defence R&D and production. In the literature on innovation and industrial performance, the defence sector has nevertheless tended to be seen as an important but largely inpenetrable, even exogenous, factor. The debates around new ICTs have been no exception. While it has been noted that military demand has influenced the nature and rate of development of new ICTs (in particular through the sponsorship of the Pentagon and NASA in the USA) there has been little detailed discussion of the nature of the defence market and its suppliers, nor of their relationship to the civil sector. Arguments over the industrial and economic impact of military R&D activity on the wider economy have been limited in similar ways. They have hinged on two issues: the opportunity cost of military technological activity (in particular the high proportion of public R&D funds devoted to defence and, in Britain, the relatively high military orientation of high technology manufacturers) and the relationship between military and civil technologies, especially the divergence of many military and civilian technological requirements and the question of technological 'spin-off' from the military to the civil sector. However, the debate has all too often been hampered by the poverty of the empirical base. There has been no clear definition of the defence electronics sector. Nor has adequate attention been paid to the wide variety of technologies which comprise 'defence electronics' — defence technology has tended to be discussed as though it were a homogeneous entity (Walker, Graham and Harbor, 1988). Finally, little attention has been paid to the organisation of military and civil activities within the firm or of the relationship between military and civil divisions and subsidiaries.

Drawing on a database of firms which has been assembled at SPRU, this chapter is an attempt to define more satisfactorily the composition of the British defence IT sector. (Our emphasis here tends to be on IT hardware, although the role of software and software suppliers is discussed. See Tim Brady's chapter in this volume for a fuller discussion of the role of software.) The relationship between the electronics industry's civil and military sectors has certainly been complicated by recent technological developments. In particular, the rapid growth of civil markets for new IT-based products has begun to change the perception of the defence sector as a technology leader. Moreover, the increasing reliance of defence contractors on suppliers of high-technology components and materials from firms (and often foreign firms) whose primary activities lie in the civil sector is gradually eroding the defence sector's traditional vertical integration.

The defence sector is defined primarily by its market. Although it includes producers of 'heartland' and 'core' ITs, as defined in the chapter by Ian Miles and Mark Matthews, it is in essence IT-using rather than IT-producing. Microelectronics now forms the basis of all weapons and military communications systems, but the defence sector is generally active in the application and integration of 'core' and 'heartland' IT products into military systems rather than with their production. In the 'heartland' technologies, and especially in computer software, this distinction becomes rather blurred — most of the major defence producers are involved in software development for embodiment in their own systems (see also Tim Brady's chapter). Others, though fewer in number, are producers of computer hardware for their own systems or as general suppliers to the military market while military telecommunications producers form an important part of the defence manufacturing sector. Nevertheless, our discussion focuses primarily on the impact of ITs on an existing industrial sector and the activities of 'core' and 'heartland' IT producers as subcontractors to the defence sector and as suppliers to the defence markets.

After many years of comparative stability the defence sector is currently undergoing great change. This is, in part, a response to the impact of new technologies on military and civil markets, but other important factors have also come into play. In particular, the attempts to create single European markets for defence equipment and civilian high-technology products, strains on defence budgets, the easing of East-West relations and progress in conventional arms control, have made the defence industries rather vulnerable and are precipitating their rapid restructuring across Europe.[1] In judging their effects on employment and industrial performance, it becomes still more important to understand what is today the underlying disposition of resources and technological activities in the industries serving defence markets.

The Maddock Report

The defence sector is not homogeneous, nor are its constitutent firms uniquely oriented towards defence markets. Sir Ieuan Maddock's 1983 report to the Electronics NEDC is one of the very few analyses which have started from this simple but necessary observation (Maddock, 1983). He identified five types of company:

Type A: companies involved in R&D, design and production which have been almost wholly committed to defence markets over several decades. For them, non-MoD work largely consists of defence exports or applying their technologies in civil aerospace markets.

Type B: companies which carry out civil and defence work side-by-side in the same design offices and production facilities, allowing considerable lateral transfer of technology. They nevertheless still give priority to defence applications (he cited software houses as the main examples).

Type C: companies which develop advanced technologies primarily for use in the civil field, and then apply them in defence. Involvement in defence markets is valued but secondary.

Type D: companies operating almost wholly in civil markets, but which often believe that the Armed Forces should make more use of civil products. They tend to be 'small, very entrepreneurial and independent of mind'.

Type E: companies which do not sell to defence markets, and often are not even in the business of selling electronic wares. However, their products and processes are deeply affected by developments in information technology.

Maddock based his remarks on a limited sample of 14 firms. In our database at SPRU we now have details on over 60 companies with interests in defence electronics, and on around one hundred of their divisions and subsidiaries. It shows that Maddock's picture of the defence sector was incomplete in some important respects.

The database

First, some brief comments on our database. It is not comprehensive. It nevertheless encompasses the major part of what most would regard as the defence electronics sector. It contains all prime contractors to MoD supplying significant items of electronics hardware and software (including that embedded in aerospace and other equipment). It also includes a substantial number of the suppliers of electronics components and sub-assemblies which have a distinctive presence in the defence market. The database deliberately excludes:

— foreign firms which supply MoD or the defence sector from abroad (their UK subsidiaries are however included). Included here are the large multinational component suppliers such as Motorola, Intel and NEC whose sales to the defence sector are substantial but a small proportion of total sales. Their military products are not significantly different from their civil products (Maddock's Type C companies);
— foreign subsidiaries of UK firms;
— firms which have some electronics design capabilities which are nevertheless minor in comparison to their core capabilities in mechanical engineering and other fields (Vickers is a notable example);
— small firms which act mainly as jobbing shops supplying low-technology sub-assemblies;
— suppliers of process or design technologies.

Variations in defence-dependence

Our database provides a clear indication of variations in firms' dependence on defence markets. As complete accuracy is seldom possible (even where firms declare their defence sales, the figures they give are often misleading),[2] firms have been placed in 10 bands according to the proportion of their sales, including exports, going to defence markets — 0–10 per cent, 10–20 per cent up to 90–100 per cent. For clarity of presentation, and to limit further the margin of error, they have been reduced to five bands in Figure 8.1. The figure shows that it is unusual for firms to be highly specialised in defence markets. Indeed, the firm that is totally attached to them is a rare bird. Firms active in defence markets are typically diversified across a range of engineering activities. However the picture is modified somewhat if the military sales of the firms in each of the five ranges of defence-dependence are summed (Figure 8.2). This shows that the majority of defence output comes from the very large firms occupying the middle of the range, having between one-fifth and four-fifths of their sales in defence.[3] This category includes the major MoD prime contractors like GEC (with about 30 per cent of its £6 billion sales in defence in 1986) and BAe (with about 70 per cent of its £4 billion sales in defence).

Whereas a high degree of specialisation in defence markets is exceptional at the level of the *company*, the reverse applies at the level of the *division* and *subsidiary* (Figure 8.3). It is normal for companies to organise their defence activities in discrete managerial and operational units, and very often on specific sites. There is thus strong *internal* specialisation in defence. The shape of the curve in Figure 8.3 is accentuated still further if the value of sales from divisions and subsidiaries in the five ranges of defence-dependence is summed (see Figure 8.4).[4] The important boundaries are less the external boundaries of the firm than those defining its internal structure.

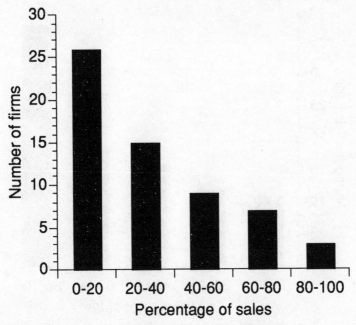

Figure 8.1 *Dependence on defence sales, corporate level*

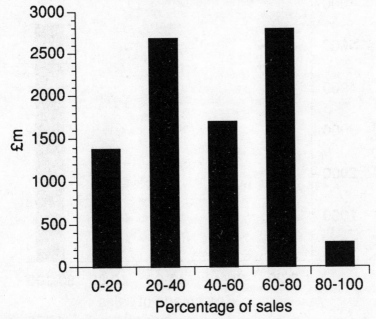

Figure 8.2 *Defence sales by firms by defence dependence*

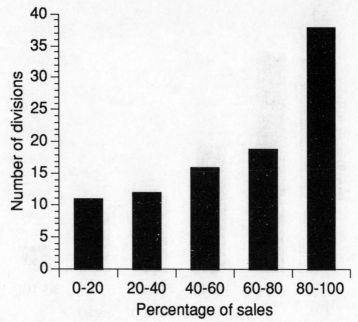

Figure 8.3 *Dependence on defence sales, divisional level*

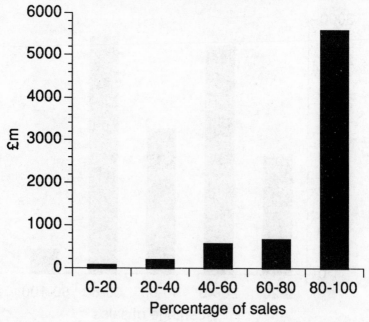

Figure 8.4 *Defence sales by division by defence dependence*

This is our first reservation about Maddock's analysis — he does not distinguish clearly enough between the firm and its component parts when assessing defence-dependence and its implications.

The very different curves contained in Figures 8.1 and 8.3 raise fundamental questions about the organisation of the defence sector. Why is it so unusual for firms to be wholly committed to defence R&D and production? Why, on the other hand, is there so little diversification at the operational level? In response to the first question, an important reason is that the cyclical nature of defence markets and cash-flows makes it hard to survive or avoid takeover without the cushion of other businesses. Thus the behaviour evinced at the divisional level is the 'natural' way of organising R&D, production and marketing, but operating units require the financial protection that only a diversified conglomerate can provide. This does not, of course, rule out the possibility that substantial benefits come in some instances (and notably in aerospace) from cross-divisional labour mobility and technology transfers.

Equally, it does not rule out other possible explanations for the relatively high incidence of defence dependence at the divisional level. Such subsidiaries may have been acquisitions of previously independent defence companies (such as Pilkington's acquisition of Barr & Stroud). More importantly, there may be real or perceived technological or cultural differences between military and civil operations which make their division seem natural.

The hierarchy of productive activities

Maddock also failed to distinguish between different types of firms according to their product and technology-bases or positions in the chain of production running from materials through to large weapon systems. In an earlier paper we identified seven levels in this product hierarchy which is reproduced in Figure 8.5 (Walker, Graham and Harbor, 1988). While we shall see below that there are firms and products (especially in the 'core' and 'heartland' IT areas) which fit very uneasily in this hierarchy, it provides a good starting-point for distinguishing the different categories of firm. We begin at level 2 — the production of materials being outside our survey.

Level 2: components

Firms active in component production can broadly be separated into four types:

2.1: the very large bulk suppliers of active electronics components (NEC, Hitachi, Texas Instruments, Intel, etc.) which serve civil and defence markets without much change in product specification.

2.2: the generally large suppliers of electronic cables and wiring, including optical fibres (the most important in Britain being BICC and, in the latter context, Pilkington). Again, civil and military products tend to be very similar, and

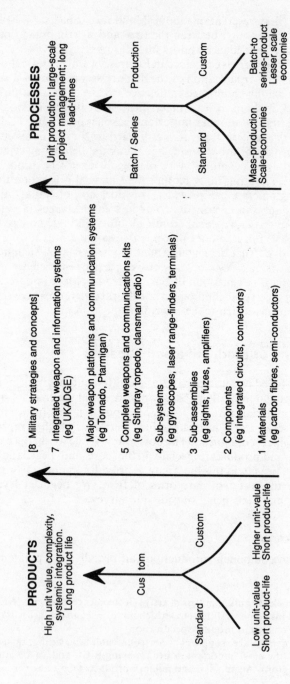

Figure 8.5 *A vertical product hierarchy*

PROCESSES

Unit production; large-scale project management; long lead-times

Production

Custom

Batch / Series

Standard

Batch-to series-product Lesser scale economies

Mass-production Scale-economies

[8 Military strategies and concepts]

7 Integrated weapon and information systems (eg UKADGE)

6 Major weapon platforms and communication systems (eg Tornado, Ptarmigan)

5 Complete weapons and communications kits (eg Stingray torpedo, clansman radio)

4 Sub-systems (eg gyroscopes, laser range-finders, terminals)

3 Sub-assemblies (eg sights, fuzes, amplifiers)

2 Components (eg integrated circuits, connectors)

1 Materials (eg carbon fibres, semi-conductors)

PRODUCTS

High unit value, complexity, systemic integration. Long product life

Custom

Custom

Standard

Higher unit-value Short product-life

Low unit-value Short product-life

where product differentiation does occur to meet military specifications
(e.g. for more extreme temperature ranges), substantial R&D is not involved.

2.3: suppliers of application-specific integrated circuits (ASICs) and other custom
or semi-custom components (including those which are specific to the
defence sector). These are produced largely by, and traded among, the major
defence contractors.[5] They engage in ASIC production partly to serve
defence needs and partly to support other industrial activities (such as the
supply of telecommunications equipment) which also require specialised
components.

2.4: suppliers of relatively low-tech passive components (which may nevertheless
involve sophisticated manufacturing and marketing techniques). They range
from small firms producing *inter alia* printed-circuit boards and capacitors
(e.g. Crystalate Holdings), to quite large multinationals producing connectors in particular (e.g. Bowthorpe, and the US firms Brintec and AMP
which have UK subsidiaries).

Level 3: sub-assemblies

This embraces a wide range of products. Here we find three categories of
suppliers:

3.1: all systems contractors produce their own sub-assemblies, especially where
sophisticated proprietary technology is involved. Moreover, as well as subcontracting, each Division tends to produce its own sub-assemblies.

3.2: small to medium-sized firms which are essentially jobbing shops, producing
batches of sub-assemblies to order, generally with low wages and
productivity.

3.3: specialised firms or divisions producing power supplies (e.g. Unitech),
amplifiers and other sub-assemblies for electronic capital goods of various
kinds, civil and military; and specific defence products such as fuzes
(e.g. Thorn-EMI) and night-sights (e.g. Pilkington, Vinten).

Level 4: sub-systems

We can again identify three categories of supplier under this heading:

4.1: the large systems-builders invariably supply sub-systems for their internal
use and under subcontract. Some firms (or divisions) also have distinct
specialisations, making them general suppliers to the market (e.g. Ferranti in
gyroscopes). These activities tend to be heavily oriented towards defence
markets, products having few civil counterparts — and where they do exist,
civil markets are usually relatively small.

4.2: suppliers of computers, terminals and other IT equipment (this is discussed
in more detail below).

4.3: specialised suppliers of control systems, instrumentation and avionic
components to civil and military aerospace markets. The principal British
examples are Dowty, Lucas Aerospace, Smiths Industries and Normalair
Garrett (which is jointly owned by Westland and the Garrett Corporation,
USA).

Level 5: complete weapons and communications kits

There are four broad product areas under this heading: sensors (radar, sonar and optical); guided and unguided weapons (missiles, bombs, torpedoes); communications (tactical radio, electronic warfare,[6] etc.); and avionics (head-up displays, fly-by-wire etc.). As is apparent below, they are the domain of the major systems contractors, or more accurately of specific divisions within them.

— *Sensors*: GEC-Marconi, British Aerospace, Ferranti, Plessey (all types). Also Dowty (sonar); Thorn-EMI, Cossor and Racal (radar); Pilkington/Barr & Stroud (optical). Only in radar is there a significant civil market, although it is much smaller than the defence market.
— *Weapons*: British Aerospace/Royal Ordnance (especially missiles); Marconi (especially torpedoes and missile guidance); Atomic Weapons Establishment. Also Ferranti-ISC (missiles); Hunting (bomb systems). Here there are no equivalent civil products.
— *Communications*: GEC-Marconi, Plessey, Racal, Ferranti. Also British Aerospace (satellites); MEL and GEC/Easams (electronic warfare); STC and British Telecom (networks). Electronic warfare apart, this is the area where there is greatest civil/military overlap, although it is usually potential rather than actual.
— *Avionics*: GEC-Avionics, Ferranti, British Aerospace. Also Lucas Aerospace, Smiths Industries, Dowty, Flight Refuelling, Plessey, Racal and others.

It should be noted that there are distinct corporate and (notably) divisional specialisations at this level of the hierarchy, across technology fields (e.g. radar or sonar), within technology fields (e.g. the different types of radar), and according to the Armed Services being provided (e.g. Ferranti provides equipment primarily for the RAF and Navy. Plessey for Army and Navy).

The above schema therefore exaggerates the degree of competition between contractors. This said, technological capabilities are seldom unique and comprehensive. On any contract awarded by MoD, there is invariably subcontracting between firms, and between divisions of firms. Although we cannot substantiate it, this subcontracting within and between the large defence contractors appears to be on a considerably more significant scale than the letting of contracts outside the 'old-boy network'. By this means, defence contractors exploit different specialisations, particularly in components and sub-systems, and ensure a degree of second-sourcing. But it also ensures that there are no outright losers, with winners in effect compensating other contractors for their lack of success, and expecting the favour to be returned in future — typical behaviour in a 'tight' oligopoly.

Level 6: major weapon platforms and communications systems

Only four electronics-related firms could truly be said to operate at this level: British Aerospace (fighter aircraft); GEC/Yarrow (frigates); Plessey (the Ptarmigan project); and Westland (helicopters). The other major platform-builders are Vickers Shipbuilding and Engineering LTD (VSEL) (submarines including Trident) and Vickers PLC (tanks). In each case there is a single UK supplier, a state of affairs which seems likely to remain despite MoD's present emphasis on competitive bidding.

Level 7: integrated weapon and information systems

This involves the coordination and integration of diverse weapon and communications systems, whether at the national level or on a NATO basis (e.g. in the NATO Air Defence Ground Environment programme). The principal actors at this level are again the main defence contractors (along with MoD's R&D Establishments and foreign manufacturers which we are not covering in this survey), which we return to below. However, other kinds of actor are here becoming more prominent.

Computer, software, and network suppliers

This brings us to the information technology suppliers, internal and external to the defence contractors, which are adopting an increasingly central role in the defence sector. Broadly speaking, there are four respects in which computer, software and communications technologies are applied in the defence sector (we are here excluding design and manufacturing processes):

i.   in information systems which are not weapon systems, such as workstations, computer simulation, databases, and project management;
ii. in communication systems ranging from early warning radar to satellites to battlefield communications;
iii. through the embedding of computer hardware and software in weapon systems and sub-systems;
iv. as instruments of increased 'systemation', whereby IT, and notably software, increasingly define the nature of and scope for combining distinct systems and sub-systems (i.e. they are the key systems integrators).

One should note that these functions are not just performed by specific items of equipment. They are also increasingly embedded in chips. Hence the great interest in very large-scale integration (VLSI) which offers possibilities for incorporating a wide range of functions in a single semiconductor device. To a degree, the hierarchy of information technologies is constantly being 'collapsed' through processes of miniaturisation. This process is likely to have profound effects on smaller producers of sub-assemblies and sub-systems where their functions will increasingly be performed by chips.

Who are the main actors in the above fields? In the first class of products — information systems — they are usually firms which are primarily oriented towards civil markets. Notable examples are DEC, which has become the principal supplier of workstations to MoD and the Armed Forces, with defence sales in excess of £25 million; and software houses such as SEMA-CAP and Logica which provide project management information systems among other services. An exception is the area of computer simulation which is dominated by the main defence contractors (notably British Aerospace) and, in particular, the specialist firm Rediffusion Simulation (now a subsidiary of the US corporation Hughes).

The second class of products (communications systems) has been covered above and is supplied mainly by the large defence contractors. However, British Telecom and other telecommunications specialists (including computer firms which are becoming telecoms specialists) are beginning to play a larger part in the market. An interesting example is STC which, through the acquisition of ICL, has attempted to gain a larger share of the military communications market.

The third class of 'embedded' products is almost entirely provided by the defence contractors which design and produce their own software and computers for use in weapon systems.

The division of labour in the fourth area of activity — what is sometimes termed 'systemation' — has become much less clear-cut. Here we find a battle being fought between the traditional defence contractors and various other IT systems suppliers, and notably the software houses which, from a very small capital base, have gained entry to the very highest level of the hierarchy set out in Figure 8.5. Having felt threatened by new entrants, however, defence contractors gradually appear to be regaining control over this activity, through development of their internal capabilities, through the acquisition of shareholdings (e.g. BAe's 24.9 per cent holding in Systems Designers), and through joint ventures (e.g. Dowty-CAP).

Finally, there is the question of VLSI. The main defence contractors are intensely interested in this technology, seeing it as a way of reducing costs and maintaining control over the design and production of weapon systems. All appear to be involved in VLSI R&D. It remains to be seen whether they will be able to control VLSI supplies to the military markets, aided by their know-how in 'configuring' chips to meet complex requirements; or whether the scale and learning advantages of semiconductor specialists will ultimately prove too great, particularly when combined with technological changes which increase flexibility in design and production and thus lower the barriers to entry in the supply of custom chips.

Military-civil technological synergy among prime contractors

Figures 8.2 and 8.3 set out in brief some of the characteristics and activities of the leading defence electronics prime contractors. They were selected from the MoD's list of UK-based contractors paid £100 million or more by the MoD in 1986–7 (Ministry of Defence, 1988).[7] Again, some reservations should be expressed at the outset. The company specialisations in Table 8.1 are, like our product hierarchy, based very much on products rather than their inherent

Table 8.1 Features of leading British defence electronics prime contractors

	BAe	Ferranti	GEC	Plessey	Racal	Thorn-EMI
Sales (m)	£3,137	£596	£5,969	£1,461	£1,266	£3,316
Sales/employees	£41,882	£27,351	£47,140	£42,512	£38,800	£38,693
UK sales dependence	44%	65%	79%	71%	40%	60%
Estimated military sales (m)	£2,280	£360	£1,930	£615	£500	£270
Main defence specialisations	Fighters Guided missiles Satellites Associated sub-systems, assemblies and electronics	Radar Navigation and display Electro-optics Sonar Naval C^2 Fuzes	Avionics C^2 Guidance Communications (land, sea, air and space) Torpedoes Radar Instrumentation Frigates	Communications Sonar** Radar Air defence Data handling EW	Radio communications EW Avionics	Fuzes Radar Electro-optics
Main civil specifications	Airliners (wings) Small aircraft Satellites Associated sub-systems, assemblies and electronics	Various industrial electronics Computer systems Components* (now Plessey)	Telecoms Power generation Consumer electronics Automation and control Medical equipment	Telecoms Semi-conductors Aerospace sub-systems and components	Security systems Telecoms Marine radar	Rental and retail Music Software Lighting Kitchen appliances
Armed Forces specialisation	RAF, (RN, Army)	RAF, Navy	RAF, (RN, Army)	Army, RN, (RAF)	Army, RN	Army, RN
Central R&D lab	Yes	No	Yes	Yes	No	Yes

Notes *These activities were sold to Plessey and have since been acquired by GEC-Siemens
**These activities have now been transferred to GEC

Table 8.2 Characteristics of the main British defence electronics prime contractors

British Aerospace	*Largest single British defence contractor *High level of collaborative work (military and civil) *High reliance on public money (especially defence) *Largely un-rationalised production base *Dominates UK aerospace **but** *Small in international industry (especially civil) *Problem of dollar-pricing in world market *High export orientation *High dependence on particular export markets *Lack of coherence in (non-aerospace) civil activities *Increasing emphasis on electronics
Ferranti	*Small by national and international standards *High defence dependence *Much product innovation but little product volume *Scattering of civil products *Civil products are all capital goods
GEC	*Largest UK defence electronics firm *High dependence on non-consumer markets *Record of problem military projects (Nimrod, Foxhunter, torpedoes, BATES) *Scattered civil activities within business areas *High involvement in European pre-competition R&D programmes *High dependence on UK markets
Plessey	*Technology-driven company *Extensive overseas links (military and civil) *Only UK firm in semiconductors *Software management expertise *Small firm by international standards (especially in civil areas) *No consumer products or markets *High dependence on UK markets **but** *Increasing emphasis on exports (especially military)
Racal	*Skilled at relatively high volume, low unit cost manufacture *High export-orientation *Dynamic diversification strategy (organic and acquisitions) *Relatively young company
Thorn-EMI	*Range of disparate activities *Engineering a minority activity *Orientation towards mass consumer markets (but not generally consumer capital goods) *Relatively low military dependence

technologies. For this reason, computer and software technologies do not feature strongly despite being integral to many of the products which do feature and despite the companies under study being active in their development and application. Thus, Table 8.1 does not capture fully either the pervasiveness of these technologies in military products or their importance to the large prime contractors. The same can be said of networking and process technologies. It should also be noted that the specialisations in Tables 8.1 and 8.2 are by no means comprehensive — they merely represent general product and technology areas. Nevertheless, the Tables reveal some interesting features.

The six companies show a striking lack of homogeneity in terms of size, product range, military dependency, behaviour and culture.[8] However, in three important respects there are great similarities across the companies. The first is that, with one exception, all are heavily oriented towards non-consumer markets. BAe, Ferranti and Plessey operate exclusively in non-consumer markets while GEC's consumer operations are insignificant compared to its 'public' operations. Racal's civil activities are highly concentrated in the security market (through its subsidiary Chubb) and in vodaphone networks and equipment — products with an actual or potential consumer market but which are presently predominantly non-consumer oriented. The exception, Thorn-EMI, concentrates its activities very much in consumer markets, but mainly in consumer services markets (retailing etc).[9] Thorn-EMI is also the only company of the six which relies on defence for less than a third of its total sales.

The second similarity is that, specialisations notwithstanding, there is much more homogeneity in military operations, both within and between companies, than in civil operations. Generally, and with the exception of telecommunications and aerospace equipment, the civil activities of the companies are more diverse than their military activities. The third similarity is that all six companies are small in international terms, with regard to their civil operations, although BAe's recent acquisition of Rover (the automobile manufacturer) has improved their position slightly.

Despite the lack of homogeneity among the prime contractors some generalisations can be made about the potential for technological synergy. We can identify four main types of product area according to their relevance to other activities:

1. *Civil products with little or no relevance to military products* Power generation, consumer electronics, music, rental and retail, standard ICs, various areas of industrial electronics; medical electronics.
2. *Military products with limited or no relevance to civil products* Sonar, fuzes, torpedoes, (some) avionics, (most) guided missile technology, (most) electronic warfare.
3. *Military and civil products with obvious potential synergy* Telecommunications, satellites, (some) airframes, (some) avionics and aircraft equipment, surveillance radar, computer hardware.
4. *Military products which may have potential relevance to civil products* Data handling,

tactical communications, target acquisition and guidance radar, software, electro-optics.

Two caveats are necessary here. Firstly, the assumption that there is a lack of potential for technological synergy in types '1' and '2' is based on the properties and applications of the *products* rather than on the technologies inherent in them. However, another study has demonstrated the lack of *technological* diffusion between large civil and military telecommunications projects where there should be substantial synergy (Harbor, 1989). The assumption that there is potential for synergy in types '3' and '4' therefore does not detract from the considerable military-civil product differentiation that occurs because of the particular demands of military specificity. Military hardening, the demands of speed and accuracy, electronic counter-measures and counter-counter-measures, stealth materials and the like, all perpetuate a clear distinction between military and civil products. However, there remain clear *technological* similarities.

Company organisation

The high degree of concentration of military activities among and within firms suggests that the internal organisation of firms can also reveal barriers to the exploitation of military and civil technological synergy. Research so far points to the existence of three types of firms:

1. Those in which there is little obvious potential synergy between existing military and civil products, technologies and operations (e.g. Thorn-EMI).
2. Those in which there already exists a considerable degree of synergy (e.g. some of the aircraft equipment companies).
3. Those in which the technology base suggests that in principle there is potential for synergy but where there are considerable organisational barriers which would have to be overcome for this to be realised (e.g. Plessey, BAe, GEC). These companies carry out both civil and defence work but with very clear distinctions, at least organisationally, between the two operations. Also, this is the most common type of company in our study.

It is useful briefly to consider the three major defence electronics-related companies — BAe, GEC and Plessey (Plessey has retained considerable autonomy despite its takeover by GEC-Siemens). Each operates in areas where there is obvious potential for military-civil technological synergy (airframes, telecommunications, satellites, etc.). Each also has large R&D budgets and facilities. All three have central research laboratories, albeit with relatively small budgets, where non-application-specific research is carried out. Often, this type of research can be expected to find applications in both military and civilian fields. However, the bulk of the R&D activity and expenditure in each firm is carried out in the operating divisions or subsidiaries and is customer-funded activity concerned primarily with product development. Invariably the customer is a government department, with work being sponsored by the MoD (defence electronics), BT (tele-communications), the CEGB (power generation) and, in the case of BAe, DTI (launch aid for civil aerospace). The development carried out may or may not have applications in other areas, but the distinct military-civilian division at this level of the firm is, we suspect, a major barrier to the diffusion of technology.

Certainly, the organisational barriers to synergy appear to be at least as considerable as the technological barriers. In any case, it appears that it is easier to facilitate synergy between the military divisions of companies than between the military and civil divisions or, indeed, between the civil divisions.

Vertical integration

That a 'hierarchy of firms' exists in defence electronics is self-evident from the above discussion. It roughly corresponds with the product hierarchy (see Figure 8.5). Those active at the top of the product hierarchy are generally large companies (or their divisions) with high defence dependence (BAe, GEC, Plessey, Racal, Ferranti, etc.). Lower down the hierarchy are smaller companies and/or divisions with lower defence dependencies. No indepen-dent firm is *both* highly defence dependent *and* an actor only at the lowest levels of the product hierarchy.[10]

The question of how firms interact at different levels of the hierarchy is also important. There seems to be a considerable element of vertical integration, whether organic or by acquisition, in the larger defence operations. Plessey, perhaps the best example, is active at level seven (Ptarmigan) right down to level two (ASICs). However, the picture is less clear for some other major contractors. What seems to be the case is that those companies that are highly defence dependent both dominate the top end of the hierarchy *and* tend to be active at many, or even most, other levels. Although we suspect that it is a reasonably good measure of vertical integration, it is by no means an accurate measure of integration in any given product, programme or technological area. It could just as easily demonstrate the 'old-boy network' referred to earlier. That is, it also shows that a company can be a prime contractor for some systems and a supplier of sub-systems and sub-assemblies or components for others. Although a more detailed understanding of subcontracting patterns would help to elucidate this, the evidence points towards a high level of vertical integration in many cases and especially among the larger and more defence-dependent companies.

It should also be noted that there is substantial vertical integration *within* defence divisions. Thus sub-assembly and sub-system (and even component) development and production are often confined within, rather than shared between, divisions. This again underlines the autonomy of individual divisions. An alternative strategy to vertical integration would be for firms to establish close links with particular suppliers. This is becoming common practice in the motor industry and may become more pronounced in defence electronics. Again, a better understanding of both acquisition and sub-contracting patterns would be useful here.

Conclusions

Faced with the easing of East-West tensions and the likely decline of defence budgets, the heavy involvement of the British electronics industry in defence is bound to decline. It seems appropriate to conclude on this point with three brief observations arising from the above discussion.

First, the amount of pain felt in adjusting to lower levels of military demand will vary greatly across the sector. Thus component suppliers for whom the defence market is a minor part of total sales will not be greatly affected, especially since the anticipated rapid growth in civil electronics markets will compensate for any decline in military consumption. Those most affected will be the systems contractors, and especially those that exhibit a high degree of vertical integration.

Second, each defence contractor has its own idiosyncracies, so that one has to beware of generalisations about reactions to the loss of defence markets. For all concerned, however, the problem of adjustment will be felt most keenly at the divisional level. There are many R&D and production sites in Britain which are dedicated to serving military requirements, without much opportunity for diversification. Thus while firms taken as a whole may be sufficiently diversified to weather a fall in defence demand, some of their divisions and sites may experience considerable pain.

Third, despite not having set out to chart firms' civil activities, it is apparent that all the British firms in our survey are minor players in global civil electronics markets, whereas they are still in the first league of defence producers. To give just one example, GEC-Avionics has over one-half of the Western world's market for head-up displays. The principal difficulty confronting these firms is to find ways of diversifying into civil high technology activities where they are already weak and face daunting competition from Japan, the United States and other advanced countries. In some degree, they are now paying the price for having been attached for so many years to protected defence markets.

Notes

1. These developments are discussed at length in Walker and Gummett, 1989, and Harbor, 1990.
2. They usually count as defence sales those divisions most heavily oriented to defence markets. Other parts of companies, such as divisions supplying components, often have significant defence sales which have to be included.
3. However, the exclusion of some major component suppliers from our sample will tend to underestimate output in the 0–20 per cent bracket.

4. Note, however, that the sales from divisions and firms with 0–20 per cent of output in defence may be significantly underestimated in Figures 8.2 & 8.4, since they (and particularly the component producers among them) are least well covered in the database.
5. There is also a small number of firms, mainly of US origin, which specialises in a narrow range of active components produced in both small and large quantities for high technology markets. The US firm Analog Devices, which produces analog-digital converters, is an example. Most of these types of components are imported from the USA.
6. Electronic warfare means interference with or disruption of an enemy's electronic systems to disable or mislead the enemy.
7. Three other companies which paid over £100 million in the same period and which are on our database are Hunting, Royal Ordnance and Westland. These, however, are less important to us as their activities are primarily outside the IT area.
8. Since this chapter was drafted, Plessey has been acquired by GEC-Siemens. Its assets in avionics and anti-submarine warfare are now controlled by GEC while Siemens controls its radar and communications operations. Its semiconductor activities are jointly controlled. However, as Plessey continues to act as a largely autonomous player in its key defence technology areas, we have continued to treat it as separate corporate entity.
9. Both Racal and Thorn-EMI announced in 1989 that they are looking to sell their defence assets. Neither has yet found a buyer.
10. Frasher-Nash and Radamec are, arguably, exceptions. The former is active at level 4 in the hierarchy and the latter at levels 2, 3 and 4; both rely on defence for 60–70 per cent of sales.

Bibliography

Harbor, B., 1989, *Technological Divergence in the Development of Military and Civil Communications Systems: the Case of Ptarmigan and System X*, paper presented to PICT National Network Conference, Brunel University, 17–19 May 1989, SPRU, Brighton.

Harbor, B., 1990, 'Defence electronics before and after 1992' in G. Locksley (ed.), *The Single European Market and the Information and Communication Technologies*, Belhaven Press, London.

Maddock, Sir I., 1983, *Civil Exploitation of Defence Technology: Report to the Electroincs EDC*, NEDO, London.

Ministry of Defence, 1988, *Statement on the Defence Estimates 1988, Vol. 2*, HMSO, London.

Walker, W., 1988, 'UK defence electronics: a review of government statistics', *PICT Policy Research Papers*, No. 4.

Walker, W., Graham, M. and Harbor, B., 1988, 'From components to integrated systems: technological diversity and integrations between the military and civilian sectors' in P. Gummett and J. Reppy (eds), *The Relations between Defence and Civil Technologies*, Kluwer Academic Press, Dordrecht, 1988.

Walker, W. and Gummett, P., 1989, 'Britain and the European armaments market', *International Affairs* **65** (3), 419–42.

Part III: The geography of information*

*Chapters prepared by Centre for Urban and Regional Development Studies

9 Communication, organisation and territory

Kevin Robins and Andrew Gillespie

This third part of the book is concerned with the geography of information and communications technologies. In the context of this agenda, it is the communications aspect of these new technologies that is particularly salient. In the first place, we are interested in the implications of new communications and information networks for organisational transformation and reconfiguration. What new forms of organisational division and integration can we see emerging, both within and between corporate structures? And what are the spatial dynamics of this process? Our subsequent focus of interest is in the ways in which this process is mapped onto and across particular territories. New organisational forms are being superimposed on already existing urban and regional systems. What are the implications of information and communications networks for these territorial formations and hierarchies? What are the threats and the opportunities for particular places and areas? It is through the articulation and interaction of organisational and territorial logics that the geography of the so-called information economy is being elaborated.

Spacing changes

Geographical agendas are fundamental in the current period of economic and social restructuring. As Doreen Massey has forcefully argued, 'social processes necessarily take place over space'; they are 'constructed, reproduced and changed in a way which necessarily involves distance, movement and spatial differentiation'. 'Spatial distributions and geographical differentiation', she continues, 'may be the result of social processes, but they also affect how those processes work. "The spatial" is not just an outcome; it is also part of the explanation' (Massey, 1984, p. 4). In the modern period we have seen enormously significant transformations in the spatial organisation of economies and societies, and contributing to these transformations has been the development of information and communications technologies. Writing of the development of the telegraph in the nineteenth century, James Carey has emphasised its considerable spatial implications. 'The innovation of the telegraph', he argues, 'can stand metaphorically for all the innovations that ushered in the modern phase of history'. The telegraph 'permitted for the first time the effective separation of communication from transportation' and it is this possibility that 'has been exploited in most subsequent developments in communications down to computer control systems' (Carey, 1989, p. 203). The telegraph afforded new possibilities for coordinating economic and political activities on an extended scale. It gave rise to 'the first forms of international business that could be called multinational' (ibid., p. 212). Manuel Castells is only developing the same insight when he describes how the 'high technologies' of the last decade or so are giving rise to new global spaces of production and to new functional linkages between organisational units. In the new space of global information flows, he suggests,

> a hierarchy of functions and power positions structures the territory across the nation and across the world, separating functions and units of production, distribution and management to locate each one in the most favourable area, yet articulating all activities through a communication network . . . We are living increasingly in a space of variable geometry where the meaning of each locale escapes its history, culture, or institutions, to be constantly redefined by an abstract network of information strategies and decisions (Castells, 1985a, pp. 14–15).

What is continuous is the development of technological systems to afford coordination and control across space.

David Harvey has described the logic at work behind these organisational and logistical imperatives, behind this desire to transcend the friction of space and to enhance the continuity of flow. He describes the apparent paradox whereby 'a portion of the total capital and labour power has to be immobilised in space, frozen in place, in order to facilitate greater movement for the remainder': 'The ability of both capital and labour power to move at short order and low cost from place to place depends upon the creation of fixed, secure, and largely immobile social and physical infrastructures. The ability to overcome space is predicated on the production of space' (Harvey, 1985a, p. 149). There is a constant tension 'between preserving the values of past commitment made at a particular place and time, or devaluing them to open up fresh room for accumulation'. It is a tension 'between fixity and motion, between the rising power to overcome space and the immobile structures required for such a purpose' (ibid., p. 150). It is this organisational logic that shapes particular territorial spaces, but then constantly undermines their integrity and coherence. And crucial to this command of organisational space, and consequently to the fate of particular territories (cities, regions, nation states), has been the development of information and communications technologies.

A key question, then, concerns the implications of the new ICTs of the 1990s — telecommunications, cable networks, computer communications, and so on — for this dynamic of fixity and mobility. Given some of the exaggerated claims being made for the revolutionary significance of these new technologies, some preliminary and cautionary observations are in order. A first point is that, however much they are associated with the hypermobility of capital, with an unprecedented organisational and locational flexibility, these new technologies by no means signal the final transcendence of spatial barriers. What they are, in fact, bringing about are new and more complex articulations of the dynamics of mobility and fixity. It is also necessary to emphasise, against the utopian scenarios of spatial transcendence, that new and emerging geographical landscapes continue to be shaped by patterns of uneven and unequal development. We need to acknowledge the spatial bias of the new ICTs, their contribution to new patterns of homogenisation and differentiation, their tendency to underpin new geographical divisions and hierarchies (Gillespie and Robins, 1989; Hepworth and Robins, 1988). Indeed, there is evidence that the current restructuring process is associated with heightened geographical differentiation, which continues to include significant regional differentials, but now also involves new kinds of inequality between localities. In considering the problem of uneven develop-ment, the question of geographical scales has become highly significant, and it may well be that it is now the case that 'the most appropriate level for analysis may be neither the region, nor the local labour market, but the level of what we might term the "urban labour market": the way in which central urban areas and regional service centres come to dominate their particular hinterland' (Savage, 1989, p. 258; see also Martin, 1989).

A second preliminary point is to emphasise that transformations associated with the new ICTs are, in fact, far less absolute and decisive than is often made out. History moves, not through abrupt breaks, but through a more complicated process of change and continuity. Technological innovation must always confront a certain intractability and inertia in the old order of things, a friction from old infrastructures and old social relations. In the course of historical development, 'new and old forms of organising pro-duction have combined to produce changing spatial division of labour and have become intertwined in different ways in different times and places' (Hudson, 1988, p. 485). Pierre Veltz describes the contradictory forces shaping the geography of post-war France:

> Social upheavals in France have been so rapid and continuous since the last war that they have been absorbed only partially and in different ways according to the region. Hence the reappearance, during the [current] crisis, of a territorial mosaic, revealing the vitality and the resistance of traditional forms of organisation and social regulation (which have not had the time to really disappear, and which are now being confronted *at the same time* by Fordist models and by the contemporary situation) (Veltz, 1983, p. 39).

The new ICTs must negotiate already complex spatial and temporal configurations. If they are, indeed, likely to bring about significant geographical transformations, then this will be under conditions shaped and constrained by earlier orders of accumulation.

Our third point is to make clear that the nature and direction of changes now being brought about by ICTs is not prescribed. Geographical transformation is not determined by technological innovations, but, rather, it is through the possibilities they offer that new spatial configurations might be elaborated. There is no single and inevitable trajectory of development. The key issue has always concerned the division and integration of labour as an essential problem in production and competition. How should production-systems be cut up and put back together? (Walker, 1988, p. 378). The contribution of ICTs has been to enhance continuously the effectiveness of organisational control and to coordinate flows of labour, materials and information across space. The new technologies of the 1990s promise to enhance organisational flexibility, but it is still the case that coordination and control may be achieved through a variety of strategies. As Walker argues, 'the ways by which integration is achieved are more numerous than generally acknowledged, and the tapestry of industrial organisation far richer' (ibid., p. 384). The nature of organisational structures may vary according to sector, according to place, according to context. Strategies for the division and integration of production systems have always centred around a 'tension between the virtues of geographical concentration to minimise spatial separation (the assembly of detail functions within the factory or the agglomeration of many firms within one urban centre) and geographical dispersal, which has the virtue of providing opportunities for further accumulation by exploiting particular geographical advantages (natural or created)' (Harvey, 1985b, p. 188). No less than ever, this tension between concentration and dispersal is at the heart of current geographical transformations. In what ways it will develop cannot be established *a priori*, but is a matter for empirical research and inquiry.

Geography and technology

What kinds of organisational restructuring are being brought about by the new ICTs? And what are the implications for particular territories, for regional economies and cultures? Where are we to look for the elements of a geographical analysis of the information economy?

Of the various theoretical approaches considered in the introductory chapter of this book, the post-industrial and neo-Schumpeterian frameworks prove to be of rather limited value. Within the post-industrial perspective there are few serious attempts to open up geographical agendas. There are some serious empirical accounts of the regional diffusion of these economic activities considered to be central to the information revolution, where the main concern is with the more or less even rate of 'modernisation' towards the post-industrial future (e.g. Keinath, 1985; Leven, 1988). For the most part, however, this approach is characterised by the naïve assumption that the information society can transcend the friction of distance, and that ubiquitous information and communications technologies will bring about a decentralised society of electronic cottages. In the evocation of a global village, we have the appeal to a utopia beyond space, a utopia in the literal sense.

Whilst some researchers within the neo-Schumpeterian perspective have developed useful insights (which we shall take up below), this approach has, for the most part dealt with geographical dynamics in a rather narrow and limited way. Attempts to delineate the geography of the so-called fifth Kondratiev wave have been restricted to a concern with the location of high-tech activities. The preoccupation is then almost exclusively with the comparative endowments and endeavours of particular regions in the interregional and international struggle for competitive advantage. In the new era of 'silicon landscapes', economic success 'lies with the country and the region and the city that innovate, that keep one step ahead of the action' (Hall, 1985, p. 5). A successful region is one that can stimulate or attract the sunrise industries associated with the emerging new wave of technological innovation and growth (Booth, 1987). Whilst this geography of technological innovation is, of course, an important contemporary phenomenon and worthy of study, it represents, in fact, only one narrow aspect of the geographical restructuring process associated with the new ICTs. The neo-Schumpeterian problematic fails to grasp broader spatial dynamics that owe more to social and political transformations than they do to technological restructuring.

It is in the various interrelated approaches associated with the 'post-Fordist hypothesis', however, that we have a real basis to explore the geographical implications of ICTs and their significance for the future of regional economies. In debates around the supposed transformation from a Fordist to a 'post-Fordist' regulation of modern capitalism, a further hypothesis is raised about the shift from Fordist to post-Fordist geographies. There have been some notable contributions within the framework of the French Regulation School (Leborgne and Lipietz, 1989). The perspectives of Regulationism have been developed, with different degrees of insight, by a number of economic geographers (e.g. Scott, 1988; Storper and Scott, 1989; Albrechts and Swyngedouw, 1989; Moulaert and Swyngedouw, 1989). A different but related line of argument has been developed within what has been called the 'institutionalist' perspective (Meegan, 1988) around the idea that ICTs under-pin the transition from an era of mass production to one of 'flexible specialisation'. Within this framework, important arguments have been put forward about the implications of flexible specialisation for the 'renaissance' of regional economies and regional policy (Piore and Sabel, 1984; Sabel, 1989; Hirst and Zeitlin, 1989a, 1989b). Whilst it is important to acknowledge the significant divergences and differences between those various researchers, what is more apparent is the shared research agenda, centred around the post-Fordist hypothesis.

We are not suggesting that this approach has all the answers. Far from it.

There has, in fact, been a strong tendency to elaborate deterministic scenarios that exaggerate the contrasts between Fordist and post-Fordist spaces (which we shall discuss in the following section). What we are saying is that the post-Fordist hypothesis begins to ask the right questions, and questions of geography have been central to its concerns. What has been significant about this perspective, particularly the work of the Regulation School, has been its 'repudiation of simple economism' and its recognition of 'the complexity and multidimensionality of modern capitalism' (Rustin, 1989, p. 54). In developing a theory of political economy, it has been concerned with the complex interrelation of economic, social and cultural forces. It is this scope that provides the basis for a more adequate and comprehensive geographical analysis. The role of technology, and of information and communications technologies in particular, can be put in the context of other factors involved in reshaping the geographical landscape. If we accept that the post-Fordist hypothesis is precisely that — a *hypothesis* about the nature of contemporary change — then it provides a valuable agenda for exploring that process of change in all its complexity. Are we now undergoing a process of decisive economic and social restructuring? Or are elements of continuity more apparent? Are we seeing the emergence of a post-Fordist geography radically different from that of Fordism? These are open questions. As Leborgne and Lipietz (1988, p. 263) stress, we cannot automatically deduce future spatial configurations from models of economic and social development; we must be sensitive to the fact that there are various feasible processes of spatial reconstruction.

Flexible production complexes?

Having emphasised the value of the post-Fordist hypothesis as a basis for opening up geographical agendas, we want now to qualify our position somewhat. As we have already suggested, the significance of this approach lies in the questions it has asked, and the debate it is stimulating, about current processes of social transformation. What is clear, however, is that within the post-Fordist camp there are important disagreements about the nature of economic, social and, consequently, geographical change. We want, in this section, to scrutinise one influential line of argument about the nature of organisational restructuring and the implications of this process for territorial development. This approach, which we shall call the neo-Marshallian hypothesis, has almost attained the status of a new orthodoxy (see Amin and Robins, 1990). While it offers some useful insights the analysis is ultimately marred by its formalism and determinism. It is an approach that has very much sought to deduce future spatial configurations from abstract models of economic development.

Perhaps the most articulate and influential exponents of this position have been the economic geographers, Allen Scott and Michael Storper. In trying to delineate what they see as the 'new geography of flexible accumulation', they draw a stark contrast between the late Fordist regime of accumulation, characterised by the dispersal and decentralisation of production to peripheral regions, and the coming post-Fordist regime, with its strong agglomerative tendencies in flexible production sectors and its 'reaffirmation of the significance of place as the foundation for efficient and effective production sectors' (Storper and Scott, 1989, p. 37). According to Scott and Storper, 'the turn towards flexibility has been marked by a decisive reagglomeration of production and the resurgence of the phenomenon of the industrial district' (ibid., p. 27). They emphasise the re-emergence of Marshallian industrial districts, of 'spatially agglomerated product complexes together with their dependent labour markets and intercalated human communities' (Scott, 1988, p. 176), as the essential feature of the new geography of production. These new industrial spaces, Scott and Storper argue, come to be characterised by 'communities of trust': 'a Marshallian "industrial atmosphere" is created and sustained in the local area as part of its overall logic of territorial reproduction' (Storper and Scott, 1989, p. 23).

The appeal of this argument derives from the tight relationship it seeks to establish between organisational and locational transformation. According to Scott and Storper, it is the vertical disintegration of organisational structures that has become the driving force reshaping the space economy of post-Fordism. Their fundamental observation is that 'vertical disintegration encourages agglomeration, and agglomeration encourages vertical disintegration' (Scott, 1986, p. 224). Basing their account on a reading of transactions cost analysis, Storper and Scott argue that the paramount and distinctive feature in the transition to flexible accumulation has been a progressive externalisation of production, and 'because of this tendency to externalisation of the transactional structures of production, selected sets of producers with especially dense interlinkages have a tendency to agglomerate locationally' (Storper and Scott, 1989, p. 26). As evidence of their thesis, they point particularly to new high-tech zones like Silicon Valley and Route 128; to the artisanal and design-intensive industries of the Third Italy; and to the clustering of producer, commercial and financial service activity in world cities. In this combined process of deverticalisation and agglomeration, Scott and Storper make clear, the new ICTs have played an unexpected role. 'The emergence of flexible production', they argue, 'has belied earlier predictions of the demise of locationally dense production systems due to the development of advanced communications technologies' (ibid., p. 27). The apparent paradox is that advanced communications technologies in fact 'encourage the appearance of new specialised production activities, which themselves then frequently cluster together in geographical space' (ibid., p. 27).

Whilst there are some notable differences, the spirit of this thesis very much converges with arguments developed within an institutionalist perspective by Charles Sabel and Michael Piore about the organisational and territorial implications of, in their terminology, the shift from mass production to flexible specialisation (Piore and Sabel, 1984). In a clear exposition of this perspective, Charles Sabel again stresses the imbrication of organisational and territorial logics, proposing that in the current period 'the relation between the economy and its territory is changing' (Sabel, 1989, p. 20). What he, in fact, argues is that the territorial implications of the new 'flexible economies' resemble those of nineteenth-century Marshallian districts in which 'the matrix of production . . . was an area, not a firm' (ibid., p. 17). For Sabel, the growth of flexible forms of organisation has been brought about by more volatile markets which have forced firms to become more adaptable and resourceful. This has led to the vertical disintegration of unwieldly mass production complexes, to new forms of subcontracting and inter-firm cooperation, to localised networks, to new forms of business culture and 'social solidarity'. Because flexibility implies specialisation, and because specialisation demands inter-firm collaboration, cooperation and trust, there has been a tendency towards 'the reconsolidation of the region as an integrated unit of production' towards the 'formation or revitalisation of regional economies that strongly resemble the nineteenth century centres of flexible specialisation' (ibid., pp. 18, 22). As with Storper and Scott, the organisational transformation of enterprise produces spatial agglomeration and reasserts the significance of place for the development process.

Whilst they do not develop a sustained position on the significance of technology, it is clear that Piore and Sabel, too, see new 'flexible' technologies as central to their future scenario of 'high technology cottage industries' (Smith, 1989; cf. Meegan, 1988). The computer, they argue, is 'an artisan's tool' (Piore and Sabel, 1984, p. 261), and it is ICTs that underpin the typical (and symbolic) geographical form of (neo-)artisanal production, the industrial district. Communications and information systems are fundamental to the coordination of transactions between the dense web of localised firms; they are crucial to the way in which the complex division of labour is articulated within the industrial district. The relations of cooperation and collaboration that characterise inter-firm networks are institutionalised through the infrastructure of localised information and communications grids. If these technologies ensure the organisational integrity of the production system, they also underpin its localisation, its containment within a particular territorial configuration. Like Scott and Storper, Piore and Sabel make the apparently paradoxical inference that these 'space-transcending' technologies in fact bring about, not global and decentralised organisational forms, but rather localised and concentrated agglomerations. What the flexible specialisation thesis asserts is that technological systems depend upon their embeddedness within the face-to-face networks, the 'clan culture', of the industrial district. Information and communications systems cannot escape or transcend the logic of (geographically specific) social institutions, norms and behaviour.

This broad post-Fordist hypothesis identifies a very precise logic of territorial development in the new phase of accumulation and, on this basis, it articulates a clear policy for regional development policy. Charles Sabel is the clearest exponent. In the present period, he argues, 'the relation between the economy and its territory is changing' (Sabel, 1989, p. 20). Sabel points to 'the ·

reconsolidation of the region as an integrated unit of production'; as in the case of the nineteenth-century industrial districts described by Alfred Marshall, 'the matrix of production [is] an area, not a firm' (ibid., pp. 17–18). In describing a 'renaissance' of local and regional economies, Sabel emphasises the new, or rather renewed, pre-eminence of area variables in the development process. Flexible production complexes are the paradigm for future growth and prosperity. Sabel sees no reason why they should not diffuse to form the basis of a new kind of federated national economy: 'To ask why flexible economies should not diffuse under competitive pressure is as reasonable as to ask why they should' (ibid., p. 52). In this version, the post-Fordist hypothesis is really the neo-Marshallian hypothesis.

This particular agenda in fact reflects a much wider contemporary concern with localities and localism. As Andrew Jonas (1988) has argued, there has been an exceptional convergence of interest in the locality as an object of inquiry. This has been the case not only in terms of economic and regional development policies, but also in the context of a resurgence of interest in social and cultural identities. What it amounts to is a geographical form of the 'small is beautiful' perspective. In our view, it is extremely problematical. As John Lovering argues, some Marshallian districts may still survive, but the overriding tendency is towards the fragmentation of local economies: 'If the local economy in the Old [Fordist] Model was a skeleton in which each part was connected to all the others, under the New Post-Fordist Model it is more like a pile of bones' (Lovering, 1988, p. 150). The locality that is being celebrated is in fact a thing of the past. 'The paradox', writes Pierre Veltz (1983, p. 42), is that ' "local" space is increasingly seen as a field of action' at a time when 'the coherence of the local, in the context of both production and reproduction, is ever more problematical'.

This new localism should be seen as a defensive and compensatory phenomenon, rather than a prefigurative one. If we are now, indeed, experiencing a process of spatial transformation then it 'involves not a single process but a compound restructuring at different spatial scales' (Smith, 1988, p. 148); it is not about a new pre-eminence of the local, but rather a new articulation of local, regional, national and global scales of activity. We should not, uncritically swallow the prevailing rhetoric of localism. Now, as it has always been, the accumulation process is about the articulation of organisational and territorial logics. As we have already argued, it is about the coordination of mobility and fixity: if capital accumulation necessitates the organisation of flows (capital, labour, materials), it also requires the territorial fix of social and physical infrastructure to make this possible. The point to be made about the present historical juncture concerns, not the pre-eminence of 'area variables', but a new relationship between organisation and territory, space and place.

Organisational transformation has, in fact, been more complex, and its territorial impact more various, than is allowed for in the approaches we have discussed in this section. The local production complex represents one expression of this new relationship. But it is only a very partial expression, and cannot carry the paradigmatic significance given to it in the neo-Marshallian hypothesis. Warning against a 'fetishism of the local', Bruno Ganne (1989) argues that the industrial district has been an exceptional, and excessively idealised, phenomenon, and that, in the case of France at least, localised industrial systems have, in fact, been undermined and eroded by the forces of concentration. What is significant is not the local, but rather an evolving local-global nexus, new articulations of local and global dynamics. The paramount tendency, we would argue, is towards corporate globalisation, expressing itself through a complex use of space and place, a compound process of deterritorialisation and reterritorialisation. This tendency, as we shall go on to argue, reflects the growing significance of new forms of corporate integration and networking made possible by the new ICTs.

Integration and globalisation

Let us begin with three apparently contradictory statements made by Carlo de Benedetti of Olivetti in a recent interview:

> Today, all businesses face one crucial economic equation: how to amortise the ever-higher costs of new products over their ever-shorter shelf-life. *Globalisation is the only possible answer.*

> Exports are becoming obsolete, because they are too slow. Marketers today must sell the latest product everywhere at once — and *that means producing locally.*

> *Technology is destroying space and time*, the last two barriers for the human race (*Observer*, 14 February, 1988, our emphases).

In these aphoristic observations, de Benedetti points to the key dynamics of the contemporary restructuring process: the relations between space and place; between global space and local space; between transcendence and control of space and territory. And he points to the strategic importance of new ICTs in this process of change.

We want to take up these insights with the research framework and agenda opened up by the post-Fordist hypothesis. In our view, they point to an alternative understanding of contemporary change and transformation. The current restructuring process, we maintain, does not mark a decisive historical break, an absolute break with the Fordist era of accumulation, but is characterised, rather, by considerable uncertainty and indeterminacy, and by strong continuities with the past. There is no clear evidence of the emergence of a radically innovative and bountiful post-Fordist era. We would argue that we have not yet progressed beyond Fordism, and that the current period can at the most be described as 'neo-Fordist'. As a general tendency we are witnessing the deepening of long historical trends towards the global concentration and centralisation of economic power. Multinational corporations remain the key shapers of the world economy, and it is the ever more extensive and intensive integration of their activities that is the primary dynamic of the present period. As Flavia Martinelli and Erica Schoenberger argue, 'despite the recent focus on "small is beautiful", the power and the importance of large corporations, increasingly multinational, is not faltering'. Indeed, 'the idea that "Big" is still "Better" seems to be comforted by the recent resurgence of industrial and financial concentration processes at a world scale' (Martinelli and Schoenberger, 1989, p. 16).

If this consolidation of corporate command and control is paramount, it is none the less the case that, to this end, there have been significant experiments in recent years in corporate restructuring and reorganisation. What we are seeing is a hugh burst of activity centred around mergers, acquisitions, joint ventures, strategic alliances, inter-firm agreements and collaborative activities of various kinds (marketing, research and development, production). The objective has been to ensure both flexibility (mobility) and control in a field of operation that has become truly global. To be, in de Benedetti's phrase, 'everywhere at once', is to develop organisational forms capable of articulating spatial and temporal coordinates on a world scale. Theodore Levitt signals the end of the multinational commercial world and the multinational corporation: 'The new reality is the globalisation of markets, and with it the powerful materialisation of the global corporation' (Levitt, 1983, p. 21). The objective now is to achieve global economies of scale through the development of universal products. And it is globalisation that makes necessary new forms of corporate alliance:

> Today you have to be in all important markets simultaneously if you are going to keep competitors from establishing their positions. Globalisation will not wait. You need alliances and you need them now. But not the traditional kind (Ohmae 1989a; cf. Ohmae 1989b).

If it is necessary to adjust to global markets and customers, it is also the case that competitive advantage is this new era of aggressive global competition, depends upon 'capturing and integrating critical inputs worldwide' (Perrino and Tipping, 1989, p. 12). Of fundamental importance here is the global management of technology, particularly through the forging of joint ventures and alliances in R&D. Perrino and Tipping describe the new 'global network' model of technology management, which 'consists of a network of technology core groups in each major market — the US, Japan and Europe — managed in a coordinated way for maximum impact' (ibid., p. 13).

ICTs clearly play a strategic role in this globalising logic. The new corporate strategies are about more effective corporate *integration* (across vertical, horizontal and territorial boundaries), and information and communications systems are important for this process. Even in the case of an early communications technology like the telegraph, as James Carey (1989) reminds us, it was clear that the 'system is the solution'. In the case of advanced ICT networks, this is all the more the case. Corporate organisation and activity must be seen in terms of systems operating across space and time coordinates. Carlota Perez, writing from a neo-Schumpeterian perspective, describes the organisational paradigm of the fifth Kondratiev long wave in terms of a process of 'systemation'. It is a process that involves the merging of all corporate activities into 'one single interactive system' (Perez, 1985, p. 453). Through the coordination of communications and 'feedback loops', the firm 'becomes a continuous flow system of activities, information, evaluations and decisions' (ibid., p. 454). With the tighter articulation of the whole chain of corporate functions — R&D, design, production, distribution, sales and marketing — what we see developing are both vertical and horizontal forms of integration, integration within the internal organisation of the firm, but also closer integration with external activities and organisations. Writing from a similar theoretical perspective, Fiorenza Belussi endorses this model of the 'network firm'. Describing the organisational structure of Benetton, she points to the 'system efficiency' that is gained by a structure that involves 'a great deal of coordination among different production units or phases, and a strong link between the firm and its market' (Belussi, 1989, pp. 5–6). In so far as the arguments put forward by Scott and Storper and by Piore and Sabel take the Italian small firm system as a paradigmatic example, Belussi's analysis is a direct confrontation. Her account of 'the emergence of new organisational "concentrated regimes" and towards new forms of oligopolistic power concentrated within a structure formed by small (often apparently independent) firms' (ibid., p. 10) explicitly challenges the flexible specialisation thesis.

The continuities with Fordist organisational structures are clear: the concentration of capital and control is not being undermined; flexible integration only moves closer to the realisation of long cherished corporate ambitions. None the less, if we are not about to enter a new post-Fordist era of flexible specialisation, it is still the case that 'integrated logistics' (Rose and Sharman, 1989) and 'dynamic networks' (Miles and Snow, 1986) do, indeed involve significant organisational innovations. Through the use of enhanced communications technologies, corporate activities are structured, not in terms of an aggregation of functions, but rather as a system of flows (Veltz, 1988). What we see is the 'increasing interpretation of the moments of production, exchange and consumption' (Veltz, 1989, p. 9). In this process, the boundaries between the firm and its external environment are also problematised: 'integrated networks not only weave firms into a common web, but also make "organisation" and "market" or "production-transactions consumption" parts of a continuum' (ibid., p. 11). Corporate transactions and interactions are rendered more versatile and responsive. The network has more capacity to reconfigure its organisational boundaries, to fragment or combine, to decentralise or recentralise.

What are the geographical implications? How are the network organisations deployed across space? Again, we distance ourselves from the flexible specialisation thesis with its exclusive emphasis upon localisation. In our view, there is no single pattern of spatial transformation, nor is there any absolute break with older geographical dynamics. According to Manuel Castells, decentralisation, considered by the protagonists of the post-Fordist hypothesis as a residual and anachronistic phenomenon of the Fordist area, persists under the new conditions: 'it seems that automation and flexible manufacturing technologies do not reverse the process of decentralisation, although multinational companies now have more options, combining automation and location to obtain an optional mix between production costs, production quality, and market accessibility' (Castells, 1989b, p. 19). The same can be said for information and communications grids: their effect is to enhance locational freedom, making possible the choice between spatial agglomeration or dispersal.

The new ICTs are bringing about a multitude of spatial possibilities (Leborgne and Lipietz, 1989). To focus upon one particular and determinate spatial logic of post-Fordism is to miss the point. What is significant is precisely the spectrum of options opened up by network technologies and systems. In some cases, there remains a commitment to old, Fordist, forms of corporate organisation (Hudson, 1989); in others, there are clear indications that new possibilities are being sought. It is a matter of a repertoire of strategies, dependent upon situated contexts and also upon balances of power. Territorial complexes may, indeed, represent one significant development, but they are by no means the only element and should not be idealised. The key issue, now as always, concerns the division and integration of labour. The logic of organisation involves fragmentation, but this is always predicated on the rearticulation and reintegration of components: 'production systems must be physically linked up; their labour processes must be coordinated; and the flows of materials, labour, and information between them must be regulated' (Walker, 1988, pp. 381–2). Integration may be achieved in a number of ways, and at a variety of spatial scales depending on the particular industry, product and phase of production. As Richard Walker makes clear, 'different production systems have characteristic degrees of integration and/or disintegration, that is, of organisational scope' (Walker, 1988, p. 382). Different production systems also have different histories, and, in the context of the present restructuring process, they face different constraints and have different options open to them. There may also be different logics at work at different levels of any production systems. Thus, it seems to be the case that higher level skills may 'involve spatially diffuse, even international, intercorporate networking, joint ventures, and the like, whereas lower order functions capable of being satisfied in-house or through subcontracting may tend increasingly to cluster in localised complexes' (Cooke, 1988, p. 287–8). The point is that there is no single, simple or general paradigm, as the neo-Marshallians would have us believe.

The nature and scope of this transformation of organisational geography can best be captured in terms of the emergence of a new global-local nexus. Network configurations afford a new mobility, a hypermobility, to global corporations. Within the global system, it becomes possible to shift activities around the network topology and across territories. If this represents a major push towards the overcoming of geographical barriers, it remains the case that space and place are not done away with, cannot be transcended in any absolute sense. As David Harvey emphasises, 'the collapse of spatial barriers does not mean that the significance of space is decreasing'. Global corporations

> are now paying much closer attention to relative locational advantages, precisely because diminishing spatial barriers give capitalists the power to exploit minute spatial differentiations to good effect. Small differences in what the space contains in the way of labour supplies, resources, infrastructures, and the like become of increased significance . . . We thus approach the central paradox: the less important the spatial barriers, the greater the sensitivity of capital to the variations of place within space, and the greater the incentive for places to be differentiated in ways attractive to capital (Harvey, 1989, pp. 294–6).

The significance of place is changed not abolished. As Ohmae reminds us, global marketing is precisely about intervention at the local level, about developing 'the capability to understand and respond to customer needs and business system requirements in each critical market' (Ohmae, 1989b, p. 159). The global must invest in the local; the local is mediated through the global. The dynamic of organisational geography is shared increasingly by these complex articulations of global mobility and local fixity.

This, of course, has important implications for the future of particular localities and regions (as John Goddard discusses more fully in Chapter 11 of this volume). It is difficult to see any substance in the neo-Marshallian vision of a world of thriving and mutually supporting industrial districts. Some localities, albeit an ever shrinking number, fortunate enough to be strategically placed in the new global networks or to contain intact local structures, will possess the means to shape their futures. However, for most places — those disadvantageously positioned through previous rounds of accumulation; those that have suffered the gradual historical erosion of skills, technologies, institutions and resources; those that have fragmented local structures — the future will be shaped by the logic of dependent and peripheral development. If, as Richard Gordon argues global organisational strategies 'involve the strategic creation of linked production complexes, each appropriate to a diverse mix of regional and social endowments and distributed as an inter-regional network in accordance with a global strategic conception', then the viability of local and regional economies will be 'a product of their ability to articulate a coherent organisational presence with a global milieu' (Gordon, 1989, p. 116). What will be crucial for particular territories is whether they can insert themselves into the network topology. In this context, the question of communications infrastructure, and of its regulation, becomes crucial (Gillespie and Robins, 1991). But technological endowments are far from decisive. There are also powerful economic forces bringing about competition between places to establish a position within the new global division of labour. The danger is that the new global order will be marked by a new segmentation of 'on-line' and 'off-line' territories, as it were; by a hierarchy that differentiates those localities that can harness territorial endowments to the network structure and those characterised by both internal fragmentation and external disarticulation from the network.

Conclusion

In this chapter, we have tried to look at the nature of contemporary economic and social transformation, and the role of ICTs in this process. We have explored the way in which the restructuring of capital is associated with a changing spatial division of labour, and we have considered the potential impact of this on particular localities. Our account has focused upon the communications aspect of the new ICTs, suggesting the centrality of communications systems to new ways of structuring organisations across space. The most appropriate framework within which to map the dynamics of change, we have argued, is that adumbrated with the 'post-Fordist hypothesis'. Having said that, we distance ourselves from the predominant neo-Marshallian argument that emphasises flexible specialisation and localised agglomerations such as industrial districts, as the paradigm for the future. Our own argument suggests a far more complex process, characterised by new forms of corporate integration, by a systems logic and the development of a network economy. This manifests itself in the development of a global order and a new global-local nexus. The future for particular localities, we argue, depends on how effectively they can position themselves within these global networks. The danger is that new hierarchies will develop dividing those territories that are 'switched' in to the network from those that are 'unswitched' or even 'unplugged'.

Bibliography

Albrechts, L. and Swyngedouw, E., 1989, 'The challenges for regional policy under a flexible regime of accumulation' in L. Albrechts, F. Moulaert, P. Roberts and E. Swyngedouw (eds), *Regional Policy at the Crossroads: European Perspectives*, Jessica Kingsley Publishers, London, pp. 67–89.

Amin, A. and Robins, K., 1990, 'The re-emergence of regional economies? The mythical geography of flexible accumulation', *Environment and Planning D: Society and Space*, **8**, 7–34.

Belussi, F., 1989, *Benetton Italy: beyond Fordism and Flexible Specialisation — The Evolution of the Network Firm Model*, Science Policy Research Unit, University of Sussex.

Booth, D.E., 1987, 'Regional long waves and urban policy', *Urban Studies*, **24**, 447–59.

Carey, J.W., 1989, *Communication as Culture: Essays on Media and Society*, Unwin Hyman, Boston.

Castells, M., 1985a, 'High technology, economic restructuring, and the urban-regional process in the United States' in M. Castells (ed.), *High Technology, Space and Society*, Sage, Beverly Hills, pp. 11–40.

Castells, M., 1985b, 'High technology and the new international division of labour', *Labour and Society*, **14**, 7–42.

Cooke, P., 1988, 'Flexible integration, scope economies and strategic alliances: social and spatial mediations', *Environment and Planning D: Society and Space*, 6, 281–300.

Ganne, B., 1989, 'La question en France de l'industrialisation diffuse des systèmes industriels localisés', Paper presented to the Conference on Districts Industriels et Systèmes de Coopération Inter-Firmes, IILS, Florence, 12–15 April.

Gillespie, A. and Robins, K., 1989, 'Geographical inequalities: the spatial bias of the new communications technologies', *Journal of Communication*, 39 (3), 7–18.

Gillespie, A. and Robins, K., 1991, 'Non-universal service? Political economy and communications geography' in J. Brotchie *et al.* (eds), *Cities of the 21st Century: New Technology and Spatial Systems*, Longman, London. Cheshire, Melbourne, pp. 159–170.

Gordon, R., 1989, 'Les entrepreneurs, l'entreprise et les fondements sociaux de l'innovation', *Sociologie du Travail*, 30 (1), 107–24.

Hall, P., 1985, 'The geography of the fifth Kondratieff' in P. Hall and A. Markusen (eds), *Silicon Landscapes*, Allen & Unwin, Boston, pp. 1–19.

Harvey, D., 1985a, 'The geopolitics of capitalism' in D. Gregory and J. Urry (eds), *Social Relations and Spatial Structure*, Macmillan, London, pp. 128–63.

Harvey, D., 1985b, *The Urbanisation of Capital*, Basil Blackwell, Oxford.

Harvey, D., 1989, *The Condition of Post-modernity*, Basil Blackwell, Oxford.

Hepworth, M. and Robins, K., 1983, 'Whose information society? A view from the periphery', *Media, Culture and Society*, 10 (3), 323–43.

Hirst, P. and Zeitlin, J. (eds), 1989a, *Reversing Industrial Decline? Industrial Structure and Policy in Britain and her Competitors*, Berg, Oxford.

Hirst, P. and Zeitlin, J., 1989b, 'Flexible specialisation and the competitive failure of UK manufacturing', *Political Quarterly*, 60 (2), 164–78.

Hudson, R., 1988, 'Uneven development in capitalist societies: changing spatial divisions of labour, forms of spatial organisation of production and service provision, and their impact on localities', *Transactions of the Institute of British Geographers*, 13, 483–96.

Hudson, R., 1989, 'Labour-market changes and new forms of work in old industrial regions: maybe flexibility for some but not flexible accumulation', *Environment and Planning D: Society and Space*, 7, 5–30.

Jonas, A., 1988, 'A new regional geography of localities?', *Area*, 20 (2), 101–10.

Keinath, F.W., 1985, 'The spatial component of the post-industrial society', *Economic Geography*, 61, 223–40.

Leborgne, D. and Lipietz, A., 1988, 'New technologies, new modes of regulation: some spatial implications', *Environment and Planning D: Society and Space*, 6 (3), 263–80.

Leborgne, D. and Lipietz, A., 1989, 'Deux stratégies sociales dans la production des nouveaux espaces économiques', Paper presented to the International Conference on Les Nouveaux Espaces Industriels: Un Survol International, Paris, 21–22 March.

Leven, C.L., 1988, 'Post-industrialism, regional change and the new urban geography' in G. Sternlieb and J.W. Hughes (eds), *America's New Market Geography: Nation, Region and Metropolis*, Rutgers University Press, New Brunswick, pp. 161–77.

Levitt, T., 1983, *The Marketing Imagination*, Collier Macmillan, London.

Lovering, J., 1988, 'The local economy and local economic strategies', *Policy and Politics*, 16 (3), 145–57.

Martin, R., 1989, 'The new economics and politics of regional restructuring: the British experience' in L. Abrechts, F. Moulaert, P. Roberts and E. Swyngedouw (eds), *Regional Policy at the Crossroads: European Perspectives*, Jessica Kingsley Publishers, London, pp. 27–51.

Martinelli, F. and Schoenberger, E., 1989, 'Oligopoly alive and well: notes for a broader discussion on flexible accumulation', Paper presented to the International Conference on Les Nouveaux Espaces Industriels: Un Survol International, Paris, 21–22 March.

Massey, D., 1984, 'Introduction: geography matters' in D. Massey and J. Allen (eds), *Geography Matters*, Cambridge University Press, Cambridge, pp. 1–11.

Meegan, R., 1988, 'A crisis of mass production?' in J. Allen and D. Massey (eds), *Restructuring Britain: The Economy in Question*, Sage, London, pp. 136–93.

Miles, R. and Snow, C., 1986, 'Organisations: new concepts for new forms', *California Management Review*, **28** (3), 62–73.

Moulaert, R. and Swyngedouw, E., 1989, 'A regulation approach to the geography of the flexible production system', *Environment and Planning D: Society and Space*, **7** (3), 327–45.

Ohmae, K., 1989a, 'The global logic of strategic alliances', *Harvard Business Review*, **67** (2), 143–54.

Ohmae, K., 1989b, 'Managing in a borderless world', *Harvard Business Review*, **67** (3), 152–61.

Perez, C., 1985, 'Microelectronics, long waves and world structural change: new perspectives for developing countries', *World Development*, **13** (3), 441–63.

Perrino, A. and Tipping, J., 1989, 'Global management of technology', *Research and Technology Management*, May–June, pp. 12–19.

Piore, M. and Sabel, C., 1984, *The Second Industrial Divide: Possibilities for Prosperity*, Basic Books, New York.

Rose, J. and Sharman, G., 1989, 'The redesign of logistics', *Mckinsey Quarterly*, Winter, 29–43.

Rustin, M., 1989, 'The politics of post-Fordism: or the trouble with "new times" ', *New Left Review*, (175), 54–77.

Sabel, C., 1989, 'Flexible specialisation and the re-emergence of regional economies' in P. Hirst and J. Zeitlin (eds), *Reversing Industrial Decline? Industrial Structure and Policy in Britain and her Competitors*, Berg, Oxford, pp. 17–70.

Savage, M., 1989, 'Spatial differences in modern Britain' in C. Hamnett, L. McDowell and P. Sarre (eds), *Restructuring Britain: The Changing Social Structure*, Sage, London, pp. 244–68.

Scott, A., 1986, 'Industrial organisation and location: division of labour, the firm, and spatial process', *Economic Geography*, **62** (3), 215–31.

Scott, A., 1988, 'Flexible production systems and regional development: the rise of new industrial spaces in North America and Western Europe', *International Journal of Urban and Regional Research*, **12** (2), 171–86.

Smith, C., 1989, 'Flexible specialisation, automation and mass production', *Work, Employment & Society*, **3** (2), 203–20.

Smith, N., 1988, 'The region is dead! Long live the region!' *Political Geography Quarterly*, **7** (2), 141–52.

Storper, M. and Scott, A., 1989, 'The geographical foundations and social regulation of flexible production complexes' in J. Wolch and M. Dear (eds), *The Power of Geography: How Territory Shapes Social Life*, Unwin Hyman, Boston, pp. 21–40.

Veltz, P., 1983, 'Fordism, rapport salarial et complexité des pratiques sociales: Une perspective critique', *Critiques de l'Economie Politique*, (23/24), 30–42.

Veltz, P., 1988, 'Informatique et "intelligence de la production" ', *Terminal*, (39/40/41), 20–6.

Veltz, P., 1989, 'Nouveaux modèles d'organisation de la production et tendances de l'économie territoriale', Paper presented to the International Conference on Les Nouveaux Espaces Industriels: Un Survol International, Paris, 21–22 March.

Walker, R., 1988, 'The geographical organisation of production-systems', *Environment and Planning D: Society and Space*, **6**, 377–408.

10 Computer networks in Britain: Communication technologies or technologies of control?

Ken Ducatel

Communication in organisations uses a range of media from direct face-to-face meetings to electronic data interchange between computers. Each communication medium has its own specific qualities making it appropriate for some communication activities and not for others: face-to-face meetings are generally regarded as the best way of getting to know people; fax is a useful way of sending graphic information quickly over a long distance. The different qualities of different media mean that none can quite replace another.

We would expect communications innovations such as computer networks to affect organisational relationships. However, the changes caused by computer network communication will be hard to predict beforehand. Any changes will be as much a reflection of organisational culture as a product of the technology in itself. Consider two extreme cases of the application of computer networks. First, computer networks might be used to facilitate the links between workers. Each workstation has its own processing power, its own store of data and by implication the ability to make decisions. The network supports devolved decision-making, by allowing access to external stores of data and by acting as a medium of information exchange between interdependent but autonomous parts of an organisation. A second model uses the computer network to channel data into a central pool. The centralised information is processed and fed into a single decision-making system. Decisions once made are issued via the computer network as commands for the rest of the organisation.

In the first case, computer networks are used to develop interactive communication, in the second the technology aids the imposition of greater order and control. In practice, of course, the interactive communication aspects of computer networks are not separate from their use as technologies of domination and control. A position midway between the two extremes is the most likely outcome. Thus, until we investigate how computer networks are actually applied we will not know whether they are technologies of domination and control, or whether they are being used to enhance the quality of working life and the opportunities for self-expression in the workplace.

The absence of an *a priori* direction in which the technology will take organisations makes the empirical investigation of how computer network technology is being implemented of the utmost importance and urgency. It is important because ways must be found to improve working conditions through the introduction of new technologies, such as computer networking. It is urgent because computer networks are not yet mature technologies; there may yet be time to intervene in the way they are implemented.

This chapter is a modest attempt to pursue the project of investigating the nature and extent of computer network usage, through an empirical description of the manner of implementation of computer networks in British workplaces. The information presented in the next section gives a rare national-level picture of the status of computer network implementation. The findings indicate the direction of the early development trajectory of computer networking in Britain. We examine, in turn, different industries and workplaces in order to probe the sorts of uses to which the computer network has been put. In the second section of the paper we consider the spatial differences in the development trajectory of computer networks in Britain. In the concluding section we examine the implications of the empirical findings, and make suggestions for policy which might make computer networking more socially responsive than it has been so far.

Computer networks in Britain

The data set

This section is an early snapshot, based on 1984 data, of the diffusion of computer network technology. The data are derived from the Workplace Industrial Relations Survey (WIRS), which is a national survey of just over 2,000 establishments in the public and private sectors (Millward and Stephens, 1987). It is the only authoritative establishment-based survey conducted on a large scale and, as such, provides a benchmark for the analysis of the general rate of change in working conditions and work relations. The 1984 survey is of special interest because it attempts to measure the diffusion of new microelectronic technology both on the shop-floor and in the office (Daniel, 1987). Computer networking between sites was recorded in the survey as one aspect of the application of microelectronic technology.

Despite its advantages as a general resource on the level of development of computer technology in British workplaces, it has to be admitted that the WIRS data has drawbacks for the measurement of computer networking. It does not indicate the intensity of use of the computer network, nor the communication activities taking place. Nor indeed does it measure the presence of on-site computer networks (Local Area Networks). Finally, there is no information on the topology of the networks which are recorded. For instance, it is impossible to know if each site has computer connections with many other sites or whether it is linked only to a mainframe at head office. Nor is there a sense of the geography of the linkages or of the spatial scale of the computer network links.

In the face of the many drawbacks of the WIRS it is worth stating the value of an analysis based on this data. The 1984 WIRS data are useful because they capture a point on the development trajectory of computer networking when a relatively small proportion of workplaces were using a computer network. By comparing workplaces which have computer networks with those that do not, according to their organisational function and across sectors and regions, it is possible to build a picture of the kinds of uses to which computer networks have initially been applied. This kind of information could not be constructed if computer networks were more widely diffused, because the variations will be smoothed out as computer networks become commonplace. It is not so important therefore that we should be able to open the black box and see how the technologies are used; the differential adoption rates from sector to sector and from region to region are revealing in themselves about the early application of computer networks.

Workplaces and computer networks

The most striking thing about the early applications of computer networks is that they are strongly biased towards internal use. The evidence for this is of two forms. First, there is the direct evidence that of the 25 per cent of establishments which had networks 80 per cent were solely internal links (see Table 10.1). Second, single-site establishments very rarely have a computer link at all, with only about 5 per cent of establishments computer networked against an average across the sample as a whole of about 30 per cent (see Table 10.2).

Table 10.1 Type of computer network link by size of establishment

Size	Internal network	External network	Both	No link
25–49	10.4	4.1	0.5	85.0
50–99	25.5	3.8	1.1	69.6
100–499	32.6	5.5	3.6	58.3
500+	44.4	8.0	12.6	35.1
Average	19.7	4.5	1.6	74.2

Base = 1326

Source: WIRS, 1984

Table 10.2 Establishment with computer network links

Type of Establishment	Manufacturing		Services	
	%	base	%	base
Single site	4.3	123	5.9	237
Head office	15.9	28	37.8	153
Admin office	65.7	5	37.1	128
Other	29.5	214	28.6	112

Source: WIRS, 1984

The inference we draw is that computer networks were, in 1984, used to solve internal communication problems, rather than maintain contacts with the outside world. Internal communication differs from external communication: it is more regular and routine and can be formalised in ways which the more anarchic external transactions cannot. It has been argued (Beniger, 1986) that hierarchical structures and the routines of organisational life were explicitly developed into bureaucratic forms of management to overcome the problems of communication, control and management as institutions and firms grew more complex. Thus, bureaucratic management, which is a rule-bound culture of management, would be expected to employ a technology such as computer networks to formalise communication within organisations still further.

Contrast internal bureaucracy with the nature of external communication. Here, the stress is upon search and signalling in the market-place (Coase, 1937; Williamson, 1975). The nature of communication may be disciplined by frequent and routine transactions, the repeated purchase of standardised products and services, but the imposition of rules is less sure. External contracts and contacts are more open to termination and renegotiation; the parties involved are less likely to share a unified organisational goal, and may even be competitors in the market-place.

The tendency for bureaucratic systems to apply computer networks to formal or routine communications is reinforced by limitations of the technology itself. Its attributes as a medium of communication make it unsuitable for contacts involving a high degree of risk and uncertainty. For instance, research by the Communications Studies Group compared the effectiveness of several telecommunications media with face-to-face meetings for different sorts of business activities (Short *et al.*, 1976). The results of their experiments indicated that even interactive person-to-person telecommunication such as audioconferences (telephone conversations between two or more people) and videoconferences (video in addition to audio) were inadequate for emotive activities such as getting to know people, negotiation, conflict resolution and persuasion. We would expect that computer networks, having fewer stimuli than either audioconferences or videoconferences, are even less likely to substitute effectively for direct interpersonal communication.

Moreover, the limits of computer networks as a medium of communication are immediately appropriable for bureaucratic management. Further research by the Communications Studies Group indicated that face-to-face meetings are no more effective, and sometimes less desirable, than telecommunication for more routine activities such as giving information and receiving orders, general maintenance of contact and disciplining employees. The advantage of telecommunication is its impersonality. It is more efficient and focused, and in the latter case less embarrassing.

We now see why internal communication is more readily converted to computer networking. The attributes of the technology and the difference between internal and external communication promote the early application of computer networks within hierarchical and bureaucratic systems of management. There is no direct evidence of this from the data, but a more detailed examination of the types of workplaces and the industries which have computer networks shows more support for this formalised model of the application of computer networks.

Head offices and administrative offices are primarily involved in informational activities within an organisation. It is undoubtedly the information role of these types of workplaces which leads to their relatively high rate of computer network linkage, with about 40 per cent of such establishments having a computer link (Table 10.2). Of course, administrative offices differ from head offices in their function within the organisation. Whilst head offices exercise a co-ordinating and decision-making role, administration is primarily providing information support services to other sites within the organisation, thus their main activities are paper processing and data processing. We can use the WIRS data to show that computer technologies in Britain have been used to further the bureaucratic model of management. From Table 10.3 it is clear that administrative offices have a generally higher rate of network linkage (40 per cent) than head offices (34.3 per cent). We suggest this is because routinised administrative functions are more readily converted to

Table 10.3 Type of computer link by type of establishment

Size	Internal network	External network	Both	No link
Single site	2.7	2.5	0.1	94.6
Head office	22.5	9.3	2.5	65.7
Admin office	33.3	3.8	3.0	59.9
Other	22.5	4.4	1.8	71.3

Source: WIRS, 1984

computerisation than the head office functions. Moreover, administrative offices are more dependent on internal computer networks, which would tend to be more routine in orientation; only 17 per cent of the administrative offices which have a computer link are connected to an external computer, as compared to 35 per cent of networked head offices.

Industrial differences in the application of computer networks

Another way to discover how computer networks are being implemented is to compare the different rates at which computer networks have been adopted in different industries. Industries with high rates of computer linkage are characterised by spatially dispersed multi-site organisations (see Table 10.4). Thus, social security departments of central government (90 per cent), banking (87 per cent) and retailing (57 per cent) have all adopted network technology to facilitate the internal co-ordination of large volumes of transaction data of a routine and repetitive nature.

Table 10.4 Computer linkage rates by industrial activity: services

Industry	% Networked				
	All Estabs	Single Site	Head Office	Admin. Office	Other
Social Security	90.3	*	*	60.6	100.0
Banking	87.0	*	84.3	99.1	91.9
Retailing	51.9	27.1	25.6	*	56.5
National Government	39.1	*	70.6	33.2	36.0
Local Government	36.5	0.0	50.4	58.2	16.6
Insurance	34.9	*	28.1	18.1	40.2
Business services	27.5	8.8	39.0	*	38.0
Wholesale	21.7	7.0	28.5	17.9	24.3
Cultural industries	20.3	*	17.3	56.1	24.5
Transport	20.2	0.0	35.1	17.4	28.2
Post and comms	17.5	*	100.0	16.1	17.2
Medical	15.9	0.0	*	55.6	13.1
Central services	15.2	0.0	52.6	49.8	11.0
Education	10.9	7.4	*	8.2	11.5
Construction	9.1	0.0	4.0	4.4	17.9
Hotels & Tourism	7.8	5.9	18.2	43.4	2.2
Associations	0.0	0.0	0.0	0.0	0.0

Note: *-No observations in this cell

Source: WIRS, 1984

The conclusion that computer networks are being applied to routine organisational co-ordination is further supported by the high levels of network linkage amongst the service outlets in banking, retailing and insurance. The overall linkage rate actually increases when head office and administrative offices are excluded from the analysis, which contrasts strongly with the general trend that information-providing establishments are more likely to be linked. All the indications are, therefore, that computer networks are deployed primarily to meet internal operating requirements.

Behind these figures, there lies an interesting contrast between the nature of communication inside a retail organisation and its external transactions. A major organisational difficulty for any consumer service is the tension between the most efficient organisational form which draws the organisation together in space, and the problem that external contact with the consumer is necessary to maintain market share. Consumers, particularly shoppers, want to be able to see, touch, try on and smell goods before buying, which means that consumer services have to locate close to the customer. The need to be located near to the market to achieve direct contact with customers, therefore, stretches the internal communication lines of retail organisations. From the WIRS data, there is a strong sense that computer networks have been seized upon mainly for this reason, as a streamlining technology to deal with the problems of stretched internal communication, not as a means of enhancing the quality of internal communication within the organisation.

Location and computer networks

The findings discussed in the previous section show that computer networks are reinforcing hierarchical structures of management. In this section we take the analysis a stage further by looking at the spatial effects of the implementation of computer networks. The WIRS data has been used in two ways: first we investigate how the use of computer networks interacts with the spread of an establishment's market; secondly we consider regional differences in the implementation of computer networks.

Market orientation

The WIRS data has some useful information on whether the primary market for the workplace is local, regional, national or international. Admittedly, these categories are vague, as everyone has a different notion of what is local or regional, but they are useful because they indicate whether the processes of centralisation of communication are identifiable in a spatial sense as well as within hierarchical organisations.

The first finding is that computer networks play an unmistakable role in overcoming the difficulties of operating in large spatial markets. The larger the spatial market the more likely it is to have a computer link (see Table 10.5). Thus, whilst less than 10 per cent of manufacturing firms with local or regional

Table 10.5 Percentage of establishments with network links by market spread

Location	Private manufacturing		Private services	
	Single Site	Other	Single Site	Other
Local	0.0	3.0	0.0	35.9
Regional	0.0	10.9	0.0	42.5
National	3.3	17.3	1.3	52.4
International	0.5	39.1	8.6	56.5
Internal	–	27.4	–	50.0

Source: WIRS, 1984

markets are networked, nearly 40 per cent of manufacturers producing for export are linked. In services, the rate of linkage rises from about 35 per cent to over 50 per cent as the scope of the market increases. The implications of these findings are twofold. First, local marketing strategies are not associated with the heavy use of information technology, in fact the reverse is the case. There is, then, little evidence that the British manufacturing scene, at least, is characterised by 'flexible production ensembles' pursuing strategies of flexible integration and just-in-time production (Storper and Scott, 1989). If tightly clustered groups of interlocked producers do exist they are not using communication technology to increase the flexibility of their production and responsiveness. Rather, it is the larger, multi-site companies, producing for international markets, which are using communication networks. We are not suggesting that the more locally orientated firms are not modernising; there is some evidence (Northcott and Walling, 1988; Ducatel and Coombes, 1989) that many smaller workplaces use stand-alone computerised machinery. They are not, however, integrating these islands of automation.

The second implication, which follows from the findings in the first section, is that the more locally orientated the workplace the more likely it is to engage in communication through direct interpersonal communication rather than the more formal links which computer networks encourage. As we have seen, external communication is less susceptible to computerisation than internal communication. If the orientation of the workplace is localised the likelihood is that commercial transactions will be less predictable, planned and formalised, than if they have to be worked out over a distance. Thus, where there are ensembles of interacting producers, the continual renegotiation of contracts and subcontracts, and the need to respond to changing local needs, militates against computer communication strategies, which are best suited to systems of transactions which can be routinised.

However, there is a counter-trend to this size-scale effect. Closer examination of the data on the scale of markets reveals that computer networks are

Table 10.6 Computer linkage rates in small private service establishments by market dispersion

Location of main market	Internal network	External network	Both	No link	Base
7a: 25 to 49 Employees					
Local	21.9	3.0	0.0	75.2	117
Regional	7.6	0.0	0.0	92.4	46
National	11.8	7.1	0.0	81.1	49
International	16.3	12.2	3.7	67.8	28
Internal	0.0	0.0	26.3	73.7	7
7b: 50 to 99 Employees					
Local	26.3	6.3	0.0	67.4	45
Regional	52.4	0.0	0.0	47.6	27
National	22.8	10.9	5.7	60.6	26
International	38.2	19.2	0.0	42.7	15
Internal	65.0	0.0	1.7	33.4	10

Source: WIRS, 1984

more common than we would expect in small locally oriented service sector workplaces. This finding is clearly related to the observation at the end of the previous section that computer networks are useful to consumer service industries which face the unavoidable problem of co-ordinating activities across dispersed markets. Consumer service organisations such as banks, building societies and shops have large numbers of small workplaces reporting to a central authority. Thus, when we look at Table 10.6, we see that where small establishments serving local markets are linked they are more than likely to be providing information to an internal co-ordination network, rather than engaging in external transactions. In contrast, as the market focus widens the chances of an establishment having an external link increase.

The geography of British computer networks

The discussion so far has considered workplaces in the abstract space of organisational hierarchies. In this section we present data on the regional variations in the implementation of computer networks in Britain. The results are important because they demonstrate how computer networks are perpetuating the existing spatial divisions of labour between regions in Britain. In the first part of the chapter we saw how computer networks are being used to deepen the dependency of administrative offices and branch establishments on the head office; how the head office is becoming the

Table 10.7 Regional variations in the rate of computer network linkage of head offices

Location	Internal network	External network	Both	No link	Base
London	31.8	6.9	5.0	56.3	94
South	23.2	6.5	1.2	69.2	52
Heartland	14.9	15.0	1.8	68.3	52
Periphery	13.3	9.1	1.0	76.7	19

Note: The regional classification scheme used in this paper was developed in CURDS, and is described in Coombes and Goddard (1987)

Source: WIRS, 1984

Table 10.8 Regional variations in the rate of computer network linkage of plants and branches of multi-site organisations

Location	Internal network	External network	Both	No links	Base
London	26.0	6.3	3.8	63.9	343
South	23.2	4.0	1.8	71.1	279
Heartland	21.6	4.2	0.9	73.3	454
Periphery	19.2	2.7	0.8	77.3	241

Source: WIRS, 1984

communications focus, the external voice of the organisation. These findings are replicated when we look at the role of the core regions, London and the South-East, in the national division of labour. This has two aspects. First, the rate of modernisation, in the sense of adoption of information technology, is generally higher in the southern core. Second, only the more dependent establishments, such as back offices and branch plants, have higher linkage rates outside the core region than within.

The rate of computer network implementation declines with increased distance from London (see Tables 10.7 and 10.8). This is specially true for head office establishments, where there is a steady drop in the rate linkage from 43.7 per cent linked in London to 23.3 per cent in the periphery. The same effect is observed in establishments manufacturing plants and service outlets, with a decline from 36.1 per cent in London to 22.7 per cent in the periphery. Moreover, less than 20 per cent of networked establishments in the periphery or the heartlands have an external link, as opposed to nearly 30 per cent of networked establishments in London.

Table 10.9 Regional variations in linkage rates of establishment with increasing size

Size	London	South	Heartland	Periphery
24–49	19.4	14.9	14.1	11.8
50–99	35.8	27.7	28.8	27.2
100–499	45.1	43.5	38.9	40.2
500+	65.0	64.9	65.7	63.5

Source: WIRS, 1984

The only evidence we find of equality in the rate of modernisation between regions is the very similar linkage rates in different regions for establishments of 500 or more employees (Table 10.9). However, work reported elsewhere (Ducatel and Coombes, 1989) shows that peripheral regions have a high proportion of large, internally linked establishments, such as branch plants or foreign-owned establishments. Once again we infer that communications technology is in place to make external control and co-ordination easier, rather than to enhance the industrial autonomy of the peripheral regions. The most remarkable corroboration of this conclusion comes from the case of administrative offices. We have already seen that administrative offices have high rates of linkage, and these tend to be internal rather than external links. When looked at in the regional context, the double dependency of peripheral regions and peripheral functions within the corporate hierarchy reinforce each other; the rate of linkage of peripheral back offices is 60 per cent compared to a national average of between 30 and 35 per cent.

The implications of computer networking

The chapter started with a discussion of how computer networks could either enhance or further degrade working conditions. The empirical evidence presented here clearly points towards degradation. The manner of implementation of networking technology indicates still further routinisation of relations within organisations, with considerably less use of computer networks to improve the efficiency of transactions between organisations.

The evidence is worrying. The tendencies we have observed are liable to produce one-way management and unbalanced growth. By one-way management, we mean systems of control and co-ordination which issue down the hierarchy on the basis of information channelled up the computer system. The opportunities to exploit the tacit skills and knowledge of managers and workers at lower levels will be inhibited, because information systems are being used to impose order, rather than as a means of interaction. The unbalanced growth encouraged by the present manner in which computer networks are being developed is a direct result of the centralisation of authority implicit in one-way management. The linkages of the dependent workplace are not constructed primarily within the local environment; it has no responsibilities to its situation beyond providing employment. The centralisation of authority also restricts the growth opportunities for autonomous workplaces outside the fast modernising core regions. Establishments outside the core are at a twofold disadvantage. They do not have the proximity to interact with decision-makers in the core regions. Also, the rate of modernisation in the non-core regions is lower, and where it is high it takes place within the ring fence of internally orientated 'dependent'establishments.

How can we address these issues of increased hierarchical rigidity and deepening regional separation? Or are they immutable? First, we have to remember that the data presented in this chapter are based on the early adoption of computer networks. The technology itself has now moved on. The increasing power-performance ratio of microcomputers and the greater acceptance of networking technology has made computer networks more accessible to smaller-scale operations and to non-technical staff. The effect is to diffuse computer networking into areas outside the routinised environments noted in this chapter. This reduces the possibility of another analysis such as we have presented here, but also breaks down the institutional rigidity implicit in the ways that the technology was originally introduced. Furthermore, increased familiarity, especially amongst more junior staff, may mean that the ability of senior managers to impose greater and greater centralisation of control is weakened.

However, if the best application of computer networking is to be achieved we have to grasp the opportunity to use the introduction of a new technology to reorganise the way we work. We cannot trust to diffusion to do the work for us. New forms of interaction should allow us to discard old forms of control based upon communication techniques inferior in speed and flexibility. The observation that reorganisation should precede new technology is never so true as in this case. If we admire the Japanese productivity miracle perhaps we should emulate them in this respect (Bowen, 1989). To undermine the processes observed in this chapter two policy directions need to be followed. First, the emancipation of personnel using computer networks will come about only by thorough training systems which allow them to use the technology properly, in the manner of a master craftsman. As long as people are trained only so far as is necessary to perform a function the full benefits of multi-purpose technology such as the microcomputer will lie undiscovered. The technology must be made a tool instead of a tyrant.

Second, areas outside the core regions need special assistance in developing the interactive infrastructure which allow them to overcome the disadvantage of being in a remote and unmodernised location. Primarily this can come through developing the communications infrastructure and giving aid in planning investments to make the best use of communications systems. Examples of brave efforts by local authorites in this area are Sheffield's Information Strategy and Manchester's plans to become a wired city. These efforts are brave rather than successful, because they face considerable obstacles in providing the finance for such schemes, without a dramatic increase in their capital budgets.

At the moment, central government support for local infrastructure development and intensive training initiatives is lacking, as is substantial support from the private sector. This is an area in which the market does not provide; the initial costs are enormous and the biggest potential benefits go to the free rider, who comes along afterwards to cash in on the infrastructure which has been established. However, the full social and economic advantages of computer networks will not be exploited unless and until we recognise the need to make them technologies of communication and not technologies of control.

Bibliography

Beniger, J., 1986, *The Control Revolution: Technological and Economic Origins of the Information Society*, Harvard University Press, Cambridge, Mass.

Bowen, W., 1989, 'The puny pay-off from office computers' in T. Forester (ed.), *Computers in the Human Context: Information Technology, Productivity and People*, Basil Blackwell, Oxford, pp. 267–71.

Coase, R.H., 1937, 'The nature of the firm', *Economica*, **4**, 386–405.

Coombes, M.G. and Goddard, J.B., 1987, 'The north/south divide: some local perspectives', *Northern Economic Review*, **15** (Summer), 20–34.

Daniel, W.W., (1987, *Workplace Industrial Relations and Technical Change*, Pinter, London.

Ducatel, K.J. and Coombes, M.G., 1989, 'Contextualising flexible accumulation: linking labour market characteristics to emerging spatial divisions of labour', Paper presented to the Conference on Industrial and Social Change in Western Europe: the Dawn of a New Era of Flexible Accumulation?, Durham University, 26–28 September 1989.

Millward, N. and Stephens, M., 1987, *British Workplace Industrial Relations 1980–1984*, Gower, Aldershot.

Northcott, J. and Walling, A., 1988, *The Impact of Microelectronics: Diffusion, Benefits and Problems in British Industry*, Policy Studies Institute, London.

Short, J., Williams, E. and Christie, B., 1976, *The Social Psychology of Telecommunications*, John Wiley, London.

Storper, M. and Scott, A.J., 1989, 'The geographical foundations and social regulation of flexible production complexes' in J. Wolch and M. Dear (eds), *The Power of Geography: How Territory Shapes Social Life*, Unwin Hyman, Boston, pp. 21–40.

Williamson, O.E., 1975, *Markets and Hierarchies: Analysis and Antitrust Implications*, Free Press, New York.

11 New technology and the geography of the UK information economy

John Goddard

Introduction

PICT can trace its origins to a growing concern amongst UK policy-makers about the role of information activities in economic development. Prior to the establishment of the Programme major decisions were having to be made in a wide range of information policy arenas in the absence of well-grounded research on the implications for economic and social development of various regulatory regimes. Examples included policy towards international trade in services, on regulation of telecommunications, and on the regulation of information intensive industries such as the media. One of the reasons for this knowledge gap was that in the past policy-makers had placed most emphasis on the 'T' of 'IT' and neglected the role of information generation, capture and transmission or communication in economic growth and change more generally. This neglect was surprising given that the demand for IT derives from a growing demand for information.

There are, however, exceptions to such generalisations about the orientation of public policy debate. One of these is closely associated with the name of Charles Read. Through the Cabinet Office's Information Technology Advisory Panel he played an important role in producing the report *Making a Business of Information*, in which many of the intersecting information policy domains and their links with the spread of new information technologies are discussed (ITAP, 1983). Amongst other things, that report called for more research on the implications of the use of the advanced information and communications technologies and systems for individuals, for organisations and for economic and social change. This challenge has been taken up by the ESRC through the PICT programme.

Unfortunately, there was not a corresponding response from the policy-making system; indeed the Information Technology Advisory Panel was wound up soon after its report was published. The regulation of the information sector has remained with a number of separate public and private bodies such as trade associations, OFTEL, the ITC (formerly IBA) and separate divisions of the DTI. The public interest questions raised by the interconnections between different policy arenas have no forum within which they can be debated.

A similar overemphasis on technology and neglect of information is apparent at the sub-national scale, particularly in relation to urban and regional development, where a great deal of attention has been paid to the location of information technology production (eg Hall *et al.*, 1987). The success of high technology corridors like the M4, fortuitously underpinned by state support for research laboratories and defence spending, has led development agencies to seek to create the conditions for high technology production in lagging regions and ailing cities — for example through the promotion of science parks and, in other countries if not the UK, the science park's big brother, the technopolis. Current debates on local economic development do consider the greater flexibility that new technology is bringing to the organisation of production in different regions and the possibility of creating industrial districts based on a new division of labour between small firms (eg Scott and Storper, 1988). However, attention has tended to focus on the *workplace* and not on the new flexible geography of multi-site *organisations* made possible by telematics.

An information economy perspective would suggest that this emphasis fails to come to grips with one of the key dynamics in contemporary economic restructuring. It is as if the fundamental economic development issue in the nineteenth century related to the ability to build steam engines and not to the spread of steam power into a wide range of products and processes and the changes in the *systems* for organising production that the rapid improvements in communication made possible.

Partly because of lack of previous research on the information economy many policy decisions are still being made with little understanding of their spatial implications. For example, few agencies promoting local or regional economic development are aware of, let alone engaged in, national debates on the regulation of telecommunications and broadcasting. Cable franchises are being established, but the first time many local policy-makers begin to appreciate the possible implications is when the franchise holder requests planning permission.

National policy debates are often equally blind to spatial issues. OFTEL's formal interest is confined to telephones in rural areas; and although the Broadcasting Bill supports the regional dimension of Channel 3 the connections between broadcasting and regional development received little discussion of substance in the preceding White Paper. And yet the spread of ICT in conjunction with the informatisation of the economy carries with it implications for the location of activities and the development of cities and regions as profound as the spread of railways, roads and electric power, the telephone and newspapers in relation to the development of the industrial economy.

The essence of the information economy from the geographical perspective can be captured in four interrelated propositions.

The first proposition is that, although it has always been an important factor, information is coming to occupy centre stage as the key strategic resource on which the effective delivery of goods and services in all sectors of the world economy is dependent. Far from a transformation from an industrial to a post-industrial economy in which the emphasis is placed upon a shift from manufacturing to services, an information economy perspective would suggest that manufacturing and services activities are becoming equally dependent on effective information management. The city is — and always has been — the focus for information processing and exchange functions; as information becomes more important in both production and distribution, so the pivotal role of certain cities is reinforced.

The second proposition is that this economic transformation is being underpinned by a technical transformation in the way in which information can be processed and distributed. The key technical development is the convergence of the information processing capacity of computers (essentially a 'within-workplace' technology) with digital telecommunications (essentially a technology linking workplaces). The resultant technology of telematics is emerging as a key spatial component in the technical infrastructure of the information economy. Because of their historic role major cities are becoming the nodes or switching centres of this network based economy.

The third proposition is that the widespread use of information and communications technologies is facilitating the growth of the so called 'tradeable information sector' in the economy. This transformation embraces traditional information activities like the media and new activities like online information services. Moreover, many information activities previously undertaken within firms can now be purchased from external sources at lower cost in the 'information market-place' — the growth of the advanced producer service sector can in part be accounted for by the externalisation of information functions from manufacturing and other firms. While the use of ICT permits an increasing volume of interorganisation transactions, inter-personal contact is still sufficiently important, particularly in relation to the development of new services and relationships, for the role of cities to be further enhanced.

The final proposition is that the growing 'informatisation' of the economy is making possible the global integration of national and regional economies. As the arena widens within which this highly competitive process of structural change is worked out, so the pattern of winners and losers amongst cities and regions is likely to become more sharply differentiated. Far from eliminating differences between places, the use of information and communications technology can permit the exploitation of differences between areas, for example in terms of local labour market conditions, the nature of cultural facilities and of institutional structures. It is therefore very important to see contemporary changes in a longer-term historical perspective and in the context of the specificities of particular national space economies. Even in the information economy, geography matters!

The last point can be illustrated by the following brief historical and geographical account of the UK urban system from an information economy perspective (Goddard, 1989). The account highlights the interconnection between the way the economy has been organised and regulated and the ability to move information over space. It also seeks to make clear that the way communications technologies have been used has been shaped by a wide range of influences prevailing in different periods. The technologies for information communication have therefore created possibilities but not determined the trajectory of development.

Within Britain the key issue relates to the dominance of London over the rest of the urban system. During the middle years of the nineteenth century cities such as Newcastle, Birmingham, Manchester, Sheffield and Liverpool emerged to challenge briefly the hegemony of London. They become not only centres of production but foci for information-based activities like finance, legal services, education and the media. Many leading British banks had their origins outside London. Universities were endowed by provincial industrialists to support local research and training needs.

The period from 1890 to 1914, however, saw London reassert its dominance (Robson, 1986). London financial institutions were able to find a ready market for the profits of northern industry in the expanding Empire. In this process London drew provincial institutions into the City; there were a spate of mergers between banks leading to the emergence of the big five by 1918. The roots of the future decline of provincial cities can thus be traced back to the particular form of British financial capital with its preference for portfolio investment overseas. A further key factor facilitating this centralisation was the emergence of the national railway system which made possible the easy transfer of information in the form of people and the mail: this system radiated from London.

The inter-war period saw further centralisation, this time in the form of the control of industrial companies. The financial crisis of the depression led to a major restructuring of such companies to eliminate excess capacity. National companies like ICI emerged to replace regionally-organised companies, the majority with corporate headquarters in London and production spread around a number of cities. A key feature of the period was the widespread introduction of the telephone into larger companies. This communications innovation, like the railways earlier, assisted the interregional separation of production and administration, a division which had previously only taken place on an interregional basis to the advantage of provincial cities.

Developments in another important part of the information economy, the mass media, further accentuated these tendencies. The establishment of the BBC as a national broadcasting organisation eventually led to the emphasis on national news and views. By 1939, the number of provincial daily newspapers had fallen to thirty, half of which were controlled from London (Robson, 1986).

The post-1945 period not only witnessed the continuation of these tendencies towards administrative centralisation but also saw the emergence for the first time of a strong process of production decentralisation and a resultant net decline in the overall economic base of London and all other major cities. This new process strengthened after the mid-1960s with the spatial scale widening to embrace first the peripheral regions of Britain and then the developing world. In this period of relatively stable products and production technologies the main emphasis was on the search for economies of scale in manufacturing through the use of capital and space-intensive assembly line methods using low-cost and less skilled labour than was available in the cities. The consequence of this shift was a widespread de-industrialisation of British cities.

In contrast to manufacturing, very few economies of scale were being reaped in the information or control sector of the economy. While computers were being introduced to assist information processing within office functions, there were few technical innovations in the ability to communicate infor-mation between sites — the telephone remained the dominant technology and it merely diffused more widely through the economic system. Because growth in productivity in information activities was so low, the increasing scale of organisation necessitated the employment of more and more co-ordination staff. And because of the limitations in the essentially paper and personal-based intra-organisational communications systems, hierarchical structures were required to connect production and distribution sites via intermediate levels to higher decision-making centres; in this process provincial cities became relays in the intra-organisational information system, housing regional or divisional office functions. It was thus possible to point to the isomorphism between the corporate hierarchy and the urban hierarchy at the national and international scales (Goddard, 1978).

Such developments need to be seen in the light of fundamental changes in the regulation of the British economy that emerged in the post-war period, particularly the growing role for the local and national state. Increased state ownership of enterprises in many sectors resulted in a centralisation of headquarters control in London. With the increasing indirect role of the state through public purchasing, through support for research and development and through grants and loans, private sector companies found it increasingly desirable to transfer their headquarters to London which was the focus for state regulatory activities. The growth of collective wage bargaining through national sector-based unions was a further centralising influence. In the sphere of personal services, local government and health services grew in provincial cities, often administering centrally determined policies. The hierarchical ordering of national space around provincial cities as adminis-trative centres for the public sphere thus paralleled developments in the private sector.

It is now widely recognised that this mode of industrial organisation and regulation of production and consumption, loosely referred to as 'Fordism', collapsed in the mid-1970s with profound implications for the development of cities in Britain and elsewhere. One way of conceptualising what happened is to view it as a 'crisis of control' in which the scale and rigidities of many organisations had *inter alia* outgrown the capacity to handle the large volumes of information necessary to maintain effective control (Roobeek, 1987). In manufacturing, for example, major problems of structural overcapacity appeared in many sectors with excessive inventories produced by rigid production technologies (the so-called 'hard' automation). Contrary to the needs of the market, these technologies allowed little flexibility in production volumes. Economies of scale needed to be accompanied by economies of scope but this required new production technology, new forms of organisation and new labour processes. Similarly, the national and international dispersal of production inevitably meant more 'travelling' capital and less contact with the market. Rigid bureaucratic corporate structures were not well placed to respond to the requirements of rapid market change.

Events over the past ten years may be interpreted in terms of a struggle to reassert control through more flexible forms of organisation. The integration of computers and telecommunications technology (ICT) has been central to this struggle. As a result of the use of ICT many of the old hierarchical structures of organisations and the related distribution of functions and management of territory have been subject to challenge. These changes have been intimately related to significant shifts in political and institutional structures, shifts which have given greater emphasis to flexible patterns of employment and a revised role for the state as regulator of the markets rather than the provider of services, including telecommunications and broadcasting. These changes have had profound implications for the management of territory and the urban hierarchy.

This chapter will now introduce some of the research findings which map out some of these contemporary changes in more detail. The research has involved investigations into the geography of three components of the UK information economy (see Figure 11.1). First, there is the adoption of telematics in organisations in the public and private sector and in manufacturing and service industries and the linking of this adoption to the geographical division of tasks between workplaces within and between organisations and the territories over which they operate. Second, spatial development of the UK telecommunications system, focusing on BT itself as a complex organisation with its own interregional relations, has been studied. And third, there has been a geographical analysis of the development of a tradeable information sector *par excellence*, the audio-visual production sector. These investigations have involved in-depth studies of individual organisations, survey research, analysis of secondary data and conceptual work on the relationship between ICTs and geographical change. Finally, by synthesising findings geographically, the research has sought to highlight the threats and opportunities for area development in the information economy in a peripheral region like the North-East of England in order to point to the possibilities and limitations for proactivity on the part of development agencies.

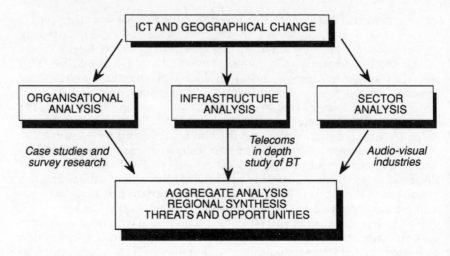

Figure 11.1 *Approaches to analysis of the geography of the information economy*

Telematics

The idea of a computer network as a spatial system has been used as a central concept in much of the analysis (Hepworth, 1987). Figure 11.2 is a highly simplified map of an intra and interorganisational network connecting different workplaces. While the network might make use of the public switched telephone system it is important to stress the fundamental difference between telematics and telephony. Telephony is an established and widely diffused technology which operates in the domain of interpersonal communications. Telematic systems are new and are in the process of becoming deeply embedded in both physical and functional structures within and between organisations. By facilitating capital and labour flows over space, telematics creates the possibility of new organisational geographies — what work is done where — and offers new possibilities for the way territories — markets or administrative areas — are managed.

A number of case studies have been undertaken to explore the trajectory of telematics development and spatial change in more detail. Three examples can be used to illustrate the changes under way. The first is for an organisation in the manufacturing sector where the change in spatial relationships are principally intranational; the second is from the public service sector where the changes are essentially local; and the third is from the private service sector where the changes are global.

The first example is a Doncaster based manufacturer of doors, windows and related components for the building industry, which has used a computer network to assist its adjustment to the changing geography of its markets (see

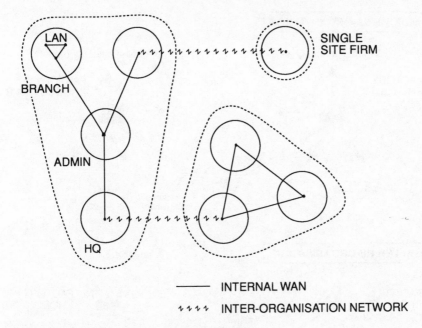

———— INTERNAL WAN

ィィィィ INTER-ORGANISATION NETWORK

Figure 11.2 *A hypothetical 'networked' organisation*

Figure 11.3). In its early development, the firm concentrated on being the least-cost producer in locally defined markets, chiefly for local authority housing. Subsequent expansion involved duplication of production across the whole product range in different areas. The use of ICTs at this stage of the firm's development was restricted to finance and cost control functions. The network was therefore used to reinforce a strategic objective of being least-cost producer.

Over a period of three years from 1979 the company's locally differentiated markets collapsed; the firm was left with an organisation suited to securing its growth in market conditions that no longer prevailed. The orientation of the firm was towards local authority markets in Northern and Western England and to manufacture on a ten-week order-to-delivery cycle. The new market conditions manifested themselves in a shift to the private sector and DIY markets in South-East England and to the manufacture of product on a three-day order-to-delivery cycle.

The response of the firm to these structural changes in its market are interwoven with the development of its computer network. The firm had to bring about the spatial reorganisation and integration of its production, as well as its sales and marketing functions, in order to achieve the requirements of a three-day order-to-delivery cycle. This reorganisation was centred upon a new information strategy capable of assembling, analysing and integrating information externally and assimilating it with information on its own

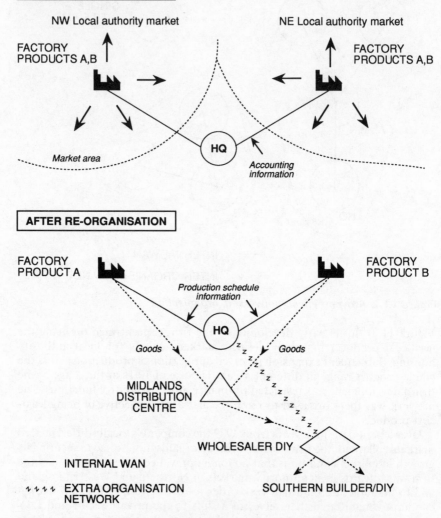

BEFORE RE-ORGANISATION

NW Local authority market

NE Local authority market

FACTORY
PRODUCTS A,B

FACTORY
PRODUCTS A,B

HQ

Market area

*Accounting
information*

AFTER RE-ORGANISATION

FACTORY
PRODUCT A

FACTORY
PRODUCT B

*Production schedule
information*

HQ

Goods

Goods

MIDLANDS
DISTRIBUTION
CENTRE

WHOLESALER DIY

——— INTERNAL WAN

ᶻ ᶻ ᶻ ᶻ EXTRA ORGANISATION
NETWORK

SOUTHERN BUILDER/DIY

Figure 11.3 *Networked base reorganisation of a manufacturing firm*

internal operations. The computer network was central to this restructuring of the firm.

In terms of production, the firm reorganised its manufacturing plants so that each had prime responsibility for a particular product range, so as to achieve economies of scale in production. Product specialisation rather than diversification at the individual plant level has now become the norm. Each branch plant despatches output to central warehouses which are responsible for deliveries to the market. The sales function was also centralised and its geographical focus re-orientated towards the market in South-East England.

The integration of these spatially fragmented functions of manufacturing, distribution and sales is now managed through the computer network. New relationships have been established whereby the activities of the company are determined by the actual uptake of product in the market. The company has also sought to align its sales activities with several of the large merchant chains through the development of intercorporate networking. In so doing it has attempted to use its computer network to exert greater influence on the market and to secure for itself the distribution of product into new geographically defined markets.

Finally, the spatial restructuring of the company has occurred within its existing locations. Through the use of information flows over the computer network the firm has managed to assert its territorial claims to markets in the South-East of England without new investment in this high-cost area. In short, the development of computer networking has allowed the spatial reorganisation of the company and ensured the integration of different functions, as well as facilitating its entry into new markets.

The second example is a county library service in North-East England (see Figure 11.4). The council has introduced a network-based circulation and control system into its multi-site library service to integrate the details of stock holding against issues, receipts, reservations, overdues, catalogue searches and the production of statistical information (for example, the recovery rate of overdue books and the success rate for different kinds of reservation, not only for each library, but for the service as a whole).

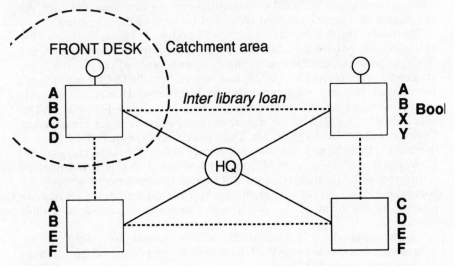

Figure 11.4 *Network structure for an information service business*

These systems had been manually based, contained within each library and committing significant labour resources to back-office activities. A network solution to circulation control has allowed the library service to remain geographically dispersed yet to be integrated around an 'information axis'. This development in the circulation control system is facilitating change in a number of ways. First, it is enabling local book stocks to be 'tailored' to local customer requirements, allowing spatial differentiation rather than duplication in the book stock. Considerable differences in consumer preferences occur in different locations and information flows are permitting these to be both formally identified and subsequently better matched to local book stocks. As a result, the number of duplicate books has been reduced and the savings made are being spent on extending the range of books available. Second, issue analysis permits 'product range' experimentation through mixing normally separately classified books, thereby increasing overall consumption. In effect the system is facilitating an intensified use of the book stock. Third, the technology is also permitting more rapid and reliable book circulation from within existing stock, further reducing the number of duplicate copies of a book and thereby releasing funds to deepen the overall stock. Fourth, the total collection is made available via the computer network to all users regardless of the location. The stock can then be conceptualised as 'virtual', permitting access regardless of the physical locations of the books and of the uses. Fifth, the emerging 'new library service' is being further enhanced by the release of staff from the back office into the front office, where broader advisory and information functions are central. In short, the adoption of a network solution to the delivery of library services has permitted new spatial structures to evolve which are increasingly sensitive to the differentiated needs of local communities yet do not deny the user the advantages of a large integrated collection because of their location.

The third example is based in the City of London. The company started life as a specialist publisher of financial magazines. Information was gathered through personal contacts and paper records and edited in the City. Magazines were printed in the UK and sold principally to City institutions. After 'Black Monday' the company's sales plummeted. However, it was able to refinance itself to provide electronic database services (see Figure 11.5). The core data are provided by the annual electoral registers which are collected from all local authorities in Britain. The registers are key punched in India and the data are then shipped to a computer bureau in one of the desert states of the USA. The files are then accessed from London by a satellite link. Information is therefore gathered in different localities within Britain, a major labour input is provided in another continent and a major capital item in the production process, in the form of the mainframe computer, is located in a third continent.

To the basic data of around 25 million records are added further information from localities in the UK, such as house prices, and from a range of institutions located in London — for example share holdings and probate information from Somerset House. Access to the data is often gained through

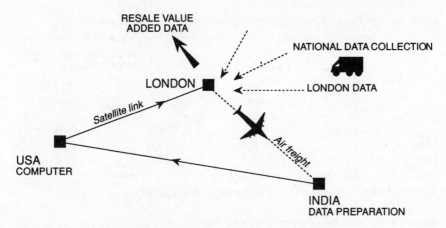

Figure 11.5 *Network structure for an information service business*

the personal contacts created through City networks. Information on individual consumer behaviour and life-styles obtained from regular market research surveys are also added to the database.

The company's clients are national and international businesses seeking to identify and size market segments for different goods and services, often for direct marketing purposes. Geography has little meaning for this type of target marketing. In marketing terms there may be more communality between, for example, Jesmond in Newcastle and Camden Town in London than between Jesmond and Wallsend or Camden and Hackney. There may also be greater affinities between Camden Town and the seventh *arrondisement* in Paris, and in pursuit of such opportunities the company is now actively exploring database construction in several European countries by establishing subsidiary operations.

From these examples it is clear that telematics can be used as a major weapon in supporting organisational and geographical change and in deriving competitive advantage. It has been closely involved in a new relationship between information flows and physical flows — 'wires' and 'wheels' are obviously related technologies. However, in other organisations networks have been 'ring-fenced' in accounting and financial control activities and have so far not been used as a basis for reconceptualising the organisation and its relation to the outside world. In order to assess the extent and significance of telematics penetration and use, 25 per cent of the organisations headquartered in four BT districts — the City of London, East Anglia, Manchester and North-East England — representing areas in the core, industrial heartland and periphery of the UK economy have been surveyed. Six hundred organisations or 40 per cent of the total approached responded. The survey has been used to identify the trajectory of telematics development since 1983 and, when linked to other data on the companies, to explore the association between network use and economic performance in different regions.

Table 11.1a Users of computer networks within organisations

	% of organisations with < 10 users		% of organisations with 100 > users	
	UK	**City of London**	**UK**	**City of London**
1982	69.4	59.2	5.9	11.2
1985	50.0	46.4	11.6	17.9
1989	23.6	15.4	28.1	40.3

Source: CURDS Computer Network Organisation Survey, 1989

Table 11.1b Volume of online transactions

	% of organisations with < 25% of transactions on-line	% of organisations with all transactions on line
1982	68.9	13.1
1985	42.6	17.8
1989	15.6	28.3

Source: CURDS Computer Networks Organisations Survey, 1989

The survey revealed an accelerating rate of network adoption, especially after 1985 (see Table 11.1a & b). In 1989, 40 per cent of all organisations were networked, half of whom had installed the network after 1985. It also revealed increasing numbers of users of the network as telematics penetrated deeper into organisations; thus in 1989 24 per cent of organisations had over one hundred users, compared with only 5 per cent in 1982; functions like purchasing, production, marketing and distribution are increasingly using telematics. A higher proportion of these users are also online, which is a further indication of integration into organisational processes. Indeed, in 1982 over 50 per cent of networked organisations had no online transactions compared with only 8 per cent in 1989. Now nearly one-third of organisations have 100 per cent of their network transactions online.

While there were no significant differences between areas in the proportions of organisations in the survey possessing a network, the contrast in network penetration within organisations between for example the North-East and the City of London is stark. In 1982 18 per cent of organisations in the City had more than one hundred users while none in the North-East reached this number. By 1989, 40 per cent of organisations in the City had over one hundred users and 41 per cent of transactions were online. The corresponding figures for the North-East were 15 per cent and 16 per cent respectively.

Table 11.2 Computer networks and company performance, 1985–87

	North-East	North-West	East Anglia	City
A. *Average employment change (%)*				
Networked	36.3	19.5	15.4	23.7
Non-networked	9.1	0.1	4.6	–4.6
B. *Average growth in turnover (%)*				
Networked	73.5	42.9	48.9	104.4
Non-networked	27.6	18.9	25.6	3.8
C. *Average growth in profitability (%)*				
Networked	17.5	4.1	9.1	11.9
Non-networked	0.7	0.6	1.4	–3.4

Source: CURDS Computer Networks Organisations Survey, 1989

By comparing firms who had adopted networking with those that have not and linking this to data on employment, turnover and profitability growth it is possible to examine the association between the presence of telematics and organisational performance (see Table 11.2). The contrasts are significant — for example a 20 per cent difference in average employment growth and an 11 per cent difference in profitability growth between networked and non-networked firms. While these differences were apparent in all regions, they are most pronounced in the North-East followed by the City of London. In the case of the North-East this would suggest the use of telematics to compensate for problems of peripherality whilst in the City of London telematics would appear to be an essential component in product innovation in the highly turbulent financial services market.

Not surprisingly the survey revealed that the size of organisation was a major factor accounting for the adoption or non-adoption of telematics (although this does not fully explain the differences between organisations and regions). In general, it is the largest companies that have adopted telematics, chiefly for intracorporate transactions. Another survey, under-taken by the Department of Employment in 1984 of 2,000 workplaces — the Workplace Industrial Relations Survey (WIRS) revealed that at that time only 5 per cent of single-site establishments in Britain had a network link compared with an average for all establishments of 26 per cent (Daniels, 1987) (see Table 10.2 p. 168). The highest incidence of links to other organisations recorded in WIRS was 14 per cent in the case of large head offices of multi-site organisations. In comparison 39 per cent of large administrative or back offices had a network link internal to the organisation. Given the concentration of head offices in London it is not surprising to find in the WIRS survey that London is the hub of computer networking in the UK, with 30 per cent of firms there having a network link compared to 20 per cent in the Northern region.

These figures suggest that the UK has a long way to progress towards a 'networked economy' in which transactions between firms, particularly between large firms and small firms and between small firms themselves are mediated by electronic means. Far from facilitating a new division of labour between firms as a basis for economic development within the peripheral regions, the analysis of WIRS suggests that telematics are being used to reinforce a long established interregional and intracorporate division between relatively low-level production tasks in the North and control tasks in the South. Whilst an increasing division of functions between small firms is emerging, especially in the South, where there is a stronger entrepreneurial tradition, the overall low incidence of networking in single-site firms suggests that this division is underpinned by traditional means of communications not telematics.

Some confirmation for these suggestions can be found by relating technical change in WIRS manufacturing establishments to the skills profile of their work-force and the characteristics of the local labour market. Such an analysis reveals that local labour markets in the peripheral regions which have a poorly qualified population are characterised by large factories employing relatively unskilled workers. Advanced technical change in production is not common but computer linkage to other parts of the organisation is. In stark contrast, rapidly growing labour markets in the outer South-East and East Anglia are characterised by small estabishments with a high skill intensity, high rates of advanced technical change but a low incidence of computer networking.

Further support for this suggestion comes from a recent survey of the use of telecommunications infrastructures by a matched sample of manufacturing establishments in the North-East, the North-West, the West Midlands and the South-East regions, undertaken for the Department of Trade and Industry by Diamond and Spence (1989). This revealed that expenditure on transport and communication as a percentage of total operating costs is highest in the South-East followed by the North-East (7.5 per cent and 7.1 per cent respectively). Breaking these figures down revealed significantly higher absolute expenditures on all forms of information transaction (business cars, air and passenger costs and telecommunications) in the South-East. These figures are indicative of a much more transaction intensive economy in the South-East region.

The growth of the information economy and interregional differences in its scale are clearly reflected in the aggregate distribution of occupations whose primary function involves the processing and exchange of information (Porat, 1977) (see Table 11.3). Applying a classification scheme developed by OECD to occupational data from the Labour Force Survey suggests that in 1984 47 per cent of the total employment in Britain was in information occupations.

Table 11.3 The distribution of information labour
(Information workers as a percentage of employment by region 1975–84)

	1975	1979	1984
South			
South-East, South-West, East Anglia	43.1	44.2	52.4
Heartland			
West Midlands, East Midlands, Yorkshire and Humberside, North-East	41.8	43.9	44.9
Periphery			..
North, Scotland, Wales, Northern Ireland	34.4	38.1	41.6
UK	40.1	42.6	47.1

Source: Labour Force Surveys

This compares with 40 per cent in 1975. In the South in 1984 this figure rises to 53 per cent whilst in the peripheral regions it is only 42 per cent. Through the teeth of the 1979–83 recession the South gained 800,000 information jobs while other regions recorded net losses as traditional industries shed both production and information labour. Part of the explanation for these figures is the South's large share of employment in what OECD calls the 'primary information sector' — information-based services and IT production — in which information occupations accounted for 78 per cent of employment in 1984. Nevertheless, over one-third of all employment in non-information goods and service sectors can also be classified as informational. The important point here is that while information activities are concentrating and growing rapidly in the South, they are significant everywhere in the UK economy.

Details on the expansion of information occupations beyond 1984 are not available. However, analysis of the growth of employment in the information-intensive financial and business services sector reveals that London has gained 273,000 jobs in this industry since 1983, a 41 per cent increase in six years. The sector now accounts for one-quarter of London's jobs. While financial and business services have grown outside London, the position of the capital is still dominant with many of the provincial centres increasing their share of this sector at the expense of smaller centres within each region. Growth rates have also been higher in office centres in the South-East outside London, reflecting the relocation of information-intensive back-office functions. According to surveyors Jones Lang and Wooton, few relocations have been beyond the South-East — of the 115 moves recorded by the company between 1979 and

1986, 78 per cent were confined to the South-East. Analyses of the trade-off for individual organisations considering relocation between rent and salary savings and the additional communication costs arising from a non-London location suggests that the communications damage can outweigh the other savings for moves beyond the Midlands (Goddard and Pye, 1977). The exception is provided by telematics based activities like BT's London directory enquiry service, parts of which have been successfully located to the North-East.

To summarise these findings, it is clear that there is a very uneven geography of information capital and information labour within the British economy. The supply and demand for information services is growing most rapidly in London and the South-East. Elsewhere it is concentrated in major provincial office centres. Nevertheless, it is clear that important opportunities exist for enterprises throughout the Northern regions, and not just in the major centres, to use telematics to gain competitive advantage and restructure their activities. Public services within the region can also become more efficient through the use of telematics. The information economy is therefore just not a phenomenon of London and the South-East.

Telecommunications infrastructure

What does this very uneven demand for telematic services, the most profitable, most rapidly growing and most competitive segment of the telecommunications market, mean for the development of the telecommunications infrastructure within the UK? (Goddard and Gillespie, 1986). This question has been addressed through an in-depth study of the evolution of BT from a public sector monopoly provider to a telecommunications business. In this study we have focused on the changing centre-periphery or field-function relationships within the company. The study has been set in the context of the evolving regulatory environment, including early attempts by development agencies in the North to promote telecommunications as part of the necessary if not sufficient conditions for regional economic development. There are some extremely complex issues here which cannot be treated fully in the space available, so what follows is an oversimplification and in the process some important points may be glossed over.

BT is charged with providing plain old telephony (POTS) throughout the UK on a uniform basis. It is evolving from a supply-led and territorial-based public service organisation towards a market-driven business seeking to address competition in various market segments. In relation to voice services this competitive environment nationally can be conceptualised in terms of a number of layers — POTS, cellular services (mobile telephony), telepoint and the personal communication network (PCN) (see Figure 11.6). Competition is structured horizontally in each layer by the presence of two or more providers and vertically by customer pressures — for example telepoint users of the PSTN. Further competition in the local loop may come from cable operators.

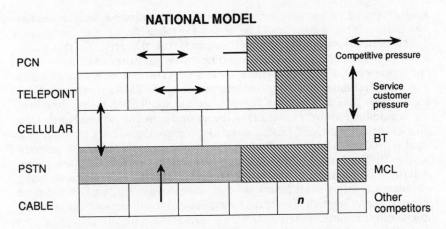

Figure 11.6 *National model for telecommunications regulation*

However, this so-called 'national model' only applies in London, the majority of the South-East and major provincial centres. Only in London are all services universally available. As one moves north availability of service within each region decreases as does the extent of competition within and between layers (see Figure 11.7). There are also intraregional differences between city centres and the surrounding areas where important parts of UK

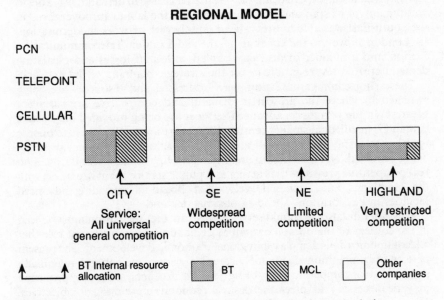

Figure 11.7 *Regional model of actual telecommunications regulation*

manufacturing industry are located but where competition is limited. Similar and more stark contrasts could be drawn for telematic services.

The national competitive model assumes that the principle regulatory forces are the vertical and lateral competitive pressures mediated where appropriate by OFTEL. In addition there are pressures from industry lobbies like the telecommunication managers association (TMA) representing the largest users generally based in London and the South-East. User pressures in the regions are however weaker — for example in the whole North-East district there are only 90 business users with more than 20 BT lines out of a total of 100,000 customers. Residential telephony is therefore the primary market. In Scotland, and by their own admission, the Telecommunications Advisory Committee established by OFTEL is not well known 'with many customers unaware of its functions'. Agencies like the Scottish Development Agency (now Scottish Enterprise) have been largely passive on telecommunications issues compared with road, rail and air transport.

As the omnipresent public service supplier, BT faces considerable tensions between its territorial inheritance and responsibility and the needs to respond to market opportunities and competitive pressures in its most rapidly growing market segments and geographical areas. A major part of its initial restructuring towards a more market orientated philosophy was to break the power of the regional divisions through a policy of 'districtisation' and functional division. This strategy had some unexpected consequences, partly because of the different labour market situations the company was facing in different parts of the country. The research suggests that the North-East district, which was experiencing only a small increase in demand, was able to retain many of its staff and in comparison with the labour turnover faced in the South-East was able to press ahead rapidly with network modernisation. In London however, the breakup of the old London Telecommunication Region into a number of districts coupled with staff losses and escalating demand created severe problems for the strategic planning of the network.

These shortcomings have now been addressed and resources are being switched to where the growth in demand and competitive pressures are greatest. In the periphery, advanced services are being provided only where demand is justified; in smaller centres where there are too few users to bundle together to justify the supply of a facility like Kilostream the service is not being provided. Nevertheless, in areas like the Highlands, where BT faces no real competitive pressures, it is acting as a public service agent in concert with the Highlands and Islands Development Board in providing advanced facilities in key locations ahead of obvious demand.

This brief discussion should serve to illustrate that regulation must be seen in the context of the uneven pattern of demand and the important role that telecommunications can play in regional economic development. The present pattern of competition is extremely complex, within and between regions. In southern areas competition may bring benefits; in others, monopoly provision may be necessary to meet the desired economic development objectives. Nevertheless it should be clear that national regulation of telecommunications in effect means regulation for London and the South-East; the costs and benefits arising in the rest of the UK are largely incidental and unplanned. The similarity with current inflationary pressures in the UK economy which have been driven by house price rises in the South-East and leading to high interest rates which severely affect investment in northern manufacturing cannot have escaped attention.

Broadcasting

This review of the geography of the information economy in Britain concludes by a brief reference to the audio-visual industries. What follows is a simple description of the regional structure of the industry and some of the factors shaping its spatial development. It is carried out with the view to drawing attention to a possible widespread ignorance or perhaps lack of interest in the regions in a part of the information economy which has been dominated by London opinion, taste and fashion.

The industry centres on the traditional broadcasting companies but includes feature film production, distribution and exhibition, independent TV production, the corporate video business, computer graphics, interactive video and post-production facilities. It is an important sector of the British economy and is playing an increasing role in regional development in terms of direct employment and as a provider of specialist services to other sectors. Less directly, as part of the cultural industries, the audio-visual sector is contributing to changing the image, identity and morale of older industrial regions. This sector is also strategically placed in relation to the convergent markets and technologies of broadcasting and telecommunications.

Most data sources indicate the absolute dominance of London as the centre of activity in the sector. The BBC has been hierarchically ordered and vertically integrated with headquarters in London and national production centres in Birmingham, Bristol and Manchester, centres in Scotland, Wales and Northern Ireland and seven regional production sites. However, over 70 per cent of employment is in London and over 70 per cent of network programming is produced there. The Corporation is now entering a period of cost cutting through contracting out various functions, freezing recruitment in selected areas and moving staff away from the high-cost South-East, partially merging BBC North-East and BBC North-West with a combined headquarters in Manchester. This will eradicate a layer of middle management, result in fewer regional opt-out programmes shown in fewer but larger combined regions.

ITV has been organised as a regional/federal group of companies divided into three sets. The five majors based in London, Manchester, Birmingham and Leeds dominate production for the network with 35 per cent of programme output compared with 12 per cent for the ten regional companies. The majors account for 60 per cent of net advertising revenues and 50 per cent of employment. Extensive reorganisation is in train involving externalisation of functions, the institution of new working practices and a programme of corporate diversification. This process is increasing demand for audio-visual services in a limited number of cities.

Channel 4 was founded in 1982 as a publishing house, making no programmes for itself but rather commissioning programmes from the ITV companies and independent producers. Its establishment has encouraged the development of a growing sector of independent production companies, associated service facilities and a free-lance labour market. The 1987 quota for independent production for the BBC and ITV with a target of 25 per cent independent production by 1992 has further boosted the sector. However, two-thirds of independent production is based in London and the South-East. The pattern which is emerging in the independent sector is one of a few large companies, which are awarded the lion's share of commissions and a fringe of small companies producing a few programmes a year.

Cable and direct broadcasting by satellite represents an alternative means of distributing television programmes. Prospects for broadband cable TV in Britain are perhaps better now than any time in the past, particularly within the higher density and concentrated industrial cities. The saturation of the US market combined with the removal of barriers to US investment in UK cable and the possibility of combining telecommunications and TV has created the possibility of rapid expansion. Cable provides an obvious system for distributing satellite programmes. Competition for cable franchises in northern industrial cities has been strong and promises to strengthen the audio-visual sector outside of London.

These various components of the audio-visual sector, together with corporate video and film production, distribution and exhibition, comprise a highly integrated sector of the information economy at global, national and local scales. Technological and regulatory change are breaking down the old vertically integrated and hierarchically structured organisations and increasing the degree of interdependence between firms. But as with telecommunications, the local interrelatedness is not always recognised in national regulatory policy. However, the significance of the audio-visual sector at the local scale is increasingly being recognised in a range of urban and regional initiatives. The sector on Tyneside is an example. At a conservative estimate it has a total turnover of £80–100 million and a direct and indirect employment of between 1,500 and 2,000 jobs. In addition to Tyne Tees Television and the BBC there are 50 independent production companies and corporate video producers. Comment Cablevision, a joint venture with US West, has established its headquarters on Tyneside. There are a range of studio and training facilities and a network of economic and particularly social linkages, the latter reflected in the formation of a Northern Media Forum. The pressure of such a range of activities has provided a search for a local economic development strategy to promote the growth of the sector on Tyneside. Schemes under discussion or in progress include bidding for the headquarters of Channel 5, publishing a guide to audio-visual production for potential purchasers of services, establishing a film office to promote the area for film production and a Northern Film Investment Fund as an offshoot of British Screen which is promoted by the Department of Trade and Industry. Other developments include the promotion of an international film festival, local programming on the cable network, the provision of training facilities and the possible establishment of a media centre in the Urban Development Corporation's 'flagship' Quayside project.

However, the scope for local action may be limited, given that many major public and private decisions affecting the area will be made outside. Tyne Tees Television may lose the Channel 3 franchise which may go to a non-local company; this may subsequently be acquired by a European media business. BBC TV has already downgraded the functions of its Newcastle studios as part of its cost-cutting exercise and Comment Cable may move its head-quarters to Manchester if it wins that franchise. Local independent companies may also be acquired by London organisations.

Conclusion

A number of conclusions emerge from the analysis that has been presented. First, far from eliminating the importance of geography, the so-called 'space-transcending' ICTs, when taken together with other factors, are supporting a more uneven pattern of regional development within the UK. Information occupations and industries have grown dramatically in London and the South-East in the past ten years, reflecting the capital's international as well as its national role. This growth has been underpinned by the rapid diffusion of computer networks; these networks are hubbed on London, serving to reinforce its dominant position in the national and international urban system.

Second, there is only limited evidence so far of ICTs contributing to more flexible ways of organising the production of goods and the delivery of services in the way that could benefit smaller enterprises and indigenous development in declining regions. Computer networks are still used primarily for intra-organisational transactions and as a means of reasserting control over organisational processes; very few small firms are networked. However, there are examples of organisations which are using ICTs to create competitive advantage, reconfigure their corporate geography and change the way in which they manage territory. Clearly ICTs have the *potential* for radically changing the face of Britain rather than simply reinforcing the old order.

Third, the intersection between sectoral and geographical considerations in relation to the development of the UK information economy is poorly articulated in the regulation of information industries or in public policy more generally. At the national level, the implications of the privatisation of BT in relation to its capacity to respond to the changing geography of demand and the fact that it is a complex territorially structured organisation, not a 'black-box', have yet to be fully assimilated. Similarly, whilst the role of broadcasting in regional development is acknowledged, the mechanisms are only dimly perceived by policy-makers. At the national and local level, there is little evidence of, but an urgent need for, coherent planning for the information economy which integrates training, infrastructure provision, technology demand stimulation measures, and so on, not only as a means of achieving more balanced regional development, but in order to ensure that the UK reaps the benefits of becoming a network-based economy.

Finally, the spread of telematics and the associated emergence of more geographically flexible and market responsive organisations raises important questions concerning methods of regulating the economy in a way which balances public and private interest. The old hierarchical order of national, regional and local governance and of sectoral and regional policy, has been irrevocably challenged. There are dangers of global integration proceeding hand in hand with regional and local disintegration, of islands of economic growth in the networked economy and economic decline of the network. These dangers may now need to be countered by a new era of re-regulation. This will require new skills in public administration and the drawing together of knowledge from a variety of sources. Better information flows between central and local government, between different departments of state and between the public and private sectors, often in a European context, will be increasingly necessary if even sharper regional disparities in the information economy are to be considered. Regional policies for the information economy will certainly be different to those for the industrial economy or the enterprise economy.

Acknowledgements

This chapter is based on research undertaken in the Centre for Urban and Regional Development Studies at the University of Newcastle upon Tyne as part of the ESRC PICT Programme. The contributions of Andrew Gillespie, Mark Hepworth, Kevin Robins, John Taylor and Howard Williams together with James Cornford, Ken Ducatel, Irene Hardill, Steve Johnson and Pooran Wynarczyk are gratefully acknowledged. Any errors of fact or interpretation are of course the author's.

Bibliography

Daniel, W.W., 1987, *Workplace Industrial Relations and Technical Change*, Frances Pinter, London.
Diamond, D. and Spence, N., 1989, *Infrastructure and Industrial Costs in British Industry*, Department of Trade and Industry, HMSO, London.
Goddard, J.B., 1978, 'Urban and regional systems', *Progress in Human Geography*, 1, 309–17.
Goddard, J.B., 1989, 'The city in the global information economy' in R. Lawton (ed.), *The Rise and Fall of Great Cities*, Belhaven Press, London.

Goddard, J.B. and Pye, R., 1977, 'Telecommunication and office location', *Regional Studies*, **11**, 19–30.

Goddard, J.B. and Gillespie, A., 1986, 'Advanced telecommunications and regional economic development', *Geographical Journal*, **152**, 383–97.

Hall, P. *et al.*, 1987, *Western Sunrise: The Genesis and Growth of Britain's Major High Tech Corridor*, Allen and Unwin, London.

Hepworth, M., 1987, 'Information technology as spatial systems', *Progress in Human Geography*, **11**, 157–80.

ITAP, 1983, *Making a Business of Information: A Survey of New Opportunities*, HMSO, London.

Porat, M., 1977, *The Information Economy: Definition and Measurement*, Special Publications, 77–12(1), Office of Telecommunications, US Department of Commerce, Washington.

Robson, B.T., 1986, 'Coming full circle: London versus the rest, 1890–1980' in G. Gordon (ed.), *Regional Cities in the UK*, Harper and Row, London.

Roobeek, A., 1987, 'The crisis in Fordism and the rise of a new technological paradigm', *Futures*, **19** (2), 129–54.

Scott, A. and Storper, M., 1988, 'Flexible production systems and regional development: the rise of new industrial spaces in North America and Western Europe', *International Journal of Urban and Regional Research*, **12**, 173–85.

Index